BigLaw

THE CHICAGO SERIES IN LAW AND SOCIETY

Edited by John M. Conley, Charles Epp, and Lynn Mather

Also in the series:

Union by Law: Filipino American Labor Activists, Rights Radicalism, and Racial Capitalism
by Michael W. McCann with George I. Lovell

Speaking for the Dying: Life-and-Death Decisions in Intensive Care
by Susan P. Shapiro

Just Words, Third Edition: Law, Language, and Power
by John M. Conley, William M. O'Barr, and Robin Conley Riner

Islands of Sovereignty: Haitian Migration and the Borders of Empire
by Jeffrey S. Kahn

Building the Prison State: Race and the Politics of Mass Incarceration
by Heather Schoenfeld

Navigating Conflict: How Youth Handle Trouble in a High-Poverty School
by Calvin Morrill and Michael Musheno

The Sit-Ins: Protest and Legal Change in the Civil Rights Era
by Christopher W. Schmidt

Working Law: Courts, Corporations, and Symbolic Civil Rights
by Lauren B. Edelman

Additional series titles follow index

BigLaw

Money and Meaning in the Modern Law Firm

Mitt Regan
Lisa H. Rohrer

The University of Chicago Press
Chicago and London

The University of Chicago Press, Chicago 60637 The University of Chicago Press, Ltd., London

Published 2021

29 28 27 26 25 24 23 22 21 20   1 2 3 4 5

ISBN-13: 978-0-226-74194-9 (cloth)
ISBN-13: 978-0-226-74213-7 (paper)
ISBN-13: 978-0-226-74227-4 (e-book)
DOI: https://doi.org/10.7208/chicago/9780226742274.001.0001

Library of Congress Cataloging-in-Publication Data

Names: Regan, Milton C., Jr., 1952– author. | Rohrer, Lisa H., author.
Title: BigLaw : money and meaning in the modern law firm / Mitt Regan, Lisa H. Rohrer.
Other titles: Money and meaning in the modern law firm | Chicago series in law and society.
Description: Chicago ; London : The University of Chicago Press, 2020. | Series: Chicago series in law and society | Includes bibliographical references and index.
Identifiers: LCCN 2020037909 | ISBN 9780226741949 (cloth) | ISBN 9780226742137 (paperback) | ISBN 9780226742274 (ebook)
Subjects: LCSH: Law firms—United States. | Practice of law—United States.
Classification: LCC KF300 .R44 2020 | DDC 338.4/73400973—dc23
LC record available at https://lccn.loc.gov/2020037909

MR:

to Nancy;

to Rebecca, Ben, and Bryan, and to Liam and Dash;

and to the memory of Sylvia Leopold

LHR:

to J.J., Gavin, and Maddie Rohrer;

and to Bill and Jan Haueisen

CONTENTS

Introduction

BigLaw

Law firm practice is not what it used to be. The significant changes over the last few decades are reflected in the following statements by two lawyers in the same firm. The first partner reflected on his experience as he entered law practice in the mid-1980s:

> I remember going to see [a late former partner] who was then the managing partner and saying, "I'm doing some accountants' liability work, I'm running around the country trying cases with [a partner] on the criminal side, I'm writing a Supreme Court cert petition, should I narrow my focus and try to do something that will help generate clients?" He said, "Don't worry about generating clients. Just be the best lawyer you can be, serve the profession, and the clients will come to you." (#257)

A second partner who graduated from law school in the early 2000s was asked about her experience in law firm practice. She replied:

> I think I thought there was less selling in it. My mom is in sales and I was talking to her about something and she said, "Oh well you're in sales," and I said, "Well if I wanted to be in sales I would have been a salesperson." . . . I don't think you really realize that you actually get to a point where you are selling a service, you are in the service industry and you've got to be a salesperson. (#241)

The first lawyer describes a world in which excellence in the craft of law defined by internal professional standards provided assurance of advancement and financial success. The second lawyer describes a world in which earning these goods requires greater reliance on business skills. This shift is commonly described by declaring that "lawyering is becoming more of a business than a profession. Some lawyers decry this. Others welcome it. Few deny it" (*Economist* 2011).

Such claims are not new. For more than a century, critics of corporate law firms have claimed that firms have steadily abandoned professional values for the sake of business success (Berle 1933; Bristol 1913; Llewellyn 1931; Stone 1934). Others have suggested that the classic partnership model of practice may have insulated some corporate firms from business pressures for the first several decades of the twentieth century (Glendon 1994; Linowitz 1994; Smigel 1964). This created an opportunity for them to draw meaningfully on professional values in fashioning their approaches to law practice.

In recent years, however, many subscribers to the second view have suggested that the market conditions underlying the classic partnership model have crumbled—that the dike has given way and that business pressures now flood unchecked into law practice. The result, many claim, is that adherence to professional values is a receding possibility. This claim is consistent with the suggestion that professions more generally are losing their traditional prerogatives to "control their own associations, to control the workplace, to control the market for their services, and to control their relation to the state" (Freidson 2013; Krause 1996, 280; Rostain 2010). To the extent this is occurring, these occupations are governed less by professional values than by either market forces or bureaucratic structures. Elliott Krause (1996, 280) poses the question: "Has capitalism finally caught up with the last remaining guilds?" He suggests that this process is under way:

> The loss of any noncapitalist values within the professions, both because of external pressures . . . and because of the surrender of positive guild values—of collegiality, of concern for the group, of a higher professional ethic beyond mere profit—that has eroded the distinction between professions and any other occupation and thus left them together as the middle-level employees of capitalism. (281)

On either view, it is clear that anxiety about lawyers losing their professional identity has been an ongoing concern since the rise of the corporate law firm and provided an impetus for periodic campaigns to reinvigorate professionalism (American Bar Association 1986; Atkinson 1995; Brandeis 1905; Gordon 1983; Hobson 1986; Levine 2013).

Few can deny that large firms are now major business enterprises. The 2019 AmLaw 100 (a list of the top 100 US firms ranked by gross revenue) reported that in 2018, thirty-seven firms generated revenues over $1 billion, ten firms earned revenues over $2 billion, and two firms produced revenues over $3 billion. Of these firms, thirty-nine firms reported profits per partner (PPP) over $2 million, twenty firms had PPP over $3 million, eight were over $4 million, three reported PPP over $5 million, and one firm reported over $6 million in profits for each equity partner (*American Lawyer* 2019).

Large law firms also have grown enormously in size in the past 30 years. The AmLaw 100 list in 1989 shows an average size of 312 lawyers; the firms in the 2019 list were over three times that size, averaging over 1,000 lawyers each (*American Lawyer* 2019). Likewise, firms in the 1989 list were relatively concentrated in just a few offices. From an average of just over three offices per firm in 1989, thirty years later, the average size was twenty-one offices per firm in the AmLaw 100 (National Association of Law Placement 1989).

This dramatic growth has brought a host of organizational challenges in 2019 that did not exist in 1989. Organizing 1,000 professionals in dozens of offices is a challenge for managing partners, most of whom began law practice in the late 1980s and early 1990s. Adding to the challenge of scale is a change in structure. In 1989, one-third of lawyers inside large law firms were equity partners—effectively "owners" of the firm; in 2019, this proportion had decreased to one-fifth, indicating what may be a shift in the balance of power within firms to a more concentrated group of senior lawyers.

At the same time, large firm lawyers belong to what traditionally was regarded as a profession. William Sullivan (2005, 21) suggests that "[a] profession is a means of livelihood that is also a way of life." He continues:

> Professionalism seeks freedom in and through significant work, not by escaping from it. In professional work, the practitioner expresses freedom by directing the exercise of carefully developed knowledge and skill toward ends that refer beyond the self and the practitioner's private satisfaction.
>
> Concern for clients or patients and for the public values for which the profession stands is essential to genuine practice. The key point is that for a genuine professional the meaning of the work derives from both what it is

and the ends toward which it is directed as much as or more than its significance comes from the return it affords.

As we elaborate in this book, we believe that gaining a full understanding of current practice requires that we abandon the assumption that business and professional concerns are inherently antagonistic. From the time that they emerged, corporate law firms have been professional organizations engaged in business. They have operated under different market conditions in different periods, and their viability has depended on both being financially successful and being able to elicit the commitment of the lawyers who work in them as market conditions have changed.

It therefore can be misleading to assume that various changes in law firm structure and policies reflect the unqualified ascent of business values. The more pertinent question is the extent to which firms are attempting to balance business and professional considerations under a new, more demanding, set of market conditions.

Historically, firms' ability to gain the kind of commitment from their lawyers that will enhance business performance rested in part on the extent to which they could credibly frame their responses to business demands as being consistent with those lawyers' understanding of themselves as professionals. Partners must regard proposed changes as aligned with their professional values to accept them, but the ways in which proposals are articulated, and the changes that gain acceptance, themselves can subtly shape the meaning of professionalism for lawyers in the firm. There is thus an ongoing dialectic between material changes in law firms and conceptions of professionalism. Understandings of professional values may serve as sources of resistance to some changes, but may also evolve to accommodate other changes whose adoption are seen as more urgently necessary.

In this book, we draw on 279 in-depth interviews conducted between 2009 and 2016 with partners in large US law firms to assess the claim that business concerns are eclipsing professional values in law firm practice.[1] All but 15 of these interviews were conducted in six firms. Five of these are in the AmLaw 100, while the sixth, before its merger with another firm, was in the AmLaw 200. We focus on the large law firm because, since its emergence in the late nineteenth century, it has had an outsized impact on the legal profession. While a relatively small percentage of lawyers work in this setting, "the corporate law firm continues to exercise an influence, both within the profession and outside it, that far exceeds its numerical strength" (Kronman 1993, 273). As Anthony Kronman observes, "[h]owever influence and power are measured—whether in raw economic terms or in subtler, political ones—these firms remain the leaders of the bar" (273). Commonly known as BigLaw (MacEwen 2013, 1), these firms attract a disproportionate amount of attention from the legal and the popular press.

We examine how large firms are responding to intensifying competition, what this means for lawyers' understandings of themselves as professionals, and the degree to which firms are attempting to fashion distinctive organizational cultures that reflect their own particular balances between business demands and professional values. We regard it as crucial to examine both lawyers and their firms because, as Michael Kelly (1994, 18) puts it, "no coherent account of professionalism, legal ethics, or the contemporary legal profession is possible without understanding the workings of practice organizations." Professionalism, Kelly writes, "is not an abstraction in an organization. It is forged in every decision of the practice" (13). The pages that follow describe how this process occurs in the daily lives of lawyers and their firms, capturing the complexity of experience beneath common stereotypes and broad generalizations about large law firms.

A crucial finding of the book is that no meaningful differences among firms explain their susceptibility to market pressures or the broad outlines of how they respond to them. The partners in our study all face the same basic business pressures regardless of their firms' practice fields, pedigree and history, geographic location, compensation policy, organizational structure, and client base. The particular form that these pressures take varies depending on some of these characteristics, but every partner faces the same competitive demands that we describe in the book. Responses from partners across all firms emphasize the common crucial challenge posed by intensifying competition and pressure for financial performance. Furthermore, the policies and practices developed in response to these demands represent prominent trends in all firms in our study.

Partners tended to answer similarly when asked what their firms needed to build and maintain a distinctive culture that balances business demands and professional values. As we describe in several chapters in the book, firms may adopt a variety of measures to accomplish this. Our research enables us to generalize, however, that these all represent different ways to meet a basic, shared challenge: the need to simultaneously solve a Prisoner's Dilemma and an Assurance Game. We did not approach our research with this conceptual framework in mind; it reflects a theory based on close analysis of roughly 5,000 pages of interview transcripts.

We believe this book makes an important contribution by providing a general analytical framework for analyzing large law firms. This framework provides a common lens through which to view the book's detailed interviews, and we hope it will guide future research on firms. In this respect, the book is written in the spirit of prior scholarship that has sought to identify some of the fundamental underlying dynamics of law firms. Two works in particular come to mind: Robert Nelson's *Partners with Power,* which focuses on the tension between bureaucracy and participation; and Marc Galanter and Thomas Palay's *Tournament of Lawyers,* which discusses the concept of the tournament as the basis for law firm organizational structure and the engine of law firm growth.

We draw three general conclusions about the modern law firm based on our research. The first is that, while law firms have faced increasing competitive pressures in the last three to four decades, those pressures have significantly intensified since the economic downturn of 2008. Many firms are facing flat or declining demand for their services along with considerable pressure from clients to minimize legal fees. At the same time, they are competing with an increasing variety of nonlegal organizations to obtain work from clients, and generally cannot count on long-term relationships with clients to provide a regular flow of business. Many partners express the view that these likely are permanent structural changes in the market for law firm services.

These trends are leading firms to emphasize that their lawyers need to be entrepreneurial in seeking out clients and business, and need to develop business skills to a greater degree than lawyers in years past. Firms are reinforcing this message by altering their compensation systems and being more willing to let go of partners and practices they regard as insufficiently profitable. They also are actively involved in recruiting lateral partners from other firms, as well as seeking to protect themselves from defection by their own productive partners. In these respects, firms are devoting attention to rationally organizing themselves as business enterprises in a more competitive market for both clients and partners.

Second, notwithstanding these trends, professional values remain meaningful to many partners as a source of satisfaction in their practices. When asked whether professionalism in current practice means simply effectively running a business that serves clients, one litigation partner in a managing role in a major firm is worth quoting at some length:

> I think there is a lot more beyond that. . . . [T]here is the craft and the professionalism of writing a Supreme Court brief or delivering an argument or a closing to a jury, conducting a cross examination, at least on the litigation side. That's a tradition of service, and people in this firm want to serve and represent individual clients whether it's me representing [unpopular defendants] in my [earlier practice] for which I took a lot of guff, or it's people today who are representing Palestinian refugees and taking some guff for that. . . .
>
> People want to do the things that drove them to go to law school in the first place. And there is room for that. . . . Making better lawyers who know how to serve people is part of the profession too, in a way I don't think it is necessarily [the case] for engineers or accountants or others who have licenses to practice. (#247)

Similarly, the *American Lawyer* noted in its 2018 report on the AmLaw 100, "Not all law firm partnerships are profit-maximizing entities; rather, many balance profits with the psychic income partners get from collegiality, intrinsic joy of the work, contained performance pressures and satisfaction drawn from developing the next generation" (Simons and Bruch 2018).

A partner's belief that his firm genuinely regards such values as important, and that it actively seeks to pursue them, can elicit commitment to the firm that is more durable than a connection based simply on financial self-interest. It can lead partners to act in the interest of their colleagues and the larger firm. To the extent this dynamic occurs, it can foster a culture that not only provides intrinsic professional rewards for partners but also enables the firm to serve clients more effectively than other firms.

If this cooperative culture creates a competitive advantage for the firm, it can generate firm-specific capital that makes it more advantageous for partners to remain at the firm than to move. This means that the firm will have more secure client relationships and a more stable partnership. In this way, a firm that gives meaningful weight to nonfinancial professional values can elicit partner commitment that also provides financial benefits for the firm.

Our third conclusion is that sustaining this sort of culture is easier said than done. Because of intense competition, a firm is likely to move increasingly in the direction of focusing on business considerations unless it deliberately seeks to do otherwise. This can lead partners to protect themselves by acting in their immediate self-interest rather than cooperating with others for the benefit of colleagues and the firm.

To avoid this default outcome, a firm must simultaneously communicate two messages to its partners. On the one hand, it must convince them that cooperative behavior will be more financially advantageous than self-interested behavior, and will produce greater returns than partners could gain at other firms. We describe this as management's need to solve a Prisoner's Dilemma. A firm that does this can create firm-specific capital by strengthening partner ties to the firm, which in turn may create a competitive advantage.

At the same time, the instrumental basis of these ties may make commitment fragile and contingent. To build even more durable ties, management must credibly communicate to partners that the firm is more than a vehicle for generating profits. It must convey that it regards the nonfinancial rewards associated with professional values as intrinsically important. This sends the message that cooperation is not simply valuable for instrumental reasons but as a way of interacting that expresses and enables partners to practice in accordance with the ideals of professionalism. We describe this management task as solving the Assurance Game. Meeting this challenge can create even stronger firm-specific capital in the form of ties between partners and the firm that are based on both financial and nonfinancial rewards that the firm provides.

As this discussion suggests, business and professional values can be complementary as well as antagonistic. Some policies that enhance a firm's business prospects can also enhance the conditions under which professional values can flourish. Similarly, measures that foster the firm's realization of professional values can elicit commitment to the firm that furthers its business success. Business and professional values—money and meaning—thus can intertwine in various ways in the modern large law firm, even though firms undeniably are more subject than ever before to the influence of market forces.

Each firm needs to negotiate this dynamic in its own way and strike a balance that takes account of the particular conditions that it confronts. Most large firms are subject to comparable economic pressures, for instance, but even within this group there are indications that distinct market segments may be emerging that will require different responses (Simmons 2018a). In addition, differences among firms in the industries and clients that they serve, the services that they offer, and their lawyers' expectations of practice will necessarily require firms to align money and meaning in their own distinctive ways. We describe how firms are doing this, either deliberately or unwittingly, and what this suggests about the future of the large law firm.

The Research

We provide details on our research design in an appendix following the conclusion, but it will be useful here to describe our general approach. About 95 percent of our interviews were in six firms of roughly 900 or more lawyers, five of which are in the AmLaw 100. The sixth firm was in the AmLaw 200 and had over 400 lawyers; it has since merged with another firm. We interviewed people from a range of practices and with different demographic and other relevant characteristics. We nonetheless cannot claim to have conducted a scientifically rigorous random sample.

As we have indicated, a major finding of our research is that the six firms in which we did the bulk of our interviews face the same business pressures and respond to them in similar ways, regardless of various differences among them. Partners across all firms also describe similarly what a firm must do to maintain a culture that elicits commitment by credibly communicating that it regards both business and professional concerns as important. As we describe above, we characterize this as simultaneously solving a Prisoner's Dilemma and an Assurance Game.

We did detect some differences in the extent to which firms explicitly seek to promote professional values and in how successfully they establish a culture that does so. Some of the six firms are more effective in instilling this sense of a common culture, although dissenting voices are heard even within these firms. We discuss this at appropriate points in the book.

Another difference that we noted, about which some partners were explicit, was the difference within firms between their New York office and other offices. A strong sense emerged that the work culture in the New York office of a firm is shaped more than the other offices by a keen sensitivity to market demands and by providing rewards to those lawyers who are most responsive to them and are most financially productive. Although New York–based lawyers experienced some camaraderie among their co-professionals, they did so mainly by participating on work teams rather than through other more informal forms of connection in the workplace. We note here this perception of the difference between the New York office and other offices in the firm, but do not discuss it further in the book.

Below is a short profile of each firm, which may be useful as a reference when we discuss any differences among firms. We have taken care to ensure that these descriptions do not include any characteristics that might be used to identify any individual firm.

Firm 1 at the time of our study was a firm of about 400 lawyers, which since has merged with another firm. Litigation was its strongest practice, although it contained some other specialized practices. The firm faced increasing competitive pressures as other firms in its market grew at a faster pace. After competitors in recent years lured away some profitable partners, the firm responded by more actively attempting to attract partners from other firms and to focus its practices on more profitable work. At the time of our interviews, Firm 1 was facing challenges because of its size, the lack of a distinctive market niche, and difficulty in leveraging work among its practices because of insufficient depth in the fields that it covered.

The remaining five firms all had more than 900 lawyers at the time of our study. Firm 2 traditionally had a strong litigation and regulatory practice. It has tried with mixed success to expand and broaden its corporate practice, although in recent years it has become strong in a specialized and highly profitable corporate field. The firm historically did a significant amount of pro bono work and encouraged its lawyers to spend time in public service, which it believes has provided a certain amount of self-selection among lawyers and helped to maintain a distinctive culture.

Firm 3 has had a strong corporate practice, and its partners traditionally regarded its culture as very collaborative. In recent years, it has engaged in a strong push for global expansion in an effort to expand corporate work along with other practices. It has had a strong managing partner in recent years, and its legacy home office continues to exert substantial influence in the firm. The firm emphasizes continuing growth, is very active in the lateral market, and is attempting to establish a more systematic process to integrate laterals into the firm.

Firm 4 historically had a wide range of practices in diverse geographical areas with differing rate structures, profitability, and partner compensation. It had especially strong relationships for several years with certain clients, which now have become less exclusive. This means competing with other firms for these clients' work. Partners spoke openly about the firm's culture, saying that it has had a more relaxed atmosphere than other large firms. Some said that the firm appropriately is moving away from this approach toward a system of greater accountability, with less tolerance for underperformers, while others expressed anxiety about the impact of this change on the firm's culture.

In the past, Firm 5 had a range of practices, which the firm is now trimming to focus on the most profitable ones. One practice area built through lateral hires has become especially profitable and now exercises considerable influence within the firm. Partners praised the firm's support for business development efforts, which they regarded as important in the firm's rise in financial performance.

Firm 6 historically formed close relationships with certain clients that are now less exclusive. It has a relatively broad range of practice areas that vary in profitability and, to some extent, it emphasizes growth less than other major firms. It disseminates information about partner compensation somewhat less widely than the other firms in our study, although partners can arrange with management to see this information. Partners spoke openly about the firm's culture. They generally regarded collaboration as an important aspect of that culture and believed that management encourages this in various ways.

With respect to differences among particular groups of partners within firms, we did not find any systematic differences in viewpoints based on seniority, department, practice group, office location, or service in a management position below top management. We did find that members of top management, such as managing partner or firm chair, generally are more likely to say that a firm has a distinctive culture and to be positive about it. There is more variation below this level, however, even among members of an executive committee or similar body. In general, lateral partners had somewhat more positive views of their firms than other partners, although the difference was not striking. Where relevant, we note within the book whether an interviewee was a lateral partner. We also found that "service partners," who generally do not generate revenues by attracting clients, held somewhat less favorable views of a firm than "rainmakers," who generate new clients. Where relevant, we note whether an interviewee was a service partner or a rainmaker.

We found more concern among women than men about opportunities to advance within firms. We discuss this finding mainly in chapter 3, but also in other chapters dealing with termination and compensation of partners. Finally, we did not have access to information about the revenues or profitability of specific practice areas in firms and so were not able to compare viewpoints based on this factor. We do offer suggestions at different points in the book, however, about how practicing in what are conventionally regarded as highly profitable and less profitable areas may affect what specific partners say about particular topics.

Our study finds that large modern firms increasingly face common pressures and deal with similar challenges. This is consistent with our suggestion that intensifying market pressures risk slowly draining firms of distinctive features beyond those based on business logic. Therefore, firms must make more deliberate efforts than in the past to preserve such distinctive features. We acknowledge that other studies with a different focus that rely on multiple methodological instruments may identify interesting differences among firms. We believe, however, that we have identified important dynamics that are common to large law firms.

Organization of the Book

Throughout the book, citations to quotations from partners indicate interview numbers. Chapter 1 sets the stage by briefly noting how the idea of a dichotomy between business and profession has shaped much of the commentary on the large law firm for more than a century. It then describes an alternative analytical model of sociologist Eliot Freidson that acknowledges that firms have always combined what can be called business and professional logics. We elaborate in this chapter on the need for a firm to solve both the Prisoner's Dilemma and the Assurance Game to sustain a culture that gives weight to both types of logic, and we describe how this task has become more challenging in the last few decades.

The remaining chapters draw on partner interviews to describe changes in the market for law firm services, how these changes are reshaping the relationship between partners and their clients and firms, and how firms' responses to these changes are shaping both lawyers' and firms' conceptions of professionalism.

Chapter 2 describes how the market for services has changed from a seller's to a buyer's market. Chapters 3 through 9 then discuss specific ways in which firms have responded to this shift, how these responses have affected partners' understandings of law practice, and the challenges that such responses pose as firms attempt to balance business and professional concerns. We tell this story largely through the words of partners themselves.

Chapter 3 discusses law firms' growing emphasis on lawyers acting as entrepreneurs and developing business skills in response to this change. Because this trend has major implications for advancement and compensation in law firms, we devote attention in this chapter to how this shift in what is valued affects the career prospects of women.

Chapter 4 analyzes the potential risk that an entrepreneurial emphasis can produce a culture in which partners focus more on their individual interests than the interests of the firm. We describe how fostering a sense of entrepreneurialism as a collaborative rather than solo effort can reduce this risk and create the conditions for both business success and professional satisfaction. Chapter 5 discusses how firms are more willing than in years past to terminate partners for what is regarded as insufficient productivity. We point out how the ways in which they do this can influence partners' sense of allegiance to the firm and their understanding of the values that it regards as important. We also note in this chapter how the entrepreneurial challenges that women may face in turn can make them especially vulnerable to termination.

Chapters 6 and 7 look at the ways in which compensation decisions play a crucial role in firms' efforts to encourage behavior that furthers financial success. Chapter 6 focuses on compensation as a material economy that allocates financial rewards. It describes the elements of typical firm compensation systems and how these elements are the product both of formal criteria and informal bargaining among partners. Chapter 7 emphasizes that compensation also represents a symbolic economy that involves the distribution of respect, in that it is seen by partners as an indication of how they are valued by the firm. As such, compensation can be critical in any effort to harmonize business and professional logics.

While chapters 2 through 7 discuss business pressures and how firms respond to them with respect to the partners in the firm, chapter 8 focuses on the lateral market. Even if a firm can create a distinctive culture that gives weight to both business and professional logics, that culture is constantly under pressure from the increasing rate of partner departures and arrivals in an active lateral market. How a firm deals with this phenomenon therefore can have a significant impact on its ability to maintain a balance of logics.

Chapter 9 focuses on the extent to which increasing business pressures are reshaping an important dimension of professionalism: lawyers' understanding of their role in society and their ability to play that role. Specifically, have changes in market conditions made partners feel less obligation to take account of concerns beyond the immediate interests of the client? Finally, a concluding chapter offers reflections on the insights from the interviews and what they can tell us about the ongoing efforts of lawyers to maintain a sense of professional identity in the face of intensifying business demands.

Business, Profession, and Ethics: A Final Note

This project began as an effort to identify what features of large law firms might promote ethical behavior. This focus led us to ask lawyers questions such as: Have you ever been asked by a client to do anything that made you feel uncomfortable? If so, did you raise your concern with someone in the firm? What was the response? Who decides whether taking on a matter would create a conflict of interest with another client? How much do ethical considerations influence that decision as compared to business concerns? Have you ever seen colleagues behave in ways that you regarded as ethically problematic? Did anyone in the firm raise any concerns about that?

Our discussions of these questions with lawyers were not entirely satisfying. We gradually realized that what lawyers regard as issues of ethical significance go well beyond matters that are conventionally defined as involving legal ethics. Questions that arise under ethics rules or the common law of professional responsibility do not exhaust the set of concerns that law firm lawyers regard as relevant when they assess the ethical environment in which they practice. Additional concerns include willingness to share billing credit with colleagues, giving up a client that poses a business conflict for the firm, taking time to mentor younger lawyers, giving up compensation for the sake of junior partners, grappling with how to deal with work and family conflicts, deciding how much time worked should be billed to the client, and considering whether to leave the firm and take clients along.

The need to make choices on these and other ethically important questions arises far more often for the typical lawyer than the need to decide whether to disclose an incriminating document or to backdate a legal opinion so that the client can gain a tax benefit. It is not the case, in other words, that lawyers in firms work in two different realms—one consisting of daily practice largely devoid of ethical significance or meaning, and the other involving more vivid occasions on which they must balance responsibilities to their clients and to the legal system in ways consistent with ethical responsibilities. Lawyers seek to live more integrated professional lives than this, infusing those lives with meaning through the creation of a normative universe that enables them to make moral judgments about a wide range of behavior. Some of this behavior may not be the subject of conventional legal ethics, but that does not mean that lawyers regard it as having no ethical significance.

In this respect, our experience has been similar to the one that Michael Kelly (2007, 4) describes:

> People in law practices with whom I talked were happy, sometimes even eager, to talk about their practice, their organization, and issues that worried them, but legal ethics was not high on the list, if it made the list at all, of what most concerned and engaged them about their practice. People had strong feelings ranging from pride to deep concern and even puzzlement about their practices. . . . I had stumbled on something different from what I had set out to find. I decided to abandon my original focus and simply describe law practices, to communicate the character, concerns, and thinking of people in the practice about their professional lives.

Thus, while chapter 9 focuses on how partners subject to increasing business pressures see their social role and its ethical obligations, it is important to emphasize that lawyers regard the issues we discuss in chapters 2 through 8 as also freighted with ethical significance. In this respect, the entire book depicts both the material and the moral worlds that large law firm partners inhabit.

1

Business and Profession: Bridging the Divide

The concern that law firm practice has changed from a profession to a business is hardly new. As Marc Galanter and Thomas Palay (1994, 908) observe, "contemporary misgivings about the commercialization of law practice are part of a long tradition of lamentation over the decline from the virtuous professionalism of an earlier day. That earlier era of virtuous professionalism always seems to lie just over the horizon of personal experience." This "declension thesis," as Robert Gordon (1984) describes it, depicts this transformation as a fall from grace. What we call the "first declension thesis" maintains that the fall occurred when large law firms serving major corporations emerged in the last third of the nineteenth century. Others subscribe to a "second declension thesis," which argues that the transformation from profession to business has occurred over the last three decades or so. Both versions therefore accept the thesis but simply differ about when the decline occurred.

This claim of professional decline, however, treats business and profession as inherently antagonistic. Every increase in attention to the business performance of a law firm then, is assumed to represent a corresponding decline in concern for professionalism. As we describe in the following chapters, the concepts of business and profession do speak to persistent important concerns about the nature of law practice in general and large firm practice in particular. When treated as dichotomous, however, they inhibit, rather than enhance, our understanding of modern practice.

This chapter first briefly describes the history of the fear that large firm law practice has changed from a profession to a business, and examines recent developments that have intensified this fear. It then describes Eliot Freidson's concept of a profession, which offers a valuable corrective to the tendency to conceive of law practice as a dichotomy between antagonistic professional and business elements. We complement Freidson's model by drawing on what is called institutional logics theory to move from the level of the legal profession to the level of the law firm.

This analytical framework highlights that until the last two or three decades of the twentieth century, many large law firms enjoyed what is called firm-specific capital based on their long-term relationships with clients. This meant that they had little need to adopt explicit measures to ensure profitability. The result was that firms had the latitude to fashion a particular combination of business and professional considerations based on their partners' views of what would provide a satisfying career.

Firms in the last few decades, however, have faced a much more competitive market. They are not able to use long-term client relationships as a form of firm-specific capital but must devote much more attention to obtaining clients and being sufficiently profitable. If a firm is to avoid being shaped solely by business demands, it now must seek alternative forms of firm-specific capital. Such capital can enable it to create a distinctive culture that strikes a balance between business and professional values under current market conditions. As we elaborate in this chapter, we describe this as the need simultaneously to solve a Prisoner's Dilemma and an Assurance Game. Simply put, a firm must convince its partners that it takes seriously the need to remain financially competitive while assuring them that the firm stands for something more than only financial success. As the chapters that follow illustrate, this is easy to state but can be very difficult to do.

Historical Background

For some observers, the large law firm has symbolized since its inception the eclipse of professional values by business imperatives (Green and Nader 1978; Strong 1914). For these critics, the profession fell from grace in the late nineteenth century.

Until the period after the Civil War, law practice in the United States was generally conducted either by solo practitioners or by two lawyers who shared office expenses while serving their own clients (Pinansky 1987). As business enterprises grew in scale and scope after the war, however, meeting their increasing and complex legal needs required larger law firms that could provide more wide-ranging and coordinated services. Such firms focused a significant amount of their time on business clients, helping to devise legal structures that could enable the emergence of economic activities of unprecedented size and complexity. Although lawyers were generalists by today's standards, they became more specialized in their attention to corporate and financial work.

The combination of law firms' larger size, their more obvious character as business enterprises in their own right, and their greater focus on work for large companies was seen as antithetical to the republican notion of lawyers as independent craftsmen who served the needs of local communities in which they were leaders. This latter conception is what Anthony Kronman (1993) calls the "lawyer-statesman." The fear emerged that this role was being effaced as law practice became assimilated into ordinary business activity. As Robert Gordon (1984, 61) observes, this anxiety was expressed in an "extraordinary outpouring of rhetoric, from all the public pulpits of the ideal—bar association and law school commencement addresses, memorial speeches on colleagues, articles and books."

An 1895 article in the *American Lawyer* (a publication unrelated to the current one of the same name), for instance, lamented that the bar "has allowed itself to lose, in large measure, the lofty independence, the genuine learning, the fine sense of professional dignity and honor. . . . For the past thirty years it has become increasingly contaminated with the spirit of commerce which looks primarily to the financial value and recompense of every undertaking" (*American Lawyer* 1895). One author noted in 1901 in the *Yale Law Journal*: "There has developed of late an idea which has found expression in the saying, 'The law is no longer a learned profession, it has become a business'" (Shelton 1901, 275; see also Berle 1933; Llewellyn 1931). Shelton continued:

> The distinction intended is not clearly defined in words, but it sufficiently appears that in the general estimate, there has been a marked decline in the standard of conduct which distinguished lawyers of a previous generation. That to the generality of the profession law is no longer a high and honorable calling, to the pursuit of which the devotion of a lifetime is demanded, and for the maintenance of whose noblest standards no sacrifice is too great. On the contrary the lawyer follows his profession as a means of earning his daily bread, he is prompted by no lofty ideals, stimulated by no particular enthusiasm, and seeks only such pecuniary rewards as will bring to him the luxuries of life before old age has deadened his powers of gratification. (275)

Another author in the same publication argued in 1913 that "the practice of law has become commercialized. It has been transformed from a profession to a business, and a hustling business at that. Financial interests have looked upon the legal profession with longing eyes, and have gradually corralled it and brought it under their domination for the profits which can be acquired from it" (Bristol 1913, 590).

The legal community responded to these criticisms by attempting to sharply demarcate law practice from commercial activity. It adopted rules prohibiting advertising, solicitation of clients, and contingent fees, and established minimum fee schedules for legal services so that lawyers would not compete for clients with one another on the basis of price. The American Bar Association Committee on Legal Education emphasized to law schools and practitioners the importance of "inculcating proper sentiments and of counteracting the evil effects of the introduction of modern business methods." Such a task, the committee said, should unite "all those who hold their profession as above price" (American Bar Association 1897, 382). Adoption of the 1908 Canons of Professional Ethics purported to express the distinctive values of the profession and obviated the need for outside regulation.

The major task of the professionalism project of the late nineteenth- and early twentieth-century elite legal community thus was to "preserv[e] . . . the distinction between a business and a profession" (Pearce 1995, 1238; see also Pearce and Wald 2012). By accepting constraints on their behavior, lawyers supposedly entered into a mythical bargain with society. Its terms were that "the profession agreed to use its skills for the good of its clients and the public. In exchange for this promise, society ceded authority to the profession, including the exclusive right to practice law and [the enjoyment of] autonomy from government and, to some extent, market regulation" (Pearce 1995; see also Rostain 2010). Lawyers were to be regulated by ethics rules adopted by the courts of the states in which they were admitted to the bar. They were committed to clients, but not beholden to them.

The claim of a dichotomy between law practice as business and as profession maintains that lawyers ideally practice in the market but are independent of its animating force, that they represent business but are able to stand apart from its influence. The fundamental premise is that "the interests of the client and the public are to take precedence over the lawyer's economic self-interest" (Solomon 1992, 147).

Proponents of the second declension thesis suggest that large law firms were able until the last two or three decades of the twentieth century to operate according to professional values beyond service to the client because limited competition for their services partly insulated them from business pressures (Glendon 1994; Linowitz 1994). For most of the twentieth century, firms and clients cultivated long-term relationships that lasted for generations. This meant that clients belonged to firms, not to individual lawyers. A 1959 Conference Board survey of almost 300 manufacturing companies, for example, revealed that companies generally were happy with their outside law firms and "have never given any thought to hiring another" (Galanter and Palay 1991, 34). One inside corporate counsel remarked in 1965 that legal service "is probably the only service we buy without some kind of survey of alternate cost" (34). Furthermore, firms generally were able to submit their bills with the simple notation "For Services Rendered" without any further detail about the basis for the charges. In addition, there was "a scarcity of information about matters such as billing rates, firm profits, partnership agreements, partner compensation, associate salaries, and even the identities of the firm's clients" (Regan 2004, 27).

These conditions effectively allowed large firms to operate as oligopolies. Oligopolistic firms have considerable ability to set prices and face only mild pressures for improving efficiency. They can eschew unseemly overt competition and explicitly focus on financial goals that characterize firms more directly subject to market forces. With a stream of predictable revenues and insulation from serious competition, they have the latitude to structure their operations with some nonfinancial considerations in mind and to establish a culture that reflects the firm's distinctive understanding of professional values. As one observer remarks of this period:

> How cases were staffed and billed, how partners were selected and paid, and how new partners were admitted to the ranks were issues based on internal considerations rather than market factors. Free to conduct their affairs as they wished, the established practices could all but ignore such boorish concerns as efficiency, productivity, marketing and competition. (Stevens 1987, 8–9)

Security with respect to the demand for their services created an opportunity to create distinctive firm cultures that reconciled business and professional concerns in particular ways. A significant measure of insulation from market pressures meant that economic considerations did not have to dominate firm policies and decisions.

Michael Trotter, for instance, describes a controversy in what is now the firm of Alston & Bird in Atlanta in the mid-1960s. Associates learned that the firm's billing clerk was not only using time slips to determine how much to bill clients but organizing them by lawyer and reporting this to management. They asked for a meeting with Philip Alston, the firm's senior partner, to protest this practice. The thrust of their complaint was that "keeping track of such information and using it to evaluate both associates and partners for the purposes of advancement and compensation would lead to competition among the lawyers to put in the most hours and that such considerations as quality of work and time spent on community service would be sacrificed" (Trotter 1997, 31).

The partners deliberated about the issue, and decided to discontinue the practice of reviewing individual lawyer billable time for what became ten years. As Trotter describes it, "because the firm had plenty of work and was growing, and because the partners were enjoying an increased level of income they had not anticipated, they agreed that such timekeeping practices would undermine the firm's close-knit culture and they saw no need to encourage competition among the lawyers" (31).

Mary Ann Glendon (1994, 37) suggests that "the concepts of professionalism promoted by bar leaders were remarkably stable and consistent from the 1920s to the mid-1960s." These created the sense in corporate practice of "certain dependable verities":

> Associates who did good work would ordinarily progress to partnership; others would be let down gently; partnership with its role divisions was a reasonably secure status; independence from clients could and should be asserted when the occasion required; economic considerations would be subordinated, if need arose, to firm solidarity or to ideals of right conduct.

As we describe in more detail in chapter 2, the conditions in the market for law firm services have changed significantly in the last three or four decades (Galanter and Henderson 2008; Galanter and Palay 1991; Regan 2004). Corporate legal departments have become increasingly large and sophisticated, with general counsel who are more attentive to the cost and efficiency of outside legal services. Clients no longer nurture long-term relationships with firms but actively encourage competition among them to provide services on particular matters. Clients also are sensitive to the cost of legal services. They actively negotiate with firms for discounts and other favorable terms, and they subject most matters to a budget.

These changes in market conditions have "encouraged a greater focus on business development and the marketing of professional services" (Brock 2006, 160; see also Brock, Hinings, and Powell 1999). Firms now tend to be more internally differentiated, "with a core staff of professional managers, and the traditional system of partnership governance giving way to a more corporate model" (163–64). In addition, "[t]he language of business—customers, market share, mergers, efficiency and profit—is increasingly the norm in contemporary professional organizations" (164). It is now common for partners to move from one firm to another, and for firms to terminate partners who are seen as insufficiently productive. A robust legal press devotes considerable attention to the financial conditions of law firms and the earnings of their partners, with information widely available on both.

Not surprisingly, these developments have led some observers to identify the last few decades as the period during which law practice declined from a profession to a business. Rebecca Roiphe (2016, 650), for instance, states, "Professionalism was a casualty of the 1970s." She argues that since that period the idea of "social professionalism" has given way to the notion of professionalism as "the delivery of services to clients in need" (652).

In 1987, Chief Justice William Rehnquist suggested that "the practice of law has always been a subtle blend between a 'calling' such as the ministry, where compensation is all but disregarded, and the selling of a product, where compensation is all important. The move over the past twenty-five years has been to increase the emphasis on compensation—to make the practice of law more like a business" (157). In 1994, law professor Mary Ann Glendon lamented that "several radical propositions that were once but minor tributaries or countercurrents have achieved respectability and prominence, if not dominance, in mainstream legal culture," among them being "that law is a business like any other; and that business is just the unrestrained pursuit of self-interest" (6).

Professionalism and Institutional Logics

As the short history above indicates, it has been common in analysis of large law firms to assume that profession and business are both distinct and antagonistic features of law practice. We argue in this section that these assumptions impair our ability to understand the complexity of large firms. Lawyers earn a living in firms that necessarily must operate as successful businesses to survive. At the same time, as the following chapters discuss in more detail, the notion that lawyers are professionals who are not simply selling services continues to resonate deeply among practitioners. We therefore need a conception of professionalism that situates it in the market to understand how lawyers and firms attempt to navigate this dynamic relationship.

One approach to the professions that provides such a perspective is Eliot Freidson's (2013) influential concept of professionalism as a "third logic" that organizes work differently from markets and bureaucracies. Freidson makes clear that the concepts of profession, market, and bureaucracy are ideal types, not representations of actual concrete phenomena. The ideal type of the market is a world in which individuals are free to buy and sell anything without regulation. Consumers are fully informed about the quality of goods and services and rationally choose those that provide them with the most satisfaction. "This world is organized around consumption, with consumer preferences and choice determining whose services will succeed" (1). The paradigm institution is the "spot market," organized solely by periodic exchanges, in which occupations emerge and disappear depending on consumer demand (46). The division of labor is based on competition among workers seeking to gain a living by satisfying consumer demand (55).

With the bureaucratic organization of work, the production and distribution of goods and services are planned and conducted by administrators in large organizations. Each organization is governed by a set of rules that specifies in detail each task, who performs it, and who can direct it, as well as the relationships among the activities (55). Executives and managers exercise control over those who produce goods and services with the goal of operating as efficiently as possible. The obligation of those who produce goods and services is to carry out the tasks that are assigned to them (67).

In contrast to the market and bureaucratic models, professionalism is an arrangement in which "workers who have the specialized knowledge that allows them to provide especially important services have the power to organize and control their work" (1–2). The occupational division of labor under professionalism "involves direct control by specialized workers themselves of the terms, conditions, goals, and content of their particularistic work" (60). The basis of this control is "discretionary specialization," in which a professional draws on abstract knowledge and specialized expertise to diagnose novel situations that require discretion and judgment in response to their unique features (23). The exercise of such discretion implies "being trusted, being committed, even being morally involved in one's work" (34).

Crucially for our purposes, Freidson notes that "[r]eality is and should be a variable mix of all three logics, the policy issue being the precise composition of that mix" (181). As he puts it, this mix should be based on an assessment of "whether the virtues of each are suppressed by emphasis on the others, and their vices excessively stimulated" (181). Furthermore, his model "assumes that the historic professions are occupations and that because, like all occupations, they cannot exist without some way of gaining an income, their position in the marketplace is the most appropriate foundation on which to erect a model" (5). All professions, in other words, are also businesses and therefore inevitably possess features of such enterprises.

Freidson thus suggests that we can place occupations on a spectrum rather than characterizing them as professions or nonprofessions. How they combine the three logics varies. Occupations may be closer or further from the professional ideal type based on the extent to which they have the ideal characteristics that Freidson identifies, and the extent to which their other features reinforce or undermine the values of the ideal professional type.

Relevant to the historical debate about the legal profession, we can conceive of the ideal types of the market and the commercial bureaucracy as particular expressions of a more general business logic. They subject workers to control by consumers and managers, respectively, in furtherance of the goal of providing goods and services. As such, they contrast with the occupational control of work that characterizes professionalism. As Freidson notes, however, all occupations must make a living. All occupations therefore inevitably must operate as effective businesses in response to particular market conditions, in the sense that they must adapt to the general dynamics of supply and demand.

This makes clear that professionalism does not, and could not, require complete independence from market forces. Instead, it reflects the extent to which an occupation under particular market conditions is (1) able to attend to the need for financial viability in light of market conditions while (2) simultaneously providing opportunities to realize the nonfinancial values of professionalism. Occupations, as well as individual organizations, should be assessed in terms of their particular mix of business and professional features rather than as falling in one category or the other.

Although Freidson focuses on professions in general, we can apply his framework to the large law firm in particular. As Kelly (1994, 17) indicates, "Global concepts of professionalism are refracted, if not replaced, by the day-to-day struggles over clients and governance and incentives within the practice organization." He continues, "We can no longer define professional values independently of specific organizational settings and cultures . . . because the particular configuration or relationship between economic and other professional values is worked out within each organization and emerges in the form of a distinct professional culture."

One framework for analyzing this phenomenon on the level of the individual organizations is "institutional logics." These are "patterns of material practices, assumptions, values, beliefs, and rules" through which individuals "provide meaning to their social reality" (Thornton and Ocasio 1999, 804; see also Besharov and Smith 2014; Thornton and Ocasio 2008). As such, institutional logics provide social actors with vocabularies of motives and understandings of identity (Lok 2010, 1308). Suddaby and Greenwood (2005, 60) suggest that in professional organizations,

> any prevailing institutional logic represents a truce or resolution, however temporary or durable, between contradictory underlying logics. That truce implies a complex of understandings—including role identities, boundaries around appropriate forms of organizing, and jurisdictions for work—that become embodied in larger mythologies of professionalism.

Scholars have tended to focus on what they call business and professional logics in their analysis of professional organizations. As we have suggested, Freidson's ideal types of market and bureaucracy can both be seen as examples of business logic, with consumers and managers respectively, rather than professionals, organizing and controlling work. As with Freidson, these logics are not distinct and antagonistic but may exist in different combinations within organizations. This directs attention to how elements of different logics may coexist in organizations and the degree to which they complement or conflict with one another (Smets et al. 2014).

The perspective of Freidson and the institutional logics approach suggests that from the late nineteenth to late twentieth century the large law firm had many characteristics that placed it on a point on a spectrum that was closer to the professional than to the business ideal type. Many firms operated in a "seller's market" that gave them considerable market power, and their lawyers directly interacted with corporate managers who had less legal expertise than they did. As a result, large firms had significant freedom to organize work and provide services without substantial client influence. This market power also made it unnecessary for firms to develop a specialized cadre of managers devoted to developing business strategy and coordinating lawyers' activities in furtherance of it. Under these competitive conditions, large firms were relatively distinct from both market and bureaucratic modes of production. This provided considerable latitude to pursue noneconomic professional goods.

As we have described, and as chapter 2 discusses in more detail, the balance of power has shifted from law firms to clients in this new "buyer's market." Firms now deal with more sophisticated general counsel and legal departments that exercise more influence over how firms are selected and how work is performed. The more intense competition for work requires that lawyers be more sensitive to client preferences than a generation ago.

In response to this development, firms are adopting more specialized and centralized management functions to formulate business strategy. As a result, lawyers face more bureaucratic controls, and clients and managers exert more influence on how lawyers perform their work.

The question therefore is to what extent modern firms can operate according to a professional mode of production that gives weight to noneconomic professional values. The notion that organizations typically reflect a mix of modes suggests that recent changes in the market for law firm services do not necessarily mean that law firms have become purely business as opposed to professional organizations. The question is rather what mix of business and professional features firms may establish in response to current market conditions, and the relative prominence of each. In the next section, we discuss an approach to thinking about the relationship between such features that moves beyond the business–profession dichotomy.

Business, Profession, and Firm-Specific Capital

That business and professional concerns might complement each other is illustrated by the work of Ronald Gilson and Robert Mnookin (1985). They analyze the operation of law firms during the period when many firms and clients had long-term relationships. They characterize these client relationships as "firm-specific capital" that helped bind lawyers to the firm (354). As they explain, individual capital represents the stream of income that a lawyer can earn in the market based on her talents, education, experience, and the like. Firm-specific capital is "the capitalized value of the difference between a firm's earnings as an ongoing institution and the combined value of the human capital of its individual partners, if this human capital were deployed outside the firm in its next most productive use" (345). As they put it:

> Because firm-specific capital can be neither easily removed from the firm nor duplicated outside the firm, the return on this capital is available to lawyers within the firm but is lost to lawyers who leave the firm. Examples of this phenomenon readily come to mind. Having IBM as a client is valuable to Cravath, Swaine & Moore, but if there is no individual partner who[,] upon leaving the firm, can take IBM with him, then the client relationship with IBM is an asset of the firm. Returns on this asset are available to individual lawyers only so long as they remain within the firm. (345–55)

Firm-specific capital is an important business asset that "allows the firm to staff more efficiently, while the investment by the client in establishing the relationship moves the firm from a competitive environment with respect to the client to one approaching bilateral monopoly." Gilson and Mnookin note, however, that "[d]eveloping and maintaining the client relationships that provide these benefits . . . requires a team effort" (369). Partners must be willing to cooperate and forgo the pursuit of immediate self-interest for the sake of maximizing the profitability of the firm. They suggest that lockstep compensation based on seniority rather than individual productivity furnished this incentive. The resulting culture of sharing not only provided financial benefits but also reinforced professional values that emphasized not shirking one's responsibility to others.

As we describe in more detail in subsequent chapters, partners in our interviews often described professionalism in terms of other-regarding behavior. This included pitching in to help colleagues without concern for personal reward, introducing clients to colleagues, being generous with sharing credit, being willing to forgo work to avoid creating a conflict of interest for another colleague, mentoring junior lawyers, taking on committee or project responsibilities for the firm, providing responsible advice to clients that does not put the firm or third parties at undue risk, adopting a reasonable interpretation of conflict of interest rules, and doing the best possible work in accordance with professional standards even if the client is less profitable than others. This type of cooperative behavior reflects some effacement of immediate self-interest for the sake of colleagues and the firm.[1] Lawyers regard firms characterized by this type of behavior as professional organizations.

Our interviews consistently suggest that Gilson and Mnookin's framework illuminates a crucial challenge for firms that foster such a cooperative culture while operating in a highly competitive market. Succeeding chapters provide an account of this challenge in more detail based on the comments of many partners across several firms.

Despite the movement toward more centralized law firm management, there are limits to the ability of management to require cooperative behavior from its lawyers. First, services to clients are provided on a decentralized basis by numerous lawyers who must exercise discretion to do their jobs well. Second, clients now tend to look to lawyers, rather than firms, for services. As we describe in chapter 8, this makes it relatively easy for partners with significant client relationships to move from one firm to another. Law firm management thus generally must persuade lawyers to engage in certain behavior rather than prescribe it.

Partners' willingness to engage in other-regarding behavior requires trust that their colleagues or the firm will not take advantage of them. A partner must believe that cooperation will be reciprocated and that frequent partner departures and arrivals will not prevent the formation of a stable cooperative culture.

How can a firm elicit such trust? At a minimum, management needs to convince partners that the cooperative behavior characteristic of professionalism will enable the firm to be a profitable and competitive business enterprise that will provide substantial financial benefits to its partners. If management can make this business case, partners will believe that the advantages of cooperation are evident to most people in the firm, which gives them confidence that if they cooperate, others will too.

Cooperative behavior thus provides a form of firm-specific capital that makes it more profitable for partners to practice at the firm than at other firms with less cooperative cultures. A firm with such capital is not simply an aggregation of discrete partner practices but a coordinated means of providing services. The ties created by such capital can reassure partners that a sufficiently large number of colleagues will remain who will reciprocate cooperative behavior over the long run. In these ways, the firm appeals to partners' long-term self-interest by emphasizing the financial benefits of professionalism.

Accomplishing this can be seen as solving the collective action problem that characterizes the Prisoner's Dilemma. In this scenario, individual preferences are ordered as follows: "(I) I do not contribute, but enough others do; (II) we all contribute; (III) no one contributes; (IV) I contribute, but not enough others do" (Lewinsohn-Zamir 1998, 387). Noncooperation thus is the dominant strategy for an individual regardless of what others do. Without any means of communicating with others or entering into an enforceable agreement to cooperate, it is rational for an individual not to cooperate. A firm that credibly communicates to its partners that cooperation serves their self-interest, and thereby generates a critical mass of cooperators, can make cooperation the dominant strategy.

The risk of this approach, however, is that it may generate only instrumental motivation to cooperate: loyalty to the firm is contingent on economic reward. Research on what is called extrinsic and intrinsic motivation illuminates the limitations of relying solely on extrinsic, or instrumental, motivation. (Lee and Martin 1991; Ryan and Deci 2000). Individuals may defect if they encounter situations in which cooperation is less valuable to them than self-interested behavior. This risk increases if partners perceive that the firm values cooperation only as a means to enhance profitability. This perception can create partner concern that cooperation could leave them at a disadvantage if the firm's real underlying concern is productivity. Furthermore, even if they regard cooperation as profitable, they may move to another firm that offers even greater financial rewards. Firm-specific capital based on financial self-interest thus can induce cooperation and enhance stability, but this behavior can be vulnerable to defection based on calculations of self-interest.

As we describe in more detail in chapter 5, our interviews indicate that many partners also regard cooperation as an intrinsically worthwhile good that expresses many of the values of professionalism. They would prefer to cooperate because they find it rewarding in itself. They are wary of doing so, however, if they believe that colleagues and management regard cooperation as only instrumentally valuable. This can inhibit the trust that is necessary to forgo immediate self-interest because others' willingness to do so is seen as variable and contingent. We are more likely to trust someone who has internalized the value of cooperation for its own sake than for the material benefits it can provide.

Management, then, must simultaneously provide assurance that the firm stands for more than profitability—that it regards the intangible nonfinancial rewards of professionalism as intrinsically, not just instrumentally, valuable. Credibly communicating this signals that it is safe to cooperate—that those who do will be rewarded because they embody important professional values, not only because such behavior enhances profitability.

This requirement can be conceptualized as the need to solve the Assurance Game. In this situation, an individual person's highest-ranked preference is that everyone contribute so that all will enjoy a common benefit. Her preference ordering is as follows: "(I) everyone contributes; (II) no one contributes; (III) I do not contribute, but others do; (IV) I contribute, but others do not" (392). This differs from the Prisoner's Dilemma, in which an individual's highest-ranking preference is "I do not contribute, but enough others do" (387).

An individual still may not cooperate, however, because she fears that others will not. This may create a sense of "hopelessness" in which people reason that "regardless of what they choose to do, the collective goal will not be achieved" (392). If they somehow had assurance that others would cooperate, they would too. The likelihood of cooperation in an Assurance Game thus "depends to a great extent on the existence and quality of information regarding the action that is likely to be taken by others (or likely to be expected by everyone to be taken by others)" (393). As we describe at various points in the pages that follow, a common term we heard that describes how a firm and its partners may credibly convey that they regard professional values as intrinsically important is that they are willing to take actions that "leave money on the table" (#52).

Solving the Assurance Game can provide a more durable form of firm-specific capital than solving the Prisoner's Dilemma. The reason it provides for staying at the firm is based on intrinsic, not simply extrinsic, motivation: that the firm has a distinctive culture that values both financial and professional goods. A firm with a culture that values cooperation for both financial and nonfinancial professional reasons can establish strong ties between partners and the firm that produce a stronger willingness to cooperate, and a more durable form of loyalty, than appeals to financial interest alone can generate. In this way, a firm's genuine commitment to professional values can provide it with a competitive advantage in the market.

A firm that seeks to balance business and professional values thus must solve the Prisoner's Dilemma by convincing its partners that it is a profitable cooperative enterprise that offers financial rewards to its partners greater than what they could obtain elsewhere. At the same time, it must solve the Assurance Game by credibly convincing them that the firm stands for more than this—that it also is a place in which professional values are regarded as intrinsically important. A firm that can achieve this balance has the opportunity to create a distinctive firm culture that can serve as a form of firm-specific capital. In this way, measures that further business objectives can vindicate professional values, and vice versa.

It was easier for a firm to satisfy these simultaneous demands in an era of long-term client relationships. Such relationships provided firm-specific capital that modern firms now must establish in some other way. This form of capital tied partners to firms, which made it rational for them to collaborate in maximizing the profitability of the organization. Lockstep compensation served the economic purpose of reinforcing this incentive. Market realities thus made it relatively easy to solve the Prisoner's Dilemma.

Secure client relationships also meant that it was less necessary for a firm to place explicit emphasis on obtaining business and boosting profitability. The absence of such pressure enhanced the credibility of assurance that the firm genuinely valued the attainment of nonfinancial professional rewards. In addition to its economic function, lockstep compensation could be seen as expressing this message. It eschewed reliance on productivity while reflecting a commitment to professional collegiality instead of competition, to the importance of high-quality work apart from profitability, and to rewarding the accumulation of professional experience and judgment. All this made it relatively easy for a firm to solve the Assurance Game.

Modern firms do not have the form of firm-specific capital that enabled firms a generation ago to simultaneously solve the Prisoner's Dilemma and the Assurance Game. They therefore must try to create it under intensely competitive market conditions. Chapters 3 through 9 draw extensively on interviews to describe what partners believe firms must do to meet this challenge.

Conclusion

This chapter suggests that the business–profession dichotomy may be best seen as a stylized account of competing values rather than an empirical description of the actual conditions of practice. That account posits that a firm organized according to professional values is insulated from the market. Its policies and decisions are based on nonmarket values that reflect its partners' aspirations about their working conditions. This allows the firm to create a particular culture with which its lawyers identify and that they wish to sustain. A clearly delineated boundary between the firm and the market thus is the prerequisite for professionalism.

The claim that law firm practice has changed from a profession to a business implicitly assumes that the boundary between the firm and the market is now completely porous. As a result, a firm's behavior reflects the operation of market forces unmediated by any consideration of nonmarket values. On this conception, the messages that a firm sends to its lawyers about what is desirable or undesirable behavior simply mirror market incentives. The firm is unable to create and sustain any culture that generates distinctive common sources of values and meaning that tie its lawyers to the firm beyond the pursuit of financial rewards. On this view, the modern firm has lost the ability to serve as an organization that balances competing business demands and professional values to forge a distinctive conception of professionalism for its lawyers.

It is true that most firms have lost the firm-specific capital based on long-term client relationships that historically provided an important form of glue. This makes the task of forging a distinctive firm culture a more formidable task than a generation ago. As we describe above, it requires firm management to solve both a Prisoner's Dilemma and an Assurance Game. A firm must convince partners that cooperative behavior serves their financial self-interest and must assure them that the firm regards such behavior as an intrinsically valuable professional reward. While this may be difficult, our interviews indicate that it is not impossible, and that, to varying degrees, firms and their parters regard it as important.

2

Clients in the Driver's Seat

As the previous two chapters suggest, modern law firms must balance business and professional logics if they wish to both succeed financially and embrace professional values. A crucial condition for accomplishing these two goals is some form of firm-specific capital that provides stability in the face of increasing competition for clients and lawyers. This chapter describes in more detail the market conditions under which firms must do so, and how those conditions reflect changes in the relationship between corporate law firms and their clients. It therefore provides a foundation for the discussion in subsequent chapters of what measures law firms are taking to respond to market pressures and the extent to which those efforts reflect business and professional logics.

Corporate clients now exert significantly more control over how law firms provide them with legal services. One important reason is that demand for many law firm services has been mostly flat or declining since the economic downturn of 2008. This has created a "buyer's market," in which clients are in a position to exercise considerable influence over how firms staff and price their work (Thomson Reuters and Georgetown Law 2019). As one article describes this shift:

> It's now commonly accepted that law firms lost their pricing power during the last recession. Up until around 2009, law firms could set their fees as they saw fit, with few clients having the audacity to push back. Annual rate increases above CPI were the norm. And while estimates might be provided

> for defined matters, they were generally ballpark indications rather than capped fees to which we were willing to be held accountable. Ah, the good old days. (Jasper and Lambreth 2016)

In addition, the market for legal services is more volatile since the financial crisis, with revenues potentially rising or falling for many firms from year to year. Observers believe that this is now a normal characteristic of that market (Cipriani 2018).

Demand for Law Firm Services

Demand for law firm services increased substantially during the early years of the twenty-first century. Between 2004 and 2008, purchases of legal services by business increased by 9.8 percent, or $15.7 billion. As one observer noted, "[E]ven when using inflation-adjusted results, and even taking into account the dot-com bust at the turn of the century, the Am Law 200 outperformed the broader economy for the nine years beginning in 1999" (Press 2014).

The astute law firm expert Bruce MacEwen (2013, 10) describes the past thirty years for law firms as "growing like clockwork at high single-digit rates, and never before September 2008 having experienced a sustained, systemic, enduring, macroeconomic downward shift in demand for . . . services."

This changed significantly with the economic crisis that began in 2008. A number of reports have documented that during the ten years following the crisis, demand for corporate legal services had not resumed the pace to which many firms had become accustomed in the previous several decades (Thomson Reuters and Georgetown Law 2018). Figure 1 shows the changes in the demand for legal services as measured by billable hours since 2007. It shows the gradual, then dramatic, decline that accompanied the economic crisis in the late 2000s, followed by an initial correction in 2010, and relatively tepid growth since then.

The year 2019 saw positive trends, with demand, rates and fees all higher than 2018 (Thomson Reuters and Georgetown 2020, 3). At the same time however, average billable hours were 123 a month, compared to 134 in 2007, which equates to 132 billable hours per year (7). For a firm of 600 lawyers, this means a difference in revenue of $35 million.[1] So even as legal spending by corporate clients has been increasing, a significant portion of that has gone to in-house corporate departments and alternative legal services providers (Thomson Reuters et al. 2019). Rate realization, or the amount that clients actually pay compared to what a firm's quoted rates would generate, contin-

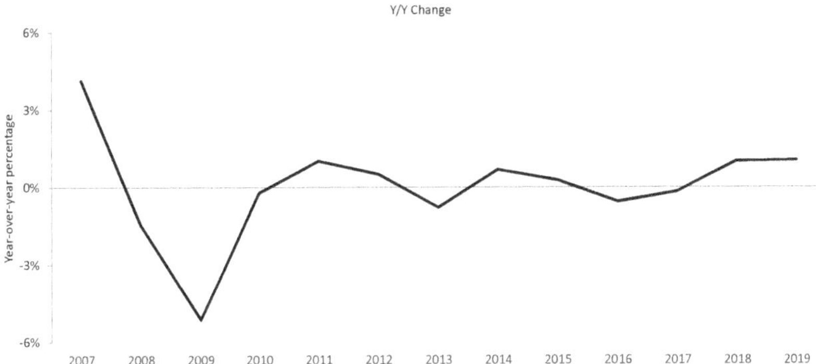

Figure 1. Growth in demand for law firm services, 2007–19. *Source:* ©Thomson Reuters, Peer Monitor®, and Georgetown Law 2019. Content reproduced with permission.

ued to decline in 2019 for AmLaw 100 firms, to approximately 81 percent. This compares to 92 percent in 2007 (Strom 2019). The difference reflects client unwillingness to pay standard rates, as well as negotiation over payment once a matter is concluded.

Our interviews indicate that many partners view the downturn as a watershed that dramatically and irreversibly increased the bargaining leverage of clients. Many also believe that it signaled a trend toward flat or only modestly increasing demand for law firm services in the foreseeable future. Indeed, some believe this market condition is likely to be permanent. One partner commented, "There is no question that the pie is shrinking for big law firms, whether you call that the top tier work or you just say the work that will pay our rates—that pie is probably shrinking. It may expand a little but we're never going back to the growth of the '90s" (#247).

As we will discuss, the increase in client bargaining power resulting from this decline has been enhanced by the growth of corporate legal departments and the expanded stature and responsibilities of the lawyers within them. A generation ago, a law firm's point of contact with a client was a business manager, who typically was not a lawyer. Now the firm's contact is an in-house lawyer who may have worked at a law firm and who often makes sophisticated assessments of the firm's work.

These changes are unsettling for lawyers in large corporate law firms. According to one partner:

> I think it's going to be like this for a while. There is a lot going on beyond just even the U.S. economy. You know it feels like there is a lot of adjustment and

> so finding a very secure place in that world for the firm . . . [is] what needs to be achieved. (#200)

As law firms and their partners attempt to adjust to these conditions, they confront both strategic challenges in meeting the demands of clients and questions about what it means to be an organization of professionals. In the sections that follow, we first describe the forces contributing to this change in demand. We then describe how this shift has affected the relationship between law firms and corporate clients.

Forces Affecting Demand

Greater scrutiny of corporate legal costs

The business climate since the 2008 economic crisis reflects increasing financial pressure on many companies from factors such as global competition, accelerating technological change, shareholder demands, and greater regulatory scrutiny. As the US economy struggled to regain buoyancy coming out of the recession, corporations relentlessly focused on containing costs (Campello, Graham, and Harvey 2010). These cost-cutting priorities have affected all business operations, including legal departments.

The pressure to minimize legal costs is a relatively new expectation for corporate legal departments. Legal services traditionally were regarded as less amenable to demands for efficiency than other types of activities because of the difficulty in predicting what services would be necessary to successfully complete a matter. A law firm generally did not provide precise estimates of what its representation would cost but simply informed the client of its hourly billing rate and the mix of partners and associates that it was likely to use. The client tended to defer to the firm's judgment about how best to provide services. The hourly rates reflected both the anticipated cost to the firm of providing an hour of service, as well as a profit margin. The result was an arrangement in which law firms had little incentive to focus on efficiency.

As legal costs sharply rose and economic conditions became more challenging, companies began to devote closer attention to what they were paying for legal services. Shortly before the economic crisis, Cisco general counsel Mark Chandler vividly described this emerging new reality in a widely reported 2007 speech. "The bottom line," he said, "is that I'm driven by the same need for productivity improvements as is the rest of the company. It's simple.

As Cisco gets bigger, the share of revenue devoted to legal expense needs to gets smaller." He continued, "Put most bluntly, the most fundamental misalignment of interests is between clients who are driven to manage expenses, and law firms which are compensated by the hour." Chandler described flat-fee arrangements he had made with various firms and noted the expectation that those fees would decline over time as the firms become more efficient in providing services. With respect to one area of legal services, he said, "We're aiming for a 20 percent cost reduction compared to our current global costs."

For corporate legal departments subject to stringent budgets, the uncertainty created by hourly billing rates is an anathema. According to one 2018 survey, over 75 percent of firms employing more than 250 lawyers report collaborating with clients on alternative fee arrangements (Clay and Seeger 2018). Furthermore, the most significant development is not such alternative arrangements, but client insistence on holding firms to a budget for a given matter. As one report notes, "the imposition of budget discipline on law firm matters forces firms to a very different pricing model than the traditional approach of simply recording time and passing the associated 'costs' through to the client on a billable-hour basis" (Thomson Reuters and Georgetown Law 2018, 10). Law firm lawyers must decide how best to organize their work under these new, more restrictive conditions. The same report underscores the demise of the pure hourly billing model by suggesting that matters subject to either a budget or an alternative fee arrangement likely constitute 80 to 90 percent of all law firm revenue (Thomson Reuters and Georgetown Law 2018, 17).

Movement of more legal services in-house

One way that companies reduce legal costs is to bring more work in-house (Sako 2010). Research conducted by ALM Intelligence suggests that as much as 75 percent of work done by legal departments is done internally, with 89 percent of respondents saying that cost and efficiency were major drivers of in-house work. "I think the big picture is . . . companies are a lot smarter about how they handle their budget," remarked one observer, who cited the recession as a key turning point (Williams-Alvarez 2017). For example, one senior law department official described to us how he reduced legal spending by focusing on who was doing the work. By increasing the number of in-house lawyers and moving away from outsourced legal work, he was able to manage his spending more effectively. He noted that this type of thinking is especially important as a company's legal needs increase.

Thus, not only are law departments able to save money, but in large businesses with a high volume of legal work, they are better able to manage their workflow in-house than by outsourcing to multiple law firms. The movement of work in-house is an ongoing process for many large companies. Clients have told us that they look at high-volume legal work such as contract management and human resources as good opportunity areas to increase internal resources—and with the souring fortunes of law firms, it is easier to convince great lawyers to come work in-house. The goal of these smart in-house leaders is to seek the optimal balance between inside and outside counsel.

The movement of work in-house reduces the overall amount of work available to outsource to law firms. As one partner remarked:

> One of the dynamics is not just about scrutinizing outside counsel bills [but] I think in many cases work [clients] used to give to outside counsel is now being done in-house and that's true across the board. And I'm keenly aware of that because I've placed a lot of the associates that have left our firm [at clients' companies] . . . and so I know their situations. And oftentimes they do send work back to the firm which is great but oftentimes they get instructed to do the work themselves you know and use internal resources to do the work. (#256)

Some partners speculate (and perhaps take some comfort in the idea) that the movement of work in-house could backfire on the clients. According to one partner with an environmental law practice:

> A lot of our associates went in-house and there is a lot of work there that is not being sent outside because of cost concerns. Environmental is never a profit center for business so it's always very carefully managed and they are way over-worked and not getting anything done. They know it and you know at a certain point something really bad will happen and that is when they call us. (#192)

Another partner, however, was more pessimistic:

> I was talking to the general counsel of a big company this week and he told me that ten years ago, of his entire legal spend 75 percent used to be outside, 25 percent inside. Now it's completely flipped. . . . So in-house counsel now

> does all the work, and the only work that remains is the highest value, highest profile work that goes to the smallest number of firms who hire the smallest number of best qualified kids. So when my son applied to law school I said, "If you don't get into a top ten law school and you're not in the top ten percent and your goal is to make a living—if your goal is to change the world, great—but if your goal is to earn a living, you're insane to be pursuing this career. (#79)

Increasing stature and responsibilities of in-house counsel

Another trend affecting the relationship between legal departments and law firms is the increasing sophistication and stature of in-house lawyers. The in-house career path has become more attractive, for instance, to midlevel and senior law firm associates. The American Bar Foundation's After the JD III study found that approximately 20 percent of lawyers entering the bar in 2000 were in business roles (with two-thirds practicing law in those roles) twelve years after their graduation (Nelson et al. 2014, 27). Attorneys move from law firms to legal departments for a number of reasons. These include an escape from billable hour demands, more predictable schedules, a more promising career path as the chances of partnership become more remote, and the opportunity to collaborate more closely with managers on addressing business issues. As lawyers move to legal departments, they often bring with them an insider's perspective on one of the company's key service providers.

These lawyers' understanding of how law firms operate gives them leverage when negotiating on behalf of the company with law firm attorneys. In particular, senior law department attorneys understand well the potential inefficiencies in law firm staffing models and which types of work provide what kind of value. They can use this knowledge to question a firm's staffing practices and make budget demands on firms. In this respect, they may intrude on some of the autonomy that law firms traditionally enjoyed in determining how to provide legal services.

Law firms have keenly felt this shift. According to one partner:

> [G]eneral counsel are becoming more and more savvy just in the eleven years I've been practicing. You see them understanding the game and they are all former partners at law firms anyway so they kind of understand the game as it is. But they also understand how to get the best service for their

> job, and especially now that there is not enough work to go around for the industry, they can choose the best because they know that really good people are willing to take on their matters. (#160)

Rationalization of legal services

Another factor affecting the demand for law firm services is a change in the relative value of different types of legal work. As professional services consultant David Maister (1997) has observed, professional work sits on a continuum between customized or "bespoke" legal work requiring complex skills and more routine work that is more akin to a "commodity."

The positions that various legal services occupy on the spectrum are not stable, however. Competitive pressures constantly push work from the higher to the lower end. As competition in a given practice area increases, firms become more cost-efficient in providing the services in that practice. They disaggregate work into many discrete routine tasks, assign them to the most efficient provider, and then reassemble the components by lawyers who add value to them by employing more sophisticated skills (Regan and Heenan 2010). Even high-end projects often have aspects that lower-cost workers can perform following a specified routine (Susskind 2008). As clients pressure firms to fixed-fee billing practices, the incentive to disaggregate increases.

Work that occupied associates twenty years ago is now done by other, less expensive sources of labor such as contract attorneys, paralegals, lawyers in lower-cost jurisdictions, or even by sophisticated software. For example, outsourcing to vendors in the United States and abroad has increased (Daly and Silver 2007). More and more, these outsourced functions include legal activities such as legal research and brief writing in addition to the more traditionally outsourced nonlegal activities such as document review.

As a result, legal work that begins as high-value, cutting-edge work done by elite firms eventually develops into a standard service that many firms can provide at a lower cost. This "legal services cycle" (Regan 2010) consists of (1) the development of an innovative service that generates above-market profits for its creator; (2) the enjoyment of premium profits by the first mover for a period of time; (3) the entry of additional firms into the market who seek to gain competitive advantage through more cost-efficient provision of the same service; (4) the standardization of many or even all facets of the service in furtherance of this goal; and (5) the transformation of the service into a commodity that corporate clients purchase mainly on the basis of price, with low profit margins for providers (Regan 2010, 115). The cycle can be found not only across different aspects of legal work but is present in other professional services firms as well. As Maister (1997, 28) has observed, "In every profession, one can point to practice areas that, in only a few short years, moved rapidly from being frontier activities handled by only a handful of innovative firms to high-volume practices offered by increasingly large numbers of competent firms."

The widespread availability of information and analysis on the Internet, innovations in global communications technology, and developments in work flow software and supply chain management have all served to shorten the length of the cycle. This means that law firm rates can be subject to ongoing pressure (Regan 2010). As one interviewee commented:

> There was a time when clients would pay a premium for folks like us because we were lawyers and we were good but it seems to me now that it has evolved more into a commodity type of service. (#147)

One example of the push toward commoditization is single-plaintiff employment litigation, a type of legal matter frequently handled by employment law firms where current or former employees are suing a company. According to one senior leader in a law firm with a large employment group:

> When the [single-plaintiff litigation] cases started, they were "bet the company" matters. But then they became a commodity and our clients told us, "We don't want to pay hourly for these—we should have greater predictability." (Rohrer and DeHoratius 2015, 6)

The realization that single-plaintiff litigation was now "commodity" work hugely affected how this firm priced and performed these services for clients. In addition, this newfound potential to routinize legal work has led to a surge in growth of alternative legal service providers, which seek to capitalize on the seeming unwillingness or inability of law firms to respond effectively to these dynamics.

Growth in alternative legal service providers

The emergence of alternative legal service providers (ALSPs) took inspiration from increased corporate offshore outsourcing of numerous functions to countries with lower labor costs (Regan and Heenan 2010). ALSPs began to analyze and isolate the steps involved in providing legal services and to offer to perform components of work being conducted by lawyers that could be performed as well and more cheaply by nonlawyers, lower-cost foreign lawyers, or lawyers in low-cost areas in the United States (Thomson Reuters and Georgetown Law 2017). A summary judgment motion, for instance, can be disaggregated into a series of steps that require only periodic review by a lawyer. To some extent, law firms had been engaging in this process by, for instance, delegating functions to paralegals that associates had previously performed. They rarely devoted intensive systematic attention to the process, however, because the hourly billing model did not create a strong incentive to do so.

As ALSPs have taken on work that otherwise would be performed by law firm associates, such as document review during discovery, large-scale contract review, or some types of legal research, they have cut into a long-established source of law firm profits. As one report observes, "Traditionally, clients looked to their law firms to provide a full range of legal and legal-related services, i.e., to handle every aspect of a matter, even including those activities that did not involve the direct provision of legal services" (Thomson Reuters and Georgetown Law 2017, 1). Now, however, companies are more apt to disaggregate services into discrete components and to assign the work to the provider who can competently perform the work at the lowest cost. One study found that 60 percent of corporate legal departments are using ALSPs for at least one type of service (2). Furthermore, ALSP as an industry is growing quickly, experiencing a compound annual growth rate of 12.9 percent from 2017 to 2019. Among the fastest growing ALSPs are the Big Four accounting firms. A survey by a group led by Thomson Reuters found that about 23 percent of large law firms report having competed for and lost business to the Big Four accounting firms within the past year (Thomson Reuters et al. 2019).

Law firms also are turning to such providers to reduce their costs in response to clients who insist on working to a budget. One report found that more than half of large law firms used ALSPs (Thomson Reuters et al. 2019, 6), and in 2019, about one-third of law firms had plans to establish their own ALSP affiliate within five years (2). As one law firm interviewee stated, "Any legal project can be broken down, and you can identify process-related elements [some of which require] . . . a different resource model" (3). As a result, firms are no longer able to rely as much on associates as a predictable source of profits. Instead, they must engage in the same type of routinization and delegation of services to low-cost providers as do their corporate clients.

Consequences for Law Firm-Client Relationships

Law departments attempt to contain costs in some of the ways we describe below. Their goal is to deliver legal services more efficiently and predictably. As one partner described this trend:

> There has been a fundamental paradigm shift in the way we do business, not [in] the law itself . . . but the economic underpinnings of our profession are changing. We need to not just hold ourselves out as being the best practitioners—we have to be the best practitioners weighed on a new scale that is the expertise that we bring to the table . . . plus how efficiently we can provide those services. So that need for efficiency . . . makes what we do not as fun as it used to be. (#182)

Greater client reliance on law firm specialists

Because law departments are populated with good generalist lawyers, they often have little need to turn to their outside lawyers for general legal advice. Clients thus tend to turn more often to outside lawyers for specialized services. One interviewee described his experience with this change in buying behavior:

> It was not uncommon in 1980 for a partner to be doing both the tax work and the corporate work on a transaction. . . . I was practicing in the '80s and I did both banking work and corporate work. I got to the point where—it was probably in the late '80s—when I just said I can't do both, I have to do one or the other, it's too complicated. . . . I think clients—especially as they get larger—really are looking for expertise in particular areas, meaning not just people that were smart but also that they had a lot of experience and prior experience. (#44)

In-house attorneys argue that they need to hire outside counsel to complement their in-house legal capability. Law firms' clients have told us that they have sought to build up competent in-house teams and then look to law firms when they need a particular expertise. With this expertise, law department leaders are looking for true experts who can identify and solve the relevant issue quickly.

One consequence of the demand for specialists is an increasing value placed on specific expertise both in the market for legal services and the internal law firm labor market. Lawyers with deep and narrow expertise are in good positions to develop close relationships with clients—relationships that may follow the partner if he moves to another firm. Clients often emphasize their relationship with a particular lawyer rather than a firm and are explicit regarding their loyalty and their intention to follow these partners to other firms, should it become necessary.

These client relationships result in rewards and recognition within the firm. At the same time, the attention given to stars can cause tensions. As one partner observed:

> Whenever you have to have established a reputation in order to provide sufficient comfort to clients particularly at the highest level of cases . . . the notion of having the reputation and providing the comfort and "stars" has become more important. And I think that inevitably that creates a little bit more of a sense of competition than has been previously because there can only be so many stars. . . . I mean you can't have everyone be a star and whereas the notion of stars was discouraged generally before, my own view is it is vital to a law firm's performance . . . [but] that cuts against the grain so you know the question is how one manages that set of issues. (#190)

Another partner from the same firm expressed a similar sentiment, sharing the impact of a star culture on the human capital of the law firm:

> The market is starting to look a little bit like almost sports teams, you know. We trade some stars, stars keep leaving and going—and the whole game if you are the coach is to temporarily get together a team and then it moves on. So I think that's the huge external pressure that law firms are facing and [the question is] how much do they succumb to that. (#213)

As we discuss in later chapters, the sense of competition that results can erode the collegial culture that large, well-established law firms typically promote among their lawyers.

Changes in purchasing policies

One of the most striking changes in the legal services market is the intensified pressure by clients on price. Firms traditionally sent letters to clients at the beginning of each year announcing increases in hourly rates and met with minimal resistance. Cisco general counsel Mark Chandler (2007) expressed how client attitudes have changed:

> Letters from law firms telling me how much billing rates are going up next year are . . . totally irrelevant to me, or as we say in Silicon Valley, orthogonal to my concerns. Think about it: not one of the CIOs of your firms expects to get a letter from Cisco explaining how much more our products will cost next year. And not one of our suppliers comes to us to tell us how much their prices will go up next year. So from my perspective, I don't care what billing rates are. I care about productivity and outputs.

Partners in law firms frequently expressed dismay at the level of pressure exerted by clients around issues of cost. As one interviewee said:

> I've been involved in several very compelling presentations to potential clients that just don't get off the ground because the price is not what they can pay and the price is already pretty low compared to what it used to be in my experience. So . . . that's a big change. (#147)

In addition, the rate that firms collect as a percentage of their standard rates (the collection realization rate) has been declining to an all-time low since the downturn (see fig. 2). This trend signals the pressure law firms are experiencing from their clients on fees because it indicates that clients are less willing to pay a firm's regular rates and have negotiated them down.

One partner commented, "I work for big corporates, they watch every dime, the notion that January 1 is an entitlement to raise rates—that's history. I mean, most clients negotiate your rates every year and will go two or three years without being able to raise any rate" (#150).

According to another partner:

> Most of them don't care about the hourly rate. All they care about is what the bottom line is going to be. So what if you charge $5,000 an hour if it's the same amount that they expect to pay. Some of them want more

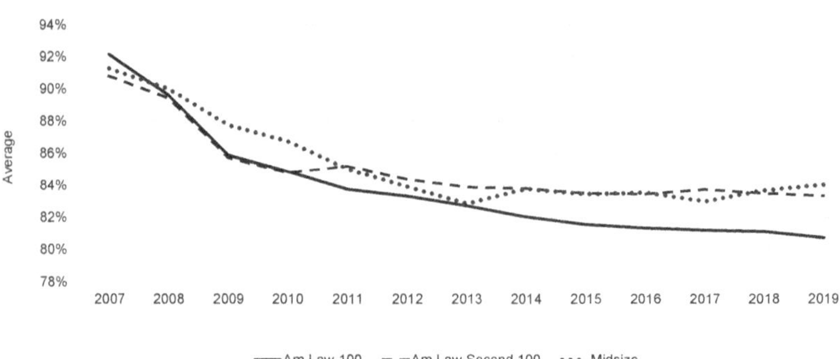

Figure 2. Collection realization against standard rates by law firm segment, 2007–19. Source: ©Thomson Reuters, Peer Monitor®, and Georgetown Law 2019. Content reproduced with permission.

> certainty from the beginning and so therefore [demand] estimates and whatnot. (#231)

One partner described the way that pricing pressures play out in conversations with clients:

> [We see it in] the amount of time spent talking about, "What is this going to cost?" and "Can't you give it to me for much less?" Or you know, "You've got to make me a special deal or I'm just going to take this to somebody else." Or, "You guys are just too expensive; I can't use you guys anymore." That kind of dialogue is just par for the course now and it really wasn't very common years ago. And it's becoming even more so now as there really is a disconnect between supply and demand much more now than there was even a couple of years ago. (#28)

Some partners acknowledged, however, that it is reasonable for clients to monitor costs more closely than they used to. As one said, "Even though it's not in my self-interest to say this, I just don't believe that it's always justified to have [a] massive legal effort on everything" (#168). Another noted, "I think clients are tired of just paying out the nose, and I think they are more savvy about what's best for the company and what's not" (#39). Still another commented, "I'm still sort of amazed by how much attorney's fees can be and when we take or do even a small matter that is resolved pretty quickly, it's still amazing; it's 'Wow, how do these companies continue to be willing to pay me so much?'" (#118).

Clients exert pressure by flexing their newfound power in the relationship. Some enhance their power by reducing the number of law firms they use and ensuring their status as an important client to the remaining firms. This process, known as convergence, often results in a "panel" of firms that do all but the most complex work for a client for a specified period of time (DuPont Case Study 2011). At the end of that period, clients often request that firms bid on membership on the panel for the next period. For example, a law department leader may look for a balanced portfolio of firms through an RFP (request for proposal) process to encourage competition. Once a panel is established, the client can distribute the majority of its work to those selected firms.

Client decisions also are based on an assessment of the importance of their work to a given firm. Some law departments can thus be quite strategic about ensuring adequate work to their panel firms to remain a significant client.

Firms may find panels attractive for at least a couple of reasons. First, panel work provides a reasonably predictable stream of revenues for a certain period of time. Second, being on a panel means that a firm has the opportunity to expand the relationship with its client by "getting its foot in the door." This may help the firm ensure that multiple lawyers provide service to the client, instead of one lawyer who may depart the firm and take the client with her. It also may enable the firm to engage in more complex and high-value work (Gardner 2016). Mitch Zuklie, global chairman and CEO of Orrick, Herrington & Sutcliffe, described the advantages of a panel to a reporter:

> Being a panel firm offers a distinct way to have a dialogue with thought leaders in an industry. These very sophisticated legal departments are the leading indicators of where an industry is headed. That relationship gives us the opportunity to know our client better. (Packel 2018)

The price of this opportunity is that a panel gives the client more influence over the law firms. Panel firms typically perform work at a discount to their standard hourly rates or work under other more unusual fee arrangements. They also typically share their work product among other members of the panel, and may collaborate with them on a given matter. Panels therefore appeal to both the business logic in the form of lower fees and more efficient delivery of services, and professional logic in the form of developing closer and more collaborative relationships with clients that are an important element of professional identity.

Clients also may limit the cost of law firm services by using procurement professionals in negotiating engagement agreements with firms. One interviewee described this trend:

> Now many of our institutional clients have turned over [the purchasing] function in part to procurement people and we have to bid. So even if we are the absolute only choice and we're very sure and confident that we are the compelling choice, we are then forced to alter [our approach]. [Clients tell us], "We would love to give this deal to you [Law Firm] but you need to show us some higher levels of efficiency. We need to structure our fee arrangements because I have firms that are lower cost providers that are not quite as good as you but they are good enough and we don't need you here."
>
> [So the situations where you can say],"Here is what we will charge on this bet-the-company litigation. If you want us to handle it, this is how much it will cost" are fewer and fewer and so that changes everything. (#182)

Despite their use of panels and procurement professionals, clients continue to insist that they "hire lawyers, not firms." This can provide law firm partners with a degree of comfort that, despite the changes going on around them, if they are able to keep their best clients close, perhaps those changes will affect them less than partners in other firms. As one partner said:

> I read all about [how] everything is changing, what the general counsels think about this and that, but frankly if you are a good lawyer and you are doing a really good job for them at the end of the day it's a human relationship and that is a relationship business and I don't think that has changed. (#177)

At the same time, this can limit the ability of law firms to create firm-specific capital because partners may leave and take clients with them. Joe Andrew, the global chairman of Dentons, which by 2018 was the largest law firm in the world, spoke to a reporter about the firm's meteoric rise since it was first formed in 2009:

> A new firm with a new name in the past might not have been competitive for 50 years because you had to build a brand. But in an era of metrics, allegedly objective valuations, and when nonlawyer professionals get involved in the process, it means that new law firms can spring out very quickly. (Packel 2018)

Andrew's remarks underscore the greater dynamism of the market for law firm services and the limits of law firm attempts to rely on historical reputation in seeking work. As we discuss in more detail in chapter 6, ties between firms and lawyers are much more fluid than before, which means that firms must strive constantly to retain the lawyers and clients that shape their reputations.

Closer supervision of law firm work

Clients are also reducing outside legal costs by more actively prescribing how law firms handle their matters. This can include directives relating to budgets, staffing, and expense recovery, as well as involvement in substantive legal decisions. Some clients, for instance, provide that a firm may recover only the cost of vendors that perform various tasks, rather than marking up the cost to include a profit. Many clients now insist that firms provide a "dashboard" showing what fees and expenses have been incurred on what tasks, and what portion of the budget remains for what services. Transparency is greatly enhanced by technology that enables legal departments to monitor and compare law firms on dimensions such as billing practices and staffing patterns.

Law firm partners acutely feel the effects of this trend. According to one partner:

> The days of . . . billing [simply "for services rendered"] are long, long, long gone. But the visibility is not just about seeing a detailed bill, the visibility is also about who is on your team. [Clients tell us], "I want to see the bios of every person you're staffing on this team. I want that to be the team and if you add or subtract anyone from that team—even a second-year, I want to know about it." [Clients also say], "I want a budget right up front, okay, and I want a run rate and I want to see if we're hitting the budget all along the way and to the extent there are deviations I want to talk about those deviations," etc. etc. And [they also dictate] what outside vendor can we use for this and what outside vendor can we use for that. There is tremendous, tremendous visibility . . . which makes it a lot more difficult. (#229)

Another partner commented:

> The banks are getting tough. In fact, I have one of the biggest investment banks that [requires that] the lawyers who work on their deals have to be approved at the beginning of the year . . . and you have to put everything [in]

> electronically and if you've got a lawyer on your bill [who] is not in their computer there are fireworks that come out. (#231)

Because much of law firm pricing is based on hourly rates, staffing practices hold significant interest for clients. Clients described to us how they look closely at who does their work; if they discover the work is too partner-heavy, they will bring this up with the firm. While some clients want fewer partners, others ask for fewer associates, especially if they value specialists. In these cases, experience becomes the most important quality. For example, when issue-spotting is the key task, delegation is not effective.

Very young associates are especially challenging to assign to client matters, particularly if the firm wants to bill for their time. Among the largest 350 US law firms, the number of entry-level associates fell from 7,703 in 2008 to 4,770 in 2012, a decline of 38 percent (National Law Journal Law Firm Rankings 2007–2012). While the stronger economy created more jobs for associates by 2018, the National Association for Law Placement estimated that firms with more than 500 lawyers hired fewer entry-level associates in 2018 as compared to 2008 (National Association of Law Placement 2019). As one lawyer observed:

> In-house counsel lawyers are happy to pay my rate for my advice because they are getting someone of sufficient expertise who has seen it before, done it before, can tell them . . . exactly what they need to do to get to where they need to go. But finding work for baby associates out of law school that will keep them busy—that's the type of work at the bottom of the food chain. Clients are saying, "I don't want it, I can do it in-house, I can do without," etc. So that I think is a problem. (#181)

The closer management of law firm work, in short, requires lawyers to adopt new skills:

> The budgeting, the insight . . . [for example, you might need to say to a client], "Hey we're going through discovery now and that's usually an incredibly painful process for you as a client but by implementing these measures I'm going to make it much less intrusive for you. I'll just work with your IT people as opposed to disrupting [your time] over this and I'm going to do it at 10 percent less than it usually costs any other firm to do it." You know, figuring out how to do that, . . . that's not how lawyers think. (#229)

With clients paying greater attention to staffing practices, law firm partners' autonomy over how work is done is increasingly constrained. One partner commented that the level of transparency that clients have is "frightening":

> [T]here are software vendors out there . . . that clients can employ who then will insist you hook up to [their] billing system because [they] want to see, for example, not so much [the number of] hours but when the hours were entered [and] take the view if a lawyer enters hours 30 days after he [performs the work] they are no good. So they want that kind of real time information. (#255)

24/7 Availability

One consistent theme in the interviews was the need to be available to clients virtually around the clock. One partner observed:

> A big change happened to the practice when Federal Express came in because it used to be you would mail stuff out, you just put it in the mail to clients. Things were much slower back then. Then [with] Federal Express the deadline was 7:00 pm and everything would go until then and now it's much more of a 24–7 kind of thing. I mean, I can get calls at nights and on the weekends. Nobody thinks a thing about calling you on your cell phone. Before we had cell phones people couldn't reach you, [but now it's] a 24–7 type commitment. (#177)

Another partner noted that a client expected an outside lawyer to treat its case as "the most important case in the world." The partner added, "It's like 'I want it and I want it now,' and it's 24/7 availability, it's no vacations really unless you are smart and can figure out a way to do it even when you are on vacation" (#157). One partner described his firm's policy on responding to clients: "Within a couple of hours we'll respond if you'll send us something, unless you are very clear with whoever you are working with or your clients, [and say] you are going to be out for a certain time, and the expectation is very high with regard to the response" (#141). Another noted that "weekend days increasingly are treated as week days where you just might not be at the office. On a typical Friday afternoon a lot of things will invariably come through, and [the client asks,] 'gee, could you let us know Monday morning or Sunday evening?'" (#104).

Such demands can create challenges for partners with significant family responsibilities. These partners often are women. One mother described how she handles these competing obligations:

> It's hard for me to have a hard stop to get home by six to let the nanny go. . . . I leave in the morning before anybody wakes up but I have to be there [in the evening] and that is very hard, even though I pick up and work after that. Even the transition [from work to home where I am] . . . unavailable for 45 minutes, . . . I take calls from a cab but you try to keep this perception going that you are available 24/7 and then you just try to work your life around it. (#254)

Conclusion

Flat or declining demand for law firm services has significantly increased corporate clients' bargaining power with law firms. As this chapter describes, clients now exercise much greater control over how law firm services are priced and provided. One partner reminisced about the period before this shift:

> The power in the relationship has completely up-ended itself I think. When I started, we were maybe at the tail end of when you could send a bill that says "January for services rendered $500,000" with no explanation. And clients had their big lawyers like a firm like [ours] up on a big pedestal and whatever they said you know was the gospel. I'm sure I'm exaggerating this as I look back at the good old days, but there was really a power relationship in which the client sort of accepted what they got. And [clients had] a very, very deferential respectful view of their lawyers and for the most part there wasn't a great deal of cost competitiveness going on. (#28)

The trends we describe clearly have increased financial pressure on law firms and forced them to focus more than ever on efficiently delivering services. In this respect, these recent trends have heightened that law firms are engaged in a business. At the same time, by reducing the asymmetry of legal sophistication between law firms and their clients, these developments have reduced the risk that firms may take advantage of clients because of firms' superior bargaining power and knowledge (Wilkins 1992, 819–20).

Some partners we interviewed were candid in questioning whether the traditional arrangement served clients' best interests. As one partner put it, "I don't think we can continue to increase rates based on the internal dynamics of a firm or based on what our competitors are doing. I mean, this is an odd situation where you don't take guidance from your customers about what the rates should be. [Acting] without too much concern about the client's reaction [can't] continue" (#78).

Some partners also suggested that the more equal relationship between firm and client that results from the involvement of in-house counsel reinforces values of professionalism: "If they need an answer now, they need an answer now and they are desperate. It's the expectation that we will get back to our clients immediately, which is good because that is the business we are in, we have to do that" (#39).

At the same time, there is no denying that law firms now face more intensive client demands and enjoy less financial stability. This means a greater role for law firm management in seeking to regulate lawyers' behavior so that a firm remains competitive. The chapters that follow describe the ways in which management has responded to these market realities and how these measures reflect and shape the balance of business and professional logics in the large law firm.

3

Encouraging Entrepreneurs

Traditionally, lawyers in major firms focused on "work that was more intellectual than purely commercial." A partner "rarely had to hustle for business. He could focus his energy on the legal pursuits that excited his analytical mind" (Scheiber 2013). Janice McAvoy, who was promoted to partner at Fried, Frank in 1995, is quoted as saying that when she was promoted the business model was "'wait for the phone to ring' and do a good job for the client on the other end" (Randazzo 2019).

Stagnant demand, unstable client relationships, and irregular flows of business have changed this. Firms now must explicitly focus on ensuring that they have enough work from clients to be competitive and even to survive. As one leader of an AmLaw 50 firm put it, "None of us are getting a huge percentage of our revenue from repeat institutional clients the way we all did 20 years ago or even 10 years ago. . . . [Y]ou have to replace work every year, every six months, every two years." Another partner explained, "You can't pay a guy writing briefs seven hundred, eight hundred, nine hundred thousand, a million dollars." Business skills have become more important. Associates eventually learn that "brainpower is only incidental to their professional advancement—the real key is an aptitude for schmoozing" (Cipriani 2018).

Today's firms therefore emphasize that their lawyers, especially partners, must continuously seek business opportunities to generate a steady stream of revenues. One partner described how his firm emphasizes this need: "We have a daily five o'clock email from our marketing department that goes out identifying all the client pitches that have been made, every client we've pitched to and then who put the presentation together, who presented and we have between two and ten a day" (#250).

Lawyers frequently use the term "entrepreneurial" to describe this orientation. Said one partner, people who are entrepreneurial "don't just sit there and wait for the phone to ring" (#184). Instead, they seek opportunities to discuss with prospective clients how the firm can meet their needs, approach current clients about increasing the amount of work done, and remain busy by seeking work from colleagues in the firm. Entrepreneurs thus have high "productivity" in that they avoid "down time" that does not contribute to generating revenues for the firm.[1]

This emphasis on being entrepreneurial makes selling one's services a much more significant feature of law practice than it used to be. One partner emphasized, "There is no doubt that the firm is going to need to be more entrepreneurial. That is the way of the world and lawyers are reacting to that in a way that goes out to try and cross-sell, to market, to have more emphasis on marketing. There is a lot more of that now than there ever was. . . . I mean, just the nature of everything has changed [in this way]" (#187). Another observed, "The practice of law is much more entrepreneurial than it used to be" (#245).

On its face, this emphasis seems a straightforward expansion of business logic in law firms. Partners in firms now must engage more actively and directly in selling their services, rather than focusing on law practice in the assurance that the firm will provide a sufficient stream of work. For those who subscribe to the business–profession dichotomy, this increase in commercial activity produces a corresponding decline in the notion of law practice as a profession.

As we will see, however, the practice of entrepreneurialism can exemplify both business and professional logics; the two complement each other. When this is the case, being entrepreneurial can align firm and individual interests, as well as financial and professional rewards.

In some instances, however, the logics may conflict. This can drive a wedge between the firm and the lawyers within it and lead to a more competitive internal culture in which business logic tends to prevail. The modern need for a lawyer to "be entrepreneurial" therefore must be understood in terms of the conditions under which business and professional logics are likely to be experienced as complementary or conflicting. Another layer of complexity is that these conditions are not static but constantly changing. Any given configuration of logics in a firm necessarily will be provisional rather than permanent.

This chapter describes these dynamics, which significantly affect firms and the lawyers within them with respect to matters such as advancement and compensation. As the chapter discusses, women may face particular challenges in an entrepreneurial culture. Women may be more vulnerable to the "pruning" that we describe in chapter 5; to receive lower compensation under the systems that we discuss in chapters 6 and 7; and to benefit less from the lateral market that we describe in chapter 8.

Being an Entrepreneur

What does it mean for a partner to be an entrepreneur? A successful entrepreneur is aware of the continuous need to seek out opportunities to sell her services:

> I think it's a realization you come to if you are cognizant of the fact that this is a business, and there is a business model, and for it to work people have to bring in clients and the way you do that is to sell your services. We're not doing billboards, but we have to market ourselves to clients and you have to go to things where you can meet more people and network and all that stuff. (#241)

This requires attention to activities that do not directly generate revenue because they cannot be billed to a client. One practice group leader described his efforts in this regard:

> You always have to be on the hunt for new clients and what that means is that you spend a lot of time every day not only doing your client billable work but also doing client development things. So yesterday was a good example. I convened a lunch with a prospective client and a couple of the new partners, so that was a couple of hours of my day. I wrote them a follow-up note; it was almost like three hours, so that eats into your billable time. There's only so much time in a day. And especially practice managers—but really everybody—has to recognize that that's very much a part of the job these days. (#256)

The need to market one's services is more pressing in some practices than in others. One junior partner, for instance, described her bankruptcy practice as one in which "it's not like these are corporate clients that have been with the firm and will be corporate clients for the firm forever. We have to build every single deal that we get from scratch, whether it's pitching, developing relationships, so in my department from a very young age you are taught that business development is a really big deal" (#178).

Another young partner recognized early in his career the need to pursue relationships with clients:

> INTERVIEWER: So in your own practice now, the work you get, is it a mix of your own origination and referrals from others?
>
> PARTNER: For me at this point there is very little that I am not originating.
>
> INTERVIEWER: And so how did you get to that point from the time you got promoted?
>
> PARTNER: A lot of aggressive marketing.
>
> INTERVIEWER: So what kinds of things can you do?
>
> PARTNER: A lot of it is mentality, even as an associate, looking for opportunities to develop relationships with people and existing clients where I had been introduced, stay in touch with people, and those people grew into roles that they could make their own decisions and call me directly or they move on to another place that is not an existing client.
>
> I mean, be nice to associates. Associates are great; people don't realize that, but a lot of those people are going to go off and become very successful at some other place. They are smart people, so I try to cultivate those relationships. (#203)

For this partner, the fact that most of his work comes from matters that he originates makes him a rainmaker. That is, most of the revenue that he generates comes from work for clients with whom he has relationships rather than clients of other partners.

Many partners at least initially aspire to be rainmakers—to enjoy a consistent flow of work based on relationships with highly profitable clients who regularly turn to them for services. For partners with this aspiration, selling their services focuses mainly on seeking additional work from existing clients and prospecting for new ones. One partner described her strategy in this way:

> For the three clients that I am currently doing the most work for, the plan is to try to meet with them in person at least twice a year outside of scheduled meetings that we're having just to discuss ongoing matters, just to have face

> time and meet with them and continue building the personal relationships I have with those people. (#201)

Even many rainmakers, however, still rely on referrals from colleagues for some of their work. The prevailing wisdom is that it is easier to obtain new work from existing clients than to acquire new ones. This makes other partners in the firm potentially valuable sources of additional work. One partner describes his efforts to market himself to other partners in the firm:

> I'll try to cross-sell to my partners, which is what you do for practice development in a big firm. You don't go out and get a brand new client, because [often] they are going to be conflicted out if you bring them in. So you meet your colleagues and you describe what you do. So [for instance] you go to a transactional practice and say, "You know, I understand there is a lot more demand to do Foreign Corrupt Practices Act due diligence in a transaction; you should think about that, [and] call me if you have a deal." (#254).

Most partners cannot realistically hope to be major rainmakers. Some may have personal relationships with only a small number of clients, while others have none. For these lawyers, the revenue they generate comes from the amount of hours that they bill. This makes having a full workload crucial. Selling their services to other partners is essential to achieving this. Hence, these service partners must be entrepreneurial by marketing themselves *within* the firm so that rainmakers will look to them to do work for their clients.

The need for such internal marketing is often especially critical for junior partners. "The reality," one such partner said, "is that for a junior partner it's going to be very difficult to bring in a matter, especially a client that is going to be willing to pay our rates" (#239). As a result, ensuring that you have enough work involves "advertising your skills and your abilities and the added value you can bring to the table to other partners in the office or the firm [who] have a book of business and clients who need service" (#239).

Even if a partner does not have experience in a specific field in which another partner needs help, she may still be able to sell general skills that contribute to the other partner's work. One partner who specializes in a particular type of litigation, for instance, described going to other practice groups and saying, "'I'm a litigator, and even though I haven't done work [in your specialized area] I can do your arbitration because I've got this package of litigation skills, so staff me on your matter'" (#239).

Becoming known to other partners in a large firm with multiple offices can take considerable effort. "You can send emails," one partner said, "but people who are very busy don't read emails . . . you're never going to get work off an email. It's getting in front of them and really attempting to develop a personal relationship with them" (#239). That's why it's important "even if you're a senior associate [to] make sure that you've got a reputation with the junior partners and build those relationships" (#239). Marketing yourself internally thus involves "getting to know partners, trying to get opportunities to work with them, and getting your name around to partners in other offices" (#252).

The need for partners to take responsibility for generating revenues can be a sharp contrast to their experience as associates. Firms make some effort to ensure that associates have enough work and, ideally, provide them with opportunities to develop various professional skills. Moreover, associates generally are not expected to develop client relationships or even to bring in new matters from existing clients. "As an associate," one junior partner commented, "you are in a regulated world" (#101).

By contrast, "as a partner, you are in a completely deregulated world. . . . It's a completely free market system" (#101). Another partner observed:

> When you're a senior associate everybody wants your time because you know what you're doing and they can turn over a lot of work to you. When you're a junior partner, you're still the same lawyer that you were two years ago before the turnover, but bringing in another partner [like you] onto the case and justifying that to the client [can be a problem]. Other partners are trying to make sure they are staying busy and they are keeping themselves fully occupied and have a good pitch to the management committee when they've got to justify themselves at the end of the year. It's much more that you're out there on your own. (#239)

Similarly, another junior partner observed:

> Maybe I should have realized it and just didn't as an associate, but once you're a partner it's hard because senior associates could do a lot of the stuff that you do and they are cheaper, and . . . you have to find someone who has work to give you. There are very few junior partners who have their own clients, who are bringing in work, so you are reliant on other people to give you work. Everybody has their person and if you are not someone's person then it's harder. (#241)

Service partners can generate considerable revenue for the firm based on their hourly billings. Some of them nonetheless are concerned that this may not be enough to provide job security. One such partner acknowledged, "I think for a lot of people, younger partners, I mean we talk about this a lot. If I don't develop business, am I going to have a job in five years, just given the nature of recent changes?" She continued, "This used to be a place where there were all sorts of service partners and I still think that that's true now, but I don't think that that's optimally where management wants us to be. I get that and I think younger partners get that. Senior associates get that and I think that is what makes people anxious" (#188).

Whether a partner is a rainmaker or a service partner, the goal of being an entrepreneur is "staying busy." Staying busy is increasingly important for job security, and partners are acutely aware of whether they are doing it. "We're aware of it on a constant daily basis," one partner said, "because we record our time and so you can see every day I'm not filling my day or I am filling my day and you've got that real time feedback" (#239). Another said, "I think lawyers at [the firm] recognize that they need to bring their A+ game in being productive here every day, and if their practice area turns down or their ability to attract business turns down I think people recognize that then the opportunities need to go to the younger people or the lawyers of their vintage who are continuing to be productive" (#196). Another observed:

> PARTNER: So the struggle is making sure there is enough work and in making sure there is always something in the pipeline.
> INTERVIEWER: And that's something you can never take for granted.
> PARTNER: You can never take for granted. (#251)

One partner who moved to a firm from a corporate legal department was generally satisfied with his move but noted the difference between the two settings:

> PARTNER: When you are in the law firm you always think about where your work is coming from. You're always thinking about, "Am I busy enough?" If you are too busy you are miserable, when you're not busy you're miserable because you would rather be busy, and so there is never that perfect level of work—there never will be—because, quite frankly, given the way we make money we just always want to be too busy.
> INTERVIEWER: I see.

> PARTNER: And this is an uncomfortable place to be, to be always thinking about wanting to eat more even if you're stuffed. And I think there are certain days where you really are operating at like peak business, where you're working maybe like 15 hours a day and then you don't think about it, but you know if you are only working 10 hours then you're thinking I could be working more. I could be doing stuff so that other people can be working more, and so you're always thinking about it. I think that's the worst part of it. (#245)

This concern has become especially prominent since the economic downturn began in late 2008. Hours billed by partners have declined since then, and projections are that demand for law firm services is unlikely to increase much in the next several years (Georgetown Law Center for the Study of the Legal Profession/Peer Monitor 2018). This makes staying busy a persistent challenge for many lawyers.

Women and Productivity

Because being entrepreneurial and productive are so important to success in the modern law firm, we provide most of our observations on women in this chapter. We also allude to some of these findings in our chapters on layoffs (chapter 5), lateral hiring (chapter 8), and compensation (chapters 6 and 7). In addition, in the chapters on compensation, we discuss women's challenges in bargaining for origination and other credits within the firm's internal market.

About 31 percent of our interviews were with women, which is higher than the percentage of female equity (20 percent) and income (30 percent) partners in the AmLaw 200, according to the latest survey by the National Association of Women Lawyers (Peery 2018, 7). Our research was not structured to focus specifically on women in large firms, nor did it involve random sampling that could rigorously identify differences in the experiences and attitudes of male and female partners. We therefore cannot offer definitive conclusions on the situation of women in large firms. Our interviews did, however, provide some support for findings in other research that suggest that women face distinctive challenges in succeeding in the law firm environment. These relate to various aspects of law firm life.

Women have comprised roughly half of law school students for over a decade, and law firms recruit them roughly in this proportion each year (Peery

2018, 2). As the NAWL data indicate, however, the percentage of female partners in large firms is considerably lower. Furthermore, a 2018 survey of the largest 350 firms by the *National Law Journal* found that just 19 percent of equity partners are female (Rozen 2018). Other research confirms that women are less likely to become partners than men with comparable credentials (Beiner 2008; Gorman and Kmec 2009; Noonan, Corcoran, and Courant 2008; Rhode 2014).

With respect to compensation, a 2018 survey of AmLaw 200, *National Law Journal* 350, and Global 100 firms by legal recruiting firm Major, Lindsey & Africa (MLA) indicated that women were six times as likely to perceive a pay gap than men (Lowe 2018). The 2018 NAWL survey showed that the median female equity partner earns 91 percent of the median male partner earnings, and the mean female equity partner earns 88 percent of that of her male counterpart. As the study noted, the lower percentage for the mean equity partner "support[s] the hypothesis that the compensation distribution skews higher for men than for women," and that "men tend to have near exclusive domain over the most highly compensated roles in the firm." Compensation data reflect this fact: in 93 percent of the firms, the highest compensated partner is a male; and, of the ten highest compensated partners in firms, on average one is a female (Peery 2018, 13). Other studies confirm these compensation disparities (Rhode 2014; Sloan 2013; Williams and Richardson 2010).

These differences exist despite no meaningful gap in the median or mean hours billed by female and male equity partners. Even though men and women have roughly the same number of billable hours, the value of the billing by the median female partner is 92 percent of the median male partner, which may reflect the fact that male partners' billing rates are about 5 percent higher than those of their female counterparts (Peery 2018, 14). This figure is consistent with other research that finds that female partners in firms with 1,000 or more lawyers bill at a rate of 10 percent less than men, and at a rate of 12 percent less than men in firms of between 500 and 999 lawyers. Some 51 percent of men in firms with 1,000 or more lawyers charge over $500 per hour, compared to 31 percent of women (Silverstein 2014). Thus, "even when women do report originating similar amounts of work, they still earn less most of the time" (Lowe 2014).

The most significant reason for the difference in male and female compensation, however, is the larger amount of credit that males receive for originating new business. The MLA survey notes, "Male partners are significantly outpacing female partners in originations. Male partners reported average originations of $2,788,000, representing an 8 percent gain over 2016. Female partners, however, after posting a 40 percent gain in originations between 2014 and 2016, are now reporting an 8 percent decrease, with average originations of $1,589,000" (Lowe 2018, 24). The value of women's originations, in other words, is 43 percent of the value of men's.

This is consistent with data from the NAWL survey indicating that women are less likely to be relationship partners in firms. On average, the total number of such partners assigned to a firm's top twenty clients was thirty-nine, of whom eight (21 percent) are women (Peery 2018, 9).

The MLA survey found that 33 percent of female partners had varying levels of dissatisfaction with their compensation, compared with 23 percent of male partners (Lowe 2018, 33). This finding of a difference between men and women is consistent with other research (Reichman and Sterling 2004), indicating that female partners who are "dissatisfied" or "extremely dissatisfied" with compensation comprise 31 percent of female equity partners and 38 percent of female income partners (Williams and Richardson 2010, 613). A 2019 American Bar Association/ALM survey of 1,262 partners in the *National Law Journal* top 500 firms with at least 15 years of seniority found that 28 percent of women and 12 percent of men were "extremely" or "somewhat" dissatisfied with their compensation (Liebenberg and Scharf 2019, 6).

The difficulties that women face in balancing work and family obligations play a role in producing these disparities. This juggling act has been the subject of extensive research and discussion (Gough and Noonan 2013; Hodges and Budig 2010; Pinnington and Sandberg 2013; Reichman and Sterling 2013). Hochschild and Machung (2012) note what they call the "second shift," which reflects the additional time working women spend taking on domestic duties such as childcare and housework. At the same time, work demands typically are based on what Joan Williams terms the model of the "ideal worker," who is someone always available because of no significant family responsibilities (Bond and Families and Work Institute 2003; Hagan and Kay 2010; Percheski 2008; Williams 2001). The ABA/ALM survey found that the top reason women gave for leaving their firms was caretaking commitments, listed by 58 percent of women (Liebenberg and Scharf 2019, 12).

Women in our study who expressed concerns about their practices tended to focus on other types of challenges, but some did describe how family demands can make it difficult to be entrepreneurial and productive. One woman, for example, contrasted her experience as a childless associate with the juggling she did after becoming a partner with children:

> The most dramatic part of it apart from lack of sleep was the lack of elasticity to your work day because as an associate you can choose to be at the office until midnight, you can respond at a moment's notice and when you have two kids, you can't. And that was just a fundamental change and at some point I may not be able to balance it. There are days that I can't. Now is that an issue because I'm a woman? I think it hits me harder because I think women tend to try to do more in the primary care giving and work environment. (#254)

Another interviewee echoed this statement with frustration: "[Women look] at the men and [say], 'They are able to work 3,000 hours because they've got a stay-at-home wife,' I don't have a stay-at-home wife so suddenly I can't compete . . . and you can't even focus on it in my view because it will drive you crazy" (#178).

The challenge may be especially acute for younger partners with less flexibility. This interviewee contrasted her own experience with her observations of younger women:

> My husband would rather cut his throat than say I'm not doing the deposition because I've got to go to the soccer game . . . and I was usually able to work it so that I didn't do it at 2:00 but I did it at 4:00. And I have still been able to do that since we entered the 24/7 culture. I think that watching younger women try and do it, in some ways it's great because they can be at home with a sick baby and they can still [work], but the horrible thing that has happened is the response time . . . and I see lawyers here just absolutely start to write somebody off if they don't get back to them within. . . . hours. . . . It's a shame and that will just tear up a woman for sure. (#146)

The time-bind that women face, particularly women with children, compounds the challenges of attracting and retaining clients:

> My kids are a little older now but I have three kids and I also have a husband who is a lawyer at a law firm here, so somebody has to be around. The amount of time it takes to be able to be both successful and bill the number of hours you need to be to be a competent lawyer, and on top of that be able to invest the number of hours that it takes to build the relationships to bring in business, to do all the lunches, to do all of that—that is difficult. (#24)

One partner described the need to reconnect with other partners after returning from maternity leave to ensure that she had enough work:

> PARTNER: So I was a partner for I think two weeks and then went out on maternity leave and then came back. And whenever you go out on leave it takes a while to ramp back up and so I think that has been my challenge.
>
> INTERVIEWER: By ramping up does that require getting plugged in again?
>
> PARTNER: Yeah, just getting plugged in again, reminding people that you're here, you've got time, getting, I would say, appropriately busy. . . . And so that, I would say, has been a challenge. (#241)

The challenge of returning from maternity leave was echoed by another female partner who has been working on women's issues in her firm:

> I actually talk to folks [about these issues] and the general consensus is, how do you strong-arm other partners into giving . . . women partners who are coming back from maternity leave work. I mean you can't. You can sensitize them to the issues and you can bring it to their attention and you can hope that it's at the forefront of their mind when they are making staffing decisions but at the end of the day it's a discretionary decision that is up to each individual. (#188)

While gendered family responsibilities undoubtedly create challenges, some research suggests that they may not substantially limit women's ability to devote as much time to their work as men (Noonan, Corcoran and Courant 2008, 173–76; Williams and Richardson 2010, 643). The 2018 NAWL survey, for instance, states, "Despite existing hypotheses to the contrary, many years of NAWL data have shown that there are no significant differences between the hours recorded by men and women attorneys at different levels and in different roles" (Peery 2018, 4).

Furthermore, there is evidence of a gender gap even among lawyers without significant family responsibilities. Studies indicate that the gap exists even for women who do not take time to care for family members and who work long hours (Dau-Schmidt et al. 2009; Noonan, Corcoran, and Courant 2008; Sommerlad 2015). In addition, a national study of lawyers with about two years of practice experience, most of whom at the time did not have children, revealed a 5.2 percent gap in compensation between male and female associates (Dinovitzer, Reichman, and Sterling 2009). This difference early in one's career, they suggest, may be magnified over time (843). After controlling for the effect of credentials, hours worked, firm characteristics, and other factors that might plausibly explain this difference, the authors found that 75 percent of the gap "is due to unexplained differences in the valuation of women's endowments" (838). Noting that the gender gap has narrowed for professions such as engineering, the authors conclude that their research suggests that "there may be something unique in the early professional work of lawyers that allows for the kind of subjective assessments and interactions that underlie differences in pay" (848).

Research in recent years has attempted to determine what lies at the root of these dynamics by focusing on "how gender interacts with the institutional mechanisms for rewarding the work that lawyers do" (Reichman and Sterling 2004, 60). One useful way of approaching this is to examine the professional "capital" that is valued in a field (Garth and Sterling 2018). As Garth and Sterling describe this concept, "[a]ctors within [a] field adopt 'strategies' oriented toward success in the field. . . . [They] internalize the rules of the game, such that it seems natural, and they try to build up the capital that is valued in the field or find ways to get the capital that they possess to be valued within the field" (127). This can call attention to the opportunities that firms make available for women to obtain such capital, the process of assessing whether women possess it, and the extent to which assumptions about men and women influence what is considered capital itself—that is, what is "valued or discounted in building lawyer careers" (128).

Research in this spirit has directed attention to how implicit gender assumptions can influence access to valuable assignments (Reichman and Sterling 2013, 9; Reichman and Sterling 2004, 62–63; Williams et al. 2018, 18–21); inclusion on "pitches" for business from prospective clients (Williams and Richardson 2010, 644); availability of assistance from associates (Reichman and Sterling 2004, 64); opportunities to obtain mentors; client relationships (Donnell, Sterling and Reichman 1998, 51–56); and receipt of credit for participating in pitches (Rikleen 2013, 12). As Sterling and Reichman (2004, 65) describe, much of this research indicates that "[i]n sum, women have a harder time reaching the big clients that offer more opportunities 'to be more productive.'" The ABA/ALM survey, for instance, found that 67 percent of women, but only 10 percent of men, said they had experienced a lack of access to business development activities (Liebenberg and Scharf 2019, 7).

One female partner emphasized that these concerns are at least as important to many women as flexibility with regard to family responsibilities:

> The women that I know at the firm . . . our general view of having a family and work-life balance is, don't talk to us about that, that's our personal issue. We're here to work, we're here to perform and we're here to succeed, don't treat us any different. If I need my kids raised, I'll get a nanny, we'll figure it out but that's my personal issue. What we want from you as a firm is to create a platform in which we can succeed.
>
> But I think that generally there is a concern among women that . . . we're not in a place where we can be successful and part of that is . . . because we are not being kept productive when we are partners. Part of it is we are not brought in on the important client relationships or . . . maybe our pictures are used for pitch materials but we're not given the work when it actually comes in, or given the credit, or . . . given access to the important clients. Or for the clients we work for we are sort of squeezed out when it comes to the important meetings and whatever else. So there is a real concern about that and it's not because we have children, it's not because we have families, it's because we're for whatever reason, we are just not able to penetrate through the glass ceiling. (#101)

Some female partners felt this opportunity gap began early, affecting the type of experience women gain as associates:

> I sat on the . . . committee that decided partners for six years. . . . [W]e would look at the candidate and people would say particularly for the corporate partner slots, less so for litigation, the guys are way more qualified and you look at it and . . . you've been giving them all the good deals for the last ten years, there is a reason.
>
> You almost [had to accept] that it was really hard to find a first rate candidate by the time they are an eighth or ninth year associate [who was a] woman, but it's because they weren't traveling with the partners they worked with, they weren't getting assigned to the great deals, they weren't given responsibility that guys were given coming up the ranks. Well, no kidding the guys are more qualified by the time they are [there for] nine years—you trained them to be more qualified. (#150)

Another female partner described the challenges for women in inheriting clients from senior partners:

> I think you had your finger on the pulse of it at the outset of the interview when you asked how the institutional clients are handed down. Those relationships are primarily male-dominated and driven, and I think that that's an issue or a concern for women partners generally. You know, how does that happen, how can I be one of those people who gets that book of business, how can I start working for that company in the first instance? So sure, I think that that is a concern. (#188)

One male partner also described how a female colleague was not awarded any credit for a successful pitch on which she played a key role:

> One of the women who worked with me identified a potential client with a problem that she was uniquely suited to handle and so she sent an email around and said it wasn't a client of the firm at that time but does anybody have a contact. So somebody in New York did and they had a joint call together but [the female partner] did all the pitch and . . . she got no credit. (#5)

This experience is reflected in the ABA/ALM survey, in which 50 percent of women, compared to 71 percent of men, were satisfied with the recognition they received for their work (Liebenberg and Scharf 2019, 5).

Scholarship also has analyzed how implicit gender stereotypes may lead firms to conclude that women lack sufficient professional capital in the form of commitment to their work (Sommerlad and Sanderson 1998; Reichman and Sterling 2004, 70–71), a sufficiently assertive temperament, or a sufficiently collaborative one (Williams and Richardson 2010, 652–53). The intangible and ambiguous character of such qualities makes them especially susceptible to the influence of gendered assumptions. As Reichman and Sterling (2004, 71) note, for instance: "Commitment is the soft side, the subjective dimension of compensation that often separates men and women. Hard to define, commitment is often measured . . . by the display of availability and conformity with the heroic worker whose business card indicates how to contact him 24/7." In the ABA/ALM survey, 63 percent of women, but only 2 percent of men, said that they had been perceived as less committed to their career (Liebenberg and Scharf 2019, 8).

One partner we interviewed described a conversation she had with a senior partner at another firm, who described her request for part-time as "arrogant." She shared his reaction:

> [He said] you shouldn't be asking to do that; you should be working every minute of every day to impress me and show me that you are committed to this job. [That you requested this] obviously means you can't possibly do [this job] unless there is nothing else in your life because that is how I run my life. (#41)

Some argue that men benefit from an assumption of competence (Williams and Richardson, 650) and tend to be evaluated more on ostensible potential, as opposed to women who must prove their competence according to defined metrics. To the extent that decisions about assignments, promotion, and compensation rest on such subjective assessments, women may suffer disadvantage. Finally, the intangibility of many qualities that ostensibly constitute professional capital means that self-promotion and putting oneself forward can play an important role in influencing how one is evaluated and regarded as entrepreneurial. Research indicates that men are more likely to engage in such behavior than women. One partner made this point when suggesting that women sometimes are hesitant to speak up about their efforts and achievements:

> I think the firm has done a lot to support women lawyers with child care and support groups and just a general awareness of the need to have women involved in business development efforts as well as work. But it is also still kind of true that women are not as comfortable promoting themselves. They want to do the best job they can and then have people recognize that. (#124)

Research indicates that women who promote themselves may face a backlash for violating gender stereotypes, thereby creating a paradox where they do not get the credit they deserve if they do not promote themselves but may face a backlash if they do (Rudman 1998).

Research also suggests that some work that women tend to do or qualities that they display may be devalued and thus not considered meaningful professional capital. Women report, for instance, that they often engage in activities that help enhance the firm, such as training associates or serving on the recruiting or diversity committee—but that this work is not valued by the firm in promotion and compensation decisions (Flom 2012; Reichman and Sterling 2002; Smith 2014; Sterling and Reichman 2016; Williams et al. 2018; Williams and Richardson 2010). One female partner compared her firm favorably with other firms:

> You'll hear a lot of law firms brag about how many women they have or women partners they have. If you dig down deeper they are mostly women on the bottom of the compensation chain, they are on the pro bono committee or the diversity committee but they never are on the compensation committee or executive committee and if they are it is one and it's always the same one. It's rare to find a woman who is on the compensation committee because that is by far the most powerful committee. (#12)

One woman described her previous firm:

> What I learned to appreciate about [the firm] were two things. Number one, if you hit your numbers the firm left you totally alone. I didn't have to do anything. I didn't have to mentor anybody, I didn't have to go join the women, I am so sick of being on the diversity committees and doing that, I didn't have to do any of that. They were very upfront [that] I had to do one thing and that was unless I was in trial or doing an argument—you had to go to the annual partners meeting, that was it. (#22)

Some women also believe that the work they do in preserving relationships with clients and keeping them satisfied is not treated as reflecting rainmaking potential; instead it is feminized as nurturing work more indicative of a service partner (Reichman and Sterling 2002, 11; Smith 2014). One female partner noted that providing good service to clients is crucial to keeping them, but that compensation tends not to acknowledge this:

> I don't see the numbers so I don't know but . . . there have been a lot of conversations among the female partners. It's my sense that the people that bring in the matters are richly rewarded. But what is the good of bringing it in if you can't hold it, if you can't deliver a quality service? I think that is where the women say, "Look, if we are the ones that are delivering the legal product that keeps the client happy that has to be weighted . . . it can't be

> that all service partners are fungible—it doesn't matter if it's Lisa, if it's not Lisa it will be somebody else—they are all the same." There has to be a sense that our contribution is important also. (#236)

Some women also described the general challenge of succeeding in an environment in which the predominant percentage of individuals with power are males, no matter how well-intentioned those men might be. This sentiment is supported by research on the effects of homophily on work relationships: one is likely to work harder at developing relationships with those who are similar to oneself. As one female partner said:

> I think the lack of seeing anyone like you . . . is harder. I mean I think people tend to look out for people who remind them of themselves so I think that . . . it can be harder for senior partners to . . . identify with . . . a black female and say, "Hey, you remind me of me [so] let me help you." (#241)

Another remarked:

> I'm not going to have that good old boy rapport, so . . . it's always something that I've been cognizant of and it's always been something I've talked to the partners about. I think other male partners can pick up the phone and go, "Hey, let's go grab a drink and watch the game." I can't really call up a client and say, "Hey, do you want to have a drink tonight," it's just a different dynamic and it's awkward. (#234)

These experiences are reflected in the ABA/ALM survey, in which 46 percent of women, but only 3 percent of men, said that they experienced a lack of access to sponsors (Liebenberg and Scharf 2019, 8).

Some women in our study said they try to ignore the challenges and politics around gender in the workplace and just focus on doing good work:

> I've got some good connections that I've formed because I've done a good job on their cases and not necessarily because I've taken them to [a sporting event]. . . . I would like to think the reason I am where I am is not because people like are [saying], "Oh she's going to bring in the next [major firm client]. It's because I do a good job and hopefully people see that and they see past the fact that she's a girl, she's young, what is she really going to bring

> to the table, and they said, "Okay, she can get the deal done, she can run it. So that's one foot in front of the other, just the best job I can do, as my mom says, "Just do the best you can do." (#234)

This might have been enough a few decades ago. In today's large firm, however, it can be a perilous strategy in light of the need to sell oneself to clients and colleagues in order to stay busy enough to be considered productive.

Our research cannot offer definitive conclusions about the experiences of female partners in the modern law firm. It does, however, provide at least some support for the findings of more systematic studies of the gender dynamics within firms. To this extent, it suggests that the challenges of law firm practice since the 2008 financial crisis may be more acute for women than for men.

Identity Work

The notion that law firm partners must be entrepreneurs was not part of the professional self-conception of most partners before the last few decades. Modern law firm partners therefore have had to shape, or in some cases reshape, their sense of identity to accommodate this relatively recent element. By now, it is commonly assumed that being an entrepreneur is part of what it means to be a partner. As one partner suggested, "the talent and willingness to be entrepreneurial from the first day you walk in is highly valued. You need to be a good technical lawyer, but that is sort of table stakes to not get fired" (#252).

For lawyers who have been in firms long enough to remember when the market was less competitive, the need to attend constantly to business matters can seem an unwelcome necessity that diverts them from the practice of law. Solo practitioners or owners of small firms may have always needed to focus on the business of the firm. Lawyers in large firms, however, for many years generally did not do so because they assumed that the firm had a stable base of clients who would provide a steady stream of work.

By contrast, those who have entered firms in the past few decades have understood that being an entrepreneur is part of being a modern law firm lawyer. One partner believes that his firm is well positioned to do well in the increasingly competitive market because "I think the lawyers in the firm have already crossed the psychological barrier of understanding that. It's not like when us older people started and you were a partner for life and you were going to get to relax a bit at the end." He pointed out "the entrepreneurial approach that everybody here seems to have," and added, "I think people get it early on that if you are going to succeed here you're going to have to have that approach." This means that "you're approaching [practice] more like a business than as a genteel provider of services" (#228).

To incorporate this relatively recent dimension into their self-understanding, partners often need to engage in "identity work." This is the process of "forming, repairing, maintaining, strengthening, or revising self-constructions" (Lok 2010). As Bévort and Suddaby (2016) describe in their study of the changing self-conceptions of accountants in accounting firms that have shifted from partnerships to corporations, it involves the creation of "identity scripts" that provide guidance on appropriate forms of behavior and interaction with others. Individuals use these scripts in an iterative process in which "individuals creatively engage in provisional interpretive reproduction in which they experiment with probable or potential scripts of identity that reconcile competing institutional pressures" (18).

The identity work of partners in the modern law firm involves developing an understanding of themselves as entrepreneurs that coheres with their understanding of the other attributes that characterize a law firm partner. This self-conception then provides a tentative sense of who they are and what is expected of them with respect to this dimension of their identity. Bévort and Suddaby suggest that the creation of a professional identity in particular "requires individuals to navigate competing institutional pressures and, periodically, to experiment with and adapt provisional identities" (21).

Note, for instance, that firms do not formally designate persons as service partners or rainmakers. Indeed, they frown upon such characterizations. All partners in a modern firm, however, are familiar with these terms as elements of identity. Nor do firms tell service partners that they need to cultivate relationships with rainmakers to be regarded as economically productive. These partners instead draw on their conception of identity to devise a script that deems this necessary to succeed in the firm.

Our interviews suggest that modern law firm partners attempt to fashion an identity that reconciles the business dimension of entrepreneurship with traditional professional values. What Greenwood and his colleagues (Cooper et al. 1996) call the "sediment" of a prior traditional understanding of partnership is visible in the ambivalence with which some partners describe the business demands of their role.

One partner commented, for instance, "Another aspect of lawyering when

I first joined the firm was that there never seemed to be any need to sell. We were sought after, and becoming a professional was sort of a refuge from the sort of ugly mercantile world where you have to actually . . . sell." Selling therefore is something "that I didn't learn when I was younger" (#27).

One partner noted the effort to reconcile the role of entrepreneur with more traditional conceptions of partnership: "Your goals as a lawyer are to be viewed as a counselor to your client, a trusted advisor, just spending time with them, so I'm constantly thinking about how I keep my clients happy, how I meet new clients" (#103).

Another partner expressed some exasperation with the demands on the modern law firm partner:

> I don't think that the business pressures have affected my sense of being a professional. I still think of myself as a professional and what I'm providing are very professional services. It's more that you have all these other additional things you have to do besides being professional.
>
> Just the business focus can be very time consuming and sometimes I'm like, if I have to make one more Power Point, I'm going to die. (#37)

One way of working through this ambivalence is to interpret the responsibility to obtain clients as an opportunity to carve out a domain of relative autonomy over one's practice. Such autonomy is one feature of the traditional notion of the professional. As one partner put it, his motivation for beginning at an early point to develop relationships with clients was that "I am just not a patient person and I have no desire to be beholden to other people" (#203). Another lawyer suggested that "the idea for a lot of partners is if you don't have your own business you are always pulled into someone else's" (#188).

An alternative way to interpret the entrepreneurial partner role is to see oneself as fulfilling a responsibility to other people in the firm. One partner observed, for instance:

> I would say one of the biggest changes is the pressure that you feel as a partner, as opposed to an associate, from a business development perspective. You really do have more of a vested ownership interest in the firm and so you are always cognizant about bringing in business. . . . So that's probably the biggest change—just putting on your business development hat and feeling responsible to keep people fed. (#178)

The responsibility to "keep people fed" involves ensuring that enough business comes in to keep everyone in the practice group busy. This partner explained, "I look around and I think, 'Wow, you know, if we're billing on average 2,000 hours a year, let's say there are 12 partners in my department, that's 24,000 partner hours that have to be generated, and that's just a very different realization of what's necessary" (#178). A partner thus is expected to generate not only enough business to keep herself busy, but to keep the associates within the practice group busy as well. Another partner remarked, "That's part of the pressure you live with, it's that, you know, you are at heart an entrepreneur and you need to feed this law firm, feed the associates and feed yourself" (#241).

In this conception of identity, being an entrepreneur involves a responsibility to help keep other people "fed." One therefore is not engaged simply in activity prompted solely by financial self-interest, but by the interests of a larger community in which one holds a position of responsibility for the welfare of others. In this way, a partner may interpret the demand to be entrepreneurial not simply as the operation of business logic, but as consistent with the notion of a professional as someone who has a responsibility for her colleagues.

Conclusion

Modern law firm partners appreciate that firms can no longer assure them of a steady stream of work based on long-term relationships with clients. As a result, partners must act as entrepreneurs who take ongoing personal responsibility for generating revenues. They must market their services to prospective clients, to other partners in the firm, or both. This means that partners must develop business skills that their counterparts a generation ago did not need to cultivate. As this chapter describes, this does not mean that partners now fully embrace business logic at the expense of professional values. Rather, it entails engaging in "identify work" in which partners seek to reconcile the need to be entrepreneurial with their understanding of themselves as professionals.

The need to be entrepreneurial can pose particular challenges for women. Some result from women's family responsibilities, but other challenges reflect fewer opportunities for contact with clients, assumptions about their availability for assignments compared to men, devaluation of the contributions that women make, fewer clients inherited from partners than men, and the risks of being seen as too assertive based on cultural expectations. The result is that intensified entrepreneurial demands on partners since the financial downturn may make it especially hard for women to advance to prominent positions in law firms.

The emphasis on being entrepreneurial may mean that partners who are successful at this will see themselves as running their own small business within the firm. This creates a risk that such partners will consider clients as theirs rather than the firm's. If this occurs, the prospect of these partners leaving with clients in tow can make it difficult for a firm to establish a stable culture that focuses on professional as well as financial rewards. The next chapter discusses this challenge and how firms may attempt to meet it.

4

Entrepreneurs and Collaboration

When lawyers are encouraged to be entrepreneurs, they may regard themselves as solo practitioners who serve as individual profit centers within the firm. From this perspective, partners build and maintain their practices and are held accountable for financial targets. They share overhead expenses with other lawyers in the firm but do not experience themselves as participating in a common enterprise. While this arrangement may benefit the individual, it may not benefit the firm. This chapter discusses this risk and how firms may attempt to minimize it.

Entrepreneurs as Solo Practitioners

One partner expressed the sense that he runs his own business within the larger firm:

> What I didn't realize was how much of a business the practice of law is. I spend a very significant percentage of my time just managing the practice and managing my relationship with the law firm and managing my relationship with my clients. And I spend a very significant portion of my time worrying about business development.
>
> I am my own sales force. I am my own marketing force. I also have to service all my clients at the same time and I am effectively my own billing department. If there is a billing dispute I can't turn it over to my

accounting department. I've got to go face the client. So you find yourself a small business within a law firm, and I had no idea that I would be [doing this]. (#250)

This sense of running your own business can lead to competition for clients among partners in the firm, who may regard a colleague's gain as their loss. One junior partner observed:

> I spend more time trying to gather up work internally than I do externally because obviously the odds are better. The problem with it is that I am competing against fellow partners, and the thing is—and this is not just the junior partners saying this; I think senior partners say this—is that you're not worried about competition outside of this building; you're worried about competition inside the building. (#101)

When a partner sees himself as the owner of a practice, the partner may regard clients as "his" clients and limit colleagues' access to them for fear of losing the relationship. One partner noted that "clients are very much protected [by some partners]." Their attitude may be, "'I will introduce you to them should I feel that you could do something and the credit should come to me" (#222). Another partner observed:

> I think when you make partner it's eye-opening. You think, "Oh, this is different, this is all about business." I think even in a partnership there can be sharp elbows in terms of people wanting to keep their clients and being reluctant to cross-sell or market. I'm not really sure this is what I expected. (#241)

Recognizing that they need to act entrepreneurially and maintain a healthy number of billable hours can lead partners to keep as much work as possible for themselves, to refrain from introducing colleagues to clients for fear they will lose their client relationships, or to not collaborate with colleagues unless they receive compensation credit for doing so. These partners want clients to develop loyalty to them, not necessarily to the firm. They know that their relationships with clients—their "book of business"—is their currency in the lateral market if they ever want or need to look elsewhere. (See chapter 8 for a full discussion of lateral markets.)

This type of behavior may serve an individual partner's self-interest, but it does not serve the interest of the firm. Any managing partner would cringe at the story that one partner told about another firm where he used to work:

> No one is going to go with you to a pitch [to try to get business from a client] until they know how much you are going to give them in the way of [compensation] credit. . . . I mean, a corporate person brought a litigator who stopped the pitch in the middle and said, "I need to talk to you outside the room." When they got outside, he said, "I'm not going back in until you give me this amount of credit." (#211)

Such behavior, however, may seem a rational reaction to the perception that the firm will hold partners strictly accountable for meeting financial targets, with failure to do so leading to compensation reductions and even termination. As one partner said, "if you make people paranoid about their future they are going to do everything in the world to protect themselves, which doesn't help with the whole philosophy that the firm is supposed to [put the] best boots on the ground." This partner continued:

> We have a lot of silos and that indicates to me that people are not taking really strong firm relationships and trying to broaden the base of practices that work for them. . . . My concern is if you make people scared enough about their compensation or their job, people will not take that chance and I think that is why we have silos where we have them." (#150)

This partner's own efforts to get colleagues to expand relationships with clients have met mainly with frustration:

> We've got big litigation clients, there is no transactional work done for them whatsoever and the litigators will tell you, "Well, I don't know the transactional guys in the company." I said, "Well, go meet them, how hard is that?" . . . Most people will not do that. . . . It's not even that it doesn't occur to them to do it; it's when you tell them they could do it they refuse to do it. I don't know what the fear is but they will not do it. (#150)

Part of the fear is that a fellow partner may not do good work for the client and thus may jeopardize the client relationship. Heidi Gardner, who has done extensive research on collaboration, describes this as an absence of "competence based trust." (Gardner 2013, 4) One partner observed:

> There is huge paranoia about opening that really important client up to somebody else. I think some of it [is] driven by the fact that if they let you in and you don't do a good job you've hurt them and they don't trust you to recognize that you are holding their reputation in your hands. (#150)

One partner described the calculus this way:

> In my view the real reasons that lawyers don't like to share client opportunities is a quality issue. So you're a lawyer, you spend God-knows how many hours building a relationship and you get a matter in a subject area that you personally don't know anything about. That means you have to go to the firm and say who is our expert on this and somebody tells you who it is and you know the person socially but you don't know anything more about that. That person can ruin your relationship with the client in a heartbeat.
>
> Many people decide, you know, it's not worth the risk. I'll just tell the client to go to [a different firm]. . . . I get brownie points with the client, I don't have any down side. (#227)

Another partner remarked, "There are people, you ask them a question, the first thing they want to do is open up a new matter to [get billing] credit" (#223).

This attitude both reflects and reinforces the sense that the firm is mainly a vehicle for each partner to pursue individual financial goals. It also reflects the perception that management sees the primary aim of the firm as maximizing financial performance. In this universe, partners are always vulnerable to actions by colleagues that threaten ownership of their clients. They are also vulnerable to management determination that their productivity is no longer acceptable.

To the extent that the firm's emphasis on entrepreneurs is seen purely as an expression of business logic, all this behavior is individually rational. From this perspective, "work is all personal, work moves; I don't care what people say. Everyone is entrepreneurial, everybody who is worth anything is out trying to get everything they can in terms of clients" (#36).

While such behavior does not promote the overall interest of the firm, it also may not promote the best interest of clients. As one partner put it, "Everything that puts more barriers within the firm is at the end of the day a loss for the client" (#222). Research generally confirms the benefits of involving multiple professionals on a matter (Gardner 2015). Competition and hoarding clients can prevent a firm from providing the best possible service to clients, from expanding the range of services that the firm provides to existing clients, and from gaining new clients by making a persuasive case that the firm offers resources that distinguish it from other firms.

Self-interested partner behavior also can impair the ability of the firm to establish the firm-specific capital that enables it to create and sustain a stable culture that gives weight to nonfinancial professional values. Clients will tend to regard their relationships as being with partners rather than with the firm. This means that it can be difficult for the firm to make the case to partners that the firm has a client base that makes practicing in the firm appreciably more financially rewarding than moving to another firm. With partners at least potentially free agents on an ongoing basis, the firm may fear that attempting to vindicate nonfinancial professional values will cost them profitable partners. The result is that a firm may not be able to establish the cultural glue that provides some protection from the vicissitudes of market forces.

Institutionalizing Clients

The challenge for a firm therefore is to encourage entrepreneurs while tempering the self-interested individualism that such an ethos can create. This requires that it solve a Prisoner's Dilemma. One important way firms seek to do this is by "institutionalizing" clients—ensuring that multiple lawyers are involved in providing service to them. Partners who primarily work with institutionalized clients find it harder to move to other firms:

> When you have client relationships . . . that are very deep with the institution if I were to go somewhere else some of those clients would call me but they also have important relationships with other people at the firm. So I don't feel like I have the ability to say I'm going to march across the street to one of our competitors and millions of dollars of business will follow me. (#33)

Another partner responded when asked what would prompt him to remain with his firm:

> The other thing that would make it hard, candidly, to leave here is whether or not I thought I could really move my book of business. I don't know. [Our firm] and firms like ours do a great job of institutionalizing clients and I don't service my clients by myself, I involve a lot of people. It makes my life

> a lot easier, but it also means those are clients of the firm now, so I've never had to go too far down the path to realize I'm not sure how easy it would be to do. (#203)

This reflects the idea of entrepreneurship as a cooperative rather than solitary activity. The greater the number of practice groups involved in serving a client, the larger the amount of new work the firm tends to receive from that client. This can provide significant financial benefits to firms that emphasize the importance of generating new business in a market with fewer long-term relationships between firms and clients.

While firms try to institutionalize clients, partners have incentives to resist these efforts. A book of business is synonymous with power in law firms (Nelson 1988). Furthermore, some firms' compensation systems are not aligned with their strategy, in that they reward partners based more on their own book of business and less on whether that partner is bringing firm resources to bear on the client's work (Lowe 2013). If clients are not institutionalized, a partner may move to another firm if the firm's fortunes begin to decline. One partner described the anxiety that attends the possibility that partners may leave and take clients with them:

> What has threatened [the firm] is the fear that some strong practice would pack up and move, and the two threats were perceived as being [Partner A's] practice and [Partner B's] practice. Both of them [are] very portable practices, prestige premier practices and I think the firm spent a lot of time worrying about how to keep that from happening. (#54)

Aside from a partner's perceived financial interest in maintaining control over clients, he may use the logic of professionalism to resist institutionalization of clients. The image of the solo practitioner retains resonance as someone who runs his own practice, exercises professional judgment about what is in the client's best interest, and answers only to himself about how to run the practice without any interference. A partner thus may claim that his resistance reflects a commitment to professional values.

To institutionalize clients, firms thus must convince partners that collaboration will be more financially rewarding than working in silos, and reassure them that cooperating will be reciprocated and not exploited. Accomplishing this can create firm-specific capital based on the financial benefits to a partner of staying at a firm compared to moving to another one.

Many partners strongly indicated that collaboration also is a source of important professional reward apart from its financial benefits. This means that a firm may be able to build even stronger firm-specific capital by solving the Assurance Game, credibly conveying to partners that the firm is a place where they can work with others who find collaboration intrinsically valuable. The next section elaborates on how collaboration can provide these financial and nonfinancial benefits.

Collaborative Culture

Research suggests that a genuinely cooperative culture can produce substantial financial benefits for an organization, an important point for firms attempting to solve the Prisoner's Dilemma. As Heidi Gardner (2013, 7) describes it, "Collaboration occurs when a group of knowledge workers integrate their individual expertise in order to deliver high-quality outcomes on complex issues." She continues, "In addition to offering up their expertise, these professionals must also help, advise, stimulate and counterbalance each other." Such activity goes beyond the reciprocal exchange involved in a referral network that may result in "cross-selling" of services. "Cross-selling," Gardner suggests, "occurs when partner A introduces partner B to her own client, so that B can provide additional services. Although A may provide some level of oversight to ensure that her client is satisfied with B's work, she is unlikely to get deeply involved in the context."

Gardner (2015, 76) describes the pressing need for collaboration by modern professional service firms:

> As clients have globalized and confronted more sophisticated technological, regulatory, economic, and environmental demands, they've sought help on increasingly complex problems. To keep up, most top-tier firms have created or acquired narrowly defined practice areas and encouraged partners to specialize. As a result, their collective expertise has been distributed across more and more people, places, and practice groups. The only way to address clients' most complex issues, then, is for specialists to work together across the boundaries of their expertise.

Gardner's (2015, 76) research indicates that when firms can accomplish this, they "earn higher margins, inspire greater client loyalty, and gain a competitive edge." Her study of three large law firms established that average annual revenues tripled when two practice groups are involved instead of one (Gardner 2016, 22–23). Furthermore, as additional groups serve a client, each group earns more on average.

Gardner (2016) argues that the reason that collaboration among several practices on client matters is profitable is because the involvement of more partners on client matters provides more information about the client's needs and goals. This can enable them to "spot opportunities that . . . less-involved competitors might overlook" (23). Her data indicate that the more practices involved on client work, the greater the number of client projects per year.

The profitability of work also can increase as a result of the involvement of multiple practices. It creates opportunities for professionals to "'move up the food chain'" with their client—that is, to gain access to more senior executives who have broader responsibilities, larger budgets, and more sophisticated needs. This complex work commands higher margins" and "makes cross-practice work subject to less price-based competition" (Gardner 2016, 23, 24).

Gardner also finds that collaboration

> enhances a professional firm's client loyalty and retention. The more partners serve a client, the longer that client remains with the firm, even when an important partner leaves. The relationship is even stronger when those outside multi-expert teams span different departments or offices in their firm, and when they serve multiple contacts within the client organization. (21)

In these ways, fostering genuine collaboration among practice groups in a firm may generate a form of firm-specific capital in an age in which long-term client relationships are difficult to sustain. As one general counsel of a Fortune 100 company remarks, "Despite what they think, most individual lawyers are actually quite replaceable. I mean, I could find a decent tax lawyer in most firms. But when that lawyer teamed up with colleagues from IP, regulatory, and ultimately litigation, I couldn't find a whole-team substitute in another firm" (Gardner 2016, 24).

Aside from its business advantages, collaboration can be a source of intrinsic professional reward for partners. It affords an opportunity to create even stronger firm-specific capital by solving the Assurance Game, fostering loyalty to the firm as an organization that is committed to providing nonfinancial rewards. Gardner (2016, 62) notes, "Many partners who had participated in collaborative client engagements reported that the most important benefit for them was the opportunity to meet new colleagues or deepen existing relationships. For example, one respondent wrote about 'the camaraderie that comes with working as a group.' [A]nother welcomed collaboration because otherwise 'being a partner can feel quite lonely sometimes.'" Still another reported that collaboration provides "the feeling that colleagues and I are working towards a common goal, namely the success and prosperity of the firm as a whole" (64).

Our own interviews confirmed this phenomenon. One partner articulated the way in which his relationships with others in the firm provide the lens through which he sees the firm:

> My connection [to the firm] is I have a number of people that I have worked with a lot and respect and enjoy working with and who I would not want to let down. . . . I feel like I've gotten a lot of good things out of [the firm] and I feel like it's a good place, it's a pretty humane place, it's a place that I think has a lot of respect for the profession, it's an ethical place that supports a lot of pro bono work, and I think those are things that . . . to the extent I have institutional loyalty, that [is] where it comes from. (#63)

One partner at Firm 3 said that the collaboration that occurs at his firm is very appealing: "I mean, it sounds sort of hokey but it's really quite meaningful." He elaborated:

> The ethos here is you come back from lunch and you return calls to your clients and your partners in the same priority. If you have a question and you call somebody, they get back to you right away, any time of night they drop what they are doing, it's fantastic. And there is no like "What's in it for me?" There is no, "Well, I'll only do this if we're going to split the origination." I mean you never even have these conversations, it's just a really nice environment for that. And that is why I think some people are so happy here versus other firms that are quite good. (#76)

Other partners at the same firm described the sense that collaboration among partners is a particularly strong element of Firm 3's culture. One commented, "There clearly is an emphasis that we don't want people in silos; it is a partnership, we're an international firm, you want people to be calling you from other offices and helping out, you are encouraged to help people out" (#82). As one partner said, "Periodically there are memos that go out about,

'This is how we should be,' but it's also more of an implicit understanding that is how we operate and this is what is special about our firm" (#93). Other partners emphasized how collaboration furnishes opportunities for intellectually satisfying exchanges of ideas with colleagues, provides chances to work with others to solve problems, and strengthens personally rewarding relationships among colleagues.

One partner commented, "The culture as I've understood it, as I've come up, has been, we are partners; [it] isn't just a title. We try to be partners and you help someone out, it's the pay it forward theory of 'look, it will all work out in the end,' I think there is a lot of that." This partner described how the culture furthers this ethos by creating expectations about sharing billing credit:

> There is a culture here of sharing originations, that if you might be the person who brought the client in the door but . . . you are a corporate lawyer and they are in the lending business and so you are going to bring in one of our lending lawyers to do a lot of work on a matter, well, then probably you are going to share some of that origination credit. . . .
>
> That is one way the firm [explicitly] talks about the culture of the place, that [this is] how we think things ought to work. That we do share and that we're stronger than the sum of our parts, that, yes, the corporate lawyer might have had the relationship, but without the firm having the ability to answer questions in a range of areas, there is a good chance we might not have gotten that work. (#70)

One partner described his experience with this emphasis on sharing when he was an associate, for whom billing credit would not affect his salaried compensation. When he learned that he had received some origination credit on a matter, he asked a partner about it. The partner replied, "This [is] the way we work; we share. You are right on some level, it doesn't [affect your compensation] but it's a good thing to have; it doesn't hurt the firm's view of you, so just say thank you" (#70).

The result for partners in firms with this culture is a strong sense of being in a genuine partnership with others in the firm. One partner described the importance to him of helping other partners:

> That means not sitting on [an] email for five days and not failing to return calls. . . . That doesn't mean that I'll necessarily have a substantive answer for

them right away but it's just, "I got your call, let me look at this and I'll get back to you in a couple days," or "I got your call, I hope it's not urgent but I'm actually going out of town with my family next week, can I call you when I get back?" Whatever it is, just being responsive to people. (#69)

Another partner said,

The nice thing for me about the firm is that over the years I have done a significant amount of outreach . . . and I've always been pleased with the other people in other parts of the firm that I got to know and work with. So you get a sense of trust of the institution, that they've hired well, and that, "Boy I'm so glad I'm at a firm [where] I talked to X; X was very responsive, and certainly you are encouraged to be responsive." . . . So I certainly try to respond to phone calls or emails [the] same day, especially emails, to at least acknowledge, "I got your email, let me give this some thought," and I think that as far as a culture [that] is pretty predominant here at [the firm]. (#93)

Another partner described a recent experience:

I had a partner in [a certain practice] group, this was right before Christmas, he called one evening I was at home. He said, "I have this crisis." He [had] gotten down to this state and really needed some corporate help and so of course I jumped in and helped him and I have had that situation before, too. Like you all of a sudden . . . have a crisis, even if it's an inconvenient time, people definitely are very willing [to help]. Sometimes it's, "I'm traveling, I'm in an all-day meeting, I can call you tonight," but it's always. "I will call you tonight," it's never, "We're going to have to speak next week"; it's never that. (#68)

Several partners at Firm 6 also said that the firm's emphasis on collegiality results in exceptional responsiveness of partners to one another. One partner commented:

When I reach outside of my practice group . . . you know, the joke is it's as if they were sitting at their desk just waiting for my call. Because I mean the response is, "Absolutely, I have time, we did a memo on that two years ago, let me send that to you, I can get somebody to update it." It's quite seamless." (#212)

A different partner at the same firm said that partners

> bend over backwards to help each other, so that is true, our reputation of being collegial. I can call someone in the corporate group and say, "I need an hour of your time," and they'll give it to me right then or later that day or stay late or whatever. (#198).

Another partner echoed this experience:

> I've never called someone up and had them not be anything less than fully willing to [say], "What can I do to help, I'm happy to help," because certainly things come up outside of your area of expertise or the expertise of people that are intimately working on the case and people are happy to lend a hand and pitch in. Same way, people call me with a question [and] I try to be as helpful as I can, helping them out with whatever their situation is. (#206)

Many partners therefore regard collaboration as intrinsically rewarding. Assuring partners that a firm appreciates this and is committed to providing such rewards signals that the firm is run according to both business and professional logics. This can help temper the risk of individualism and narrow self-interested behavior that can arise by encouraging partners to be entrepreneurs. It can create an even stronger tie to the firm, and a more durable form of firm-specific capital, than appreciation of the financial benefits that collaboration provides.

A culture in which partners seek such intrinsic professional rewards in turn can generate economic benefits for the firm, in a type of virtuous circle. As Gardner (2016, 64) notes, "Psychological research has convincingly demonstrated that when employees feel that their work has meaning and is important to their organization—and by extension, to clients—then they exert more effort and become more committed, both to the team and to the organization." This underscores that a firm that balances financial and nonfinancial rewards may be able to create a culture in which business and professional values complement one another.

Despite the potential benefits of collaboration, firms can find it challenging to convince people to engage in it:

> [F]or the professionals involved, the financial benefits of collaboration accrue slowly, and other advantages are hard to quantify. That makes it

> difficult to decide whether the investment in learning to collaborate will pay off. Even if they value the camaraderie of collaborative work, many partners are hard-pressed to spend time and energy on cross-specialty ventures when they could be building their own practices instead. (Gardner 2015, 76–77)

In addition, movement of partners in and out of the firm, along with law firm mergers, can inhibit collaboration. As Gardner (2013, 9) reports, one partner in an international firm noted that "I used to know enough about my partners' work that it would take me only one or perhaps two phone calls to locate even the most esoteric expertise I needed." After a series of mergers, however, "the firm has a lot more experts available, but finding them is exponentially trickier. Plus, people no longer feel the same personal accountability to each other that makes them interrupt their own agenda to help on another partner's client. I feel like I need to negotiate or incentivize, whereas before people would just do the right thing for each other."

Finally, consistent with our earlier point, Gardner (2013, 6) emphasizes that collaboration requires trust: "both a deep respect for a colleague's competence ('I trust you not to make a blunder') and a belief in his integrity ('I trust you won't undermine my relationship with my client')." She notes that "firms' rapid growth and internationalization, along with heightened individual mobility, makes it more challenging than ever for lawyers to develop mutual trust." Relational trust in particular develops only through "shared experiences, reciprocal disclosure, and demonstrations that individuals will not take advantage of each other" (8).

Gardner's work suggests that fostering a culture of collaboration may hold particular promise for creating firm-specific capital under modern market conditions. Doing so, however, can be especially challenging. In the next section, we discuss some steps firms may take to meet this challenge.

Fostering Collaboration

Aside from institutionalizing clients, a firm also can attempt to solve the Prisoner's Dilemma by assuring lawyers that they will benefit financially by helping colleagues. This signals the importance of collaboration by rewarding it as a valuable contribution to the firm—even when helping someone else may divert a partner from generating more revenue on his own. We describe how firms attempt to do this in more detail in chapter 7, but here mention briefly the measures used by firms whose partners described their culture as especially collaborative.

Firm 6, for instance, asks partners on their annual compensation forms to identify which partners have been helpful to them and whom they have helped. One partner described this as a "really meaningful part of the evaluation," and said, "People want to know who is helpful to other people, they want to know who is really the glue to the place, and so people want to get on that list." It is notable that this firm "does a great job of institutionalizing clients," according to the same partner (#203).

One partner in this firm noted that he "didn't worry about it" when he basically ran a particular transaction even though he did not get any credit for managing the matter. He reported that he was confident the compensation committee would appreciate his role (#204).

Morgan Lewis, a firm not in our study, follows a similar approach. As a 2018 article in the *American Lawyer* describes, "'We use phrases that relate to individual accountability to the firm,' [management partner Steven] Wall says. They include the term 'responsible partner' rather than billing or originations partner, and 'attorney-in-charge,' with regard to the person running a particular matter for a client. Base salary is determined in part by who drives revenue, Wall says, while bonus determination is more focused on collaborative aspects" (McLellan 2018).

A partner in Firm 3, whose partners also described a strong collaborative culture, described how the firm uses compensation decisions to reinforce this ethos:

> [We may say to someone], "Well, I don't know who you think you're kidding but you didn't produce all this business yourself. . . . [W]e know you have a team, we know you had a big environmental matter you took 80 percent of the credits for that when you should have only had 50 percent of that. You took advantage of this poor guy who came over here from X and he's good enough not to have complained about you, but you know what, you're not helping us and you're not helping yourself." (#105)

Measures such as these attempt to solve the Prisoner's Dilemma by communicating that cooperation will be rewarded rather than exploited. Management signals that being entrepreneurial is a collective rather than a solitary enterprise, and that this orientation will benefit both the firm and its partners more than narrowly self-interested efforts to build a self-contained practice.

While underscoring the financial benefits of collaboration is important, a firm can elicit even stronger loyalty by solving the Assurance Game—by credibly conveying to partners that it regards collaboration as intrinsically valuable. One way it can do this, which we discuss more in chapter 7, is by rewarding collaborative behavior that is not immediately financially remunerative. This involves giving weight, for instance, to firm "citizenship" activities such as mentoring junior lawyers, helping devise professional development training programs, advising on and adjudicating business conflicts, working to help strengthen the firm's data security system, leading a department or practice group, actively participating in the firm's pro bono program, or serving on various administrative committees. None of these directly generate revenue, but all are important forms of cooperative behavior. In these ways a firm "leaves money on the table" in that compensation is not strictly tied to the revenues that a partner directly generates.

Our interviews suggest that another way a firm can help solve the Assurance Game while encouraging an entrepreneurial orientation is by supporting partners in developing new practices, even when this means that a partner will be less profitable for a period of time. A firm, for instance, may provide more compensation to a partner developing a practice than he ordinarily would receive according to financial metrics. This approach carries a business logic, in that it can be seen as an investment in the partner's long-term ability to generate greater profits. It also expresses the professional logic that the firm supports an individual as someone other than simply an immediate profit center; the firm supports that person's desire to advance his career. In this respect, the firm leaves money on the table, at least in the short term.

One partner in Firm 6, for instance, described how the firm was patient in allowing him to develop a new practice area:

> I've been highly encouraged and given a lot of flexibility. . . . There have been years where I wasn't billing any hours because I was out just developing and I'm not sure that they want everybody doing that, but I guess they trusted me enough or gave me enough rope to sort of hang myself, but yeah, I've been very fortunate that I was encouraged.
>
> I was also a bit unique in that we historically did not have a strong practice [in a particular field] and even as an associate I said, "This is crazy we're

> missing a whole boatload of truly loyal clients because that is one client base that actually still remains quite loyal to its legal purveyors." . . . I said I liked the work, I've done some of it and we had already done some; we just never branded it, packaged it, and sold it appropriately. I said "I would like to go do that," and they said, "Okay." So that was where I identified a hole and was willing to take the risk to try to mine it. (#203)

The partner believed the firm would not penalize him for temporarily generating fewer profits, and thus he could pursue this opportunity.

Another partner said that her current firm "recognizes much more so than did [her previous firm] the sheer value of a good marketing person, if you are willing to market not just yourself but your partners." She elaborated:

> At [this firm] they are hugely supportive of marketing efforts. I had a sense even from the interview process and I still think it's very true that if they have somebody who is really good at that they are perfectly happy for you to bill 1,000 hours and market for 1,000 hours. That may be a little bit overstated, but if you are successful at it [they support it].
>
> And they are willing to pay for it not only out of pocket but recognizing that that's a valuable contribution. That's different; not every firm has that. So it's not like, "Did you bill 2,500 hours and now where is your 500 or 600 hours of marketing?" It's, "You put in 2500 hours total." (#150)

Partners also can help solve the Assurance Game by helping even when they will receive no financial benefit from doing so. This sends a powerful message that colleagues regard collaboration as intrinsically valuable, thereby furnishing especially meaningful assurance that the firm operates according to professional as well as business logic. One partner in Firm 6 characterized his colleagues' responsiveness as "universally terrific," and described a recent experience:

> I had a pitch this week with a partner who I work with a lot; we went out to pitch a prospective new client. Even though [he and I would get billing credit on the matter], we had several of our partners who we reached out to who could not have been more enthusiastic about trying to help us bring in the work. Contacting people they knew, shooting emails to people who knew the general counsel there, saying, "These two partners are great. What

> can we do? How can we help?" I think [a focus on] how can we help bring in business for the firm is very much the overall perspective here, so I'm always very pleased with the generosity of my partners in wanting to just help bring the work in. (#207)

Another partner in the same firm said, "I would say one of the good things about being here is [that] most people are not overly concerned with getting credit; they are concerned, 'Hey let's just get the job done,' and they are glad to be brought into a project" (#223).

A partner in Firm 3 expressed the view of many of the partners about the firm:

> We have a culture where people will pitch in to assist client needs basically at any time, for any reason. So you can send an email out to a half dozen people and say, "I just got this question; the client would like to have a meeting on this Saturday night at 6:00; who can do this?" and four out of six people will respond and say, "Yeah, I'm happy to help out," even though they are not going to get paid for it, they don't know the client, and even though it's Saturday night at 6:00. (#75)

Partners who do this leave money on the table in that they otherwise could be using their time for activities that will benefit them financially.

To be sure, it can be difficult to disentangle instrumental and intrinsic rewards from collaboration. People might well not collaborate if they believe that it would generate no tangible rewards; after all, collaboration seeks to attain something other than simply collaboration. At the same time, it is common to distinguish between people who help others in expectation of a benefit and those who do so because they want to help. One Firm 3 partner's description of his connection to his firm illustrates this:

> When my wife, who I married in the midst of law school, and I had our first child they thought he might die the first couple of days. . . . At the time they thought he had a seizure and might have some sort of brain aneurism or tumor, so [I was] with him down in the NICU. Oh my, I still remember people just fell over themselves to take away a massive case that I was involved in at the time. Not saying, "Well it's ours now," but "Just forget about this—we're going to fire you if you come in here. You go handle life, this is all going to

> be waiting for you when you get back, and you've got a hell of a lot more important things to worry about." That made a real impression on me at the time early in my career. (#100)

At the same time, the size of modern large firms means that, even within a firm committed to supporting practice development, the effectiveness of such initiatives can vary among practice groups. As one partner in Firm 6 said:

> In theory there are supposed to be practice group heads and I think it really does vary from practice group to practice group how strong those leaders are and how much they are invested in making sure that the people within their groups stay busy and are progressing. . . . I think some groups do a great job at that and they are very supportive and can have a long-term succession plan. [In others,] the leaders of the practice groups are [people] who have great client relationships but they may not be people who were selected for that position because they were great mentors or sponsors for people within their groups. (#239)

Another Firm 6 partner interested in selling his services internally indicated that in his firm, "Nobody is teaching you how to do that. . . . [T]hey'll put you in a setting like a partners meeting and say, 'Go meet each other,' but I mean, you just became partner and there are 500 of your colleagues there, so that can be intimidating" (#254). Ultimately, even in firms with a generally collaborative culture, it is up to partners in the modern law firm to take the initiative and forge their own path. As one partner put it:

> There isn't necessarily going to be anybody else looking out for you anymore. It's kind of up to you to keep yourself busy. . . . For whatever kind of practice group structure there is going to be . . . at the end of the day the only person who is going to care about you is you. And, you know, other people are going to make the decisions that are right for them and so you've got to be your own advocate. (#239)

Conclusion

Law firms now operate in a legal market in which they must continuously focus on obtaining work from clients. One consequence is an emphasis on being "entrepreneurial" as a crucial attribute of a modern law firm partner. This ethos reflects a more explicit focus on law firm practice as a business, both for the firm and for each of its partners. This creates the risk that a partner who is an especially successful entrepreneur may come to see himself as running his own business and may seek to maximize its profits with minimal regard for colleagues or the firm. The result may be a firm that is perceived by its partners to be dominated by business logic, in which commitment to the firm is contingent on the financial reward that it provides.

Firm management may be able to avoid this outcome if it makes an effort to institutionalize clients and to take credible steps to emphasize that being entrepreneurial is a collaborative rather than solitary enterprise. While this serves the firm's business interests, it can also generate deeper loyalty to the firm if partners believe that colleagues are not rewarded for narrowly self-interested behavior and that management values collaboration as a core professional value. The result may be a balance of business and professional logics that provides some measure of firm-specific capital in the form of a distinctive organizational culture with which partners identify.

Striking this balance can be a challenge for law firm management. Partners must believe that other partners are pulling their weight, and market pressures mean that firms can be patient with below-average partner performance for only so long. At some point, a firm must respond to these concerns by insisting that partners meet productivity standards or seek opportunities elsewhere. The next chapter discusses how the traditional stigma against law firm layoffs has evaporated in recent years, especially since the economic downturn in 2008.

5

Pruning for Productivity

Since the 2008 economic downturn, law firms have become much more willing to lay off lawyers, including partners, whom they regard as unproductive. Firms historically eschewed layoffs due to fluctuations in the business cycle, out of concern that doing so would hurt their reputations with prospective recruits and the public. As one observer noted, "Layoffs are a brutal reality of corporate America. During fallow periods, publicly traded companies, including the big banks, routinely cull their ranks. The country's largest law firms, by contrast, have historically taken a kinder, gentler approach, rarely firing employees en masse" (Lattman 2013).

The downturn, however, sharply reduced demand for law firm services and left many firms with little work for a good number of their lawyers. Firms responded by laying off lawyers in unprecedented numbers. On a single day in February 2009 known as "Bloody Thursday," six major firms announced the termination of a total of almost 1,000 lawyers and staff. For that month, law firms laid off 2,000 lawyers and staff (Harper 2013). During all of 2009, law firms laid off 12,259 lawyers and staff (Moliterno 2012, 336).

While those cuts occurred in the midst of an especially sharp economic downturn, layoffs have lost their traditional stigma as a way to maintain profitability even in the face of more modest fluctuations. As one former partner who is an observer of the law firm sector described, "Even a single year of relatively minor decline can create concerns. Cutting costs through layoffs and getting more billable hours out of the survivors has become a typical, businesslike response" (Harper 2013). A law firm consultant described the role that layoffs need to play in fashioning a strategy to deal with economic uncertainty. "In a word, [firms] need to get lean. They need to reduce chronic underperformers, they need to reduce fixed overhead both in terms of attorney and staff overhead. . . . Firms that get lean can come through this and have a lot of opportunity on the other side" (Cassens Weiss 2012).

The New Normal

In June 2013, Weil Gotshal & Manges, a notable global law firm based in New York with 1,200 lawyers, announced that it was laying off 60 associates and 110 staff members, as well as reducing compensation for about 10 percent of the firm's partners. Profits per partner in the firm were $2.2 million the year before, which led it to rank seventeenth among US firms. That figure, however, represented an 8 percent decline from the year before. The firm generated over $1.2 billion in revenue for the same year, ranking thirteenth, but that was essentially the same amount of revenue as in the preceding year. These figures were published in the *American Lawyer* and raised concern within the firm that they would signal a lack of dynamism and growth by the firm.

Two months later, about 20 percent of bankruptcy associates were let go because of a decline in demand for such work. The firm's managing partner described the market conditions that led the firm to adopt these measures:

> As we have discussed during various town hall meetings over the last few years, the market for premium legal services has entered into a "new normal" after the 2008 financial crisis. Many firms have been forced to take actions over the last few years to reduce costs to deal with this new reality. . . . As the restructuring and litigation work relating to the 2008 financial crisis winds down, and as the overall market for transaction activity remains at the lower levels which we believe is the new normal, we must now make the adjustments we avoided over the last few years to position the Firm to continue to thrive. . . .
>
> From a revenue perspective we will continue to take significant steps to further increase our market share. However, it appears that the market for premium legal services is continuing to shrink. Therefore, actions to enhance revenue alone will not be sufficient to position the Firm as necessary for these new market conditions. (Lat 2013)

The managing partner's memo stated that in addition to the layoffs that had been announced, "There will have to be meaningful compensation adjustments for certain partners in light of the economic realities of the new normal. It may well be that some of these partners will decide to pursue other opportunities" (Lat 2013). In some firms, such adjustments have taken the form of demoting equity partners to salaried partner status.

A partner therefore knows that how successful she is as an entrepreneur will affect not only compensation but ultimately her future at the firm. "If you are not productive for a few years," one partner said, "firms don't carry their wounded that long anymore." It used to be that "you could give somebody a chance to retool if he or she lost a client or two." Now, "it can happen but it's rare" (#14). A partner at another firm echoed this:

> I think it's inevitable when people are asked, "What have you done for [the firm] lately and are you billing, are you handling enough work?" I mean, if you are a worker bee partner, if your hours are high enough you're okay, but if you don't have the hours, you don't have the business, you're going to have some issues and you're not going to be able to stick around for 20 years." (#199)

As one partner succinctly put it to a reporter, "You're only as secure as the amount of money you bring in. The job is to make money for the firm" (Rogers 2013). When asked whether there have been cultural changes since he joined the firm, one partner responded:

> Yeah, well I certainly think that things changed as a result of the downturn. [This] was a place that prided itself on never having done economic layoffs, and that changed when things went south starting in '09. There is much less tolerance for people who aren't busy, both on the associate side but on the partner side as well. I think the idea that if you make partner, you can kind of glide out your career as long as you were minimally busy is gone. Partnership is not a guarantee of a lifetime appointment. (#189)

Partners in law firm management are aware that greater willingness to lay off people and to let go of less-profitable practice areas can lead some people to say that "the firm has become too bottom-line oriented, that business is being put first, and this was a more humane and social place in the past" (#228).

They see the need to take such measures as unavoidable, however, because of unforgiving competitive conditions. As one partner put it:

> We try to balance [it with] preserving our culture . . . but the reality is that we have to adapt to the way that the economics of the law firm industry are moving. . . . You can't just put your head in the sand and plug your ears and say, "No, no, we're just going to keep doing it the way that we did it ten years ago because that is how we like to do it; we don't change." You do that, then eventually you'll just be a dinosaur. So you have no choice but to adapt. (#71)

Another partner commented on a firm that was having significant problems at the time of the interview. (The firm eventually was acquired by another firm.) "Our firm," he said, "could have found itself in deep, deep water the way [this firm] is now, for instance, if it wasn't as forward-thinking as it is. If it hadn't taken steps to deal with under-performance, or just good performance but in practice areas that just don't fit with this kind of . . . platform. You can't be all things to all people, you just can't" (#228).

One partner described the situation at a firm where he and some colleagues previously had worked that was eventually acquired by another firm after what looked like a death spiral:

> We realized pretty quickly that there was going to be some financial turmoil, they were going to have to let lots of people go. The productivity level of the partners was dismal. I had heard at one point that . . . [l]ess than 50 percent of the partners billed more than 1,000 hours a year. And it wasn't because they were rainmakers; it was just people who had been around for a while and it was hard to get rid of people. (#253)

Firms believe that failure to acknowledge these realities will imperil not only their competitiveness but their very survival. A 1994 account of the dissolution of what was then New York's oldest law firm—Lord, Day, founded in 1818—provides a cautionary tale. It reflects the dramatic shift in the law firm market over the last few decades, whose lessons law firm leaders see as central to their situation today. As the *New York Times* reported at the time the firm closed, "The old values of being true, quiet professionals still held. Lord, Day's lawyers served the same clients for generations. The aggressive pursuit of new business and old bills was considered unseemly. Gentility counted for a lot—colleagues uniformly described one another as 'nice.' It was a lovely way to run a law firm. It turned out to be a terrible way to run a business" (Hoffman 1994).

By the late 1980s, "senior partners were waking up with a start. They realized that if the firm did not expand rapidly, it would die. With scarcely 100 lawyers, it could not assign 30 or 40 bodies necessary for the complex mergers and acquisitions that were bringing windfalls to larger firms." Ultimately, "like many firms, Lord, Day refused for so long to adapt to the new legal market that when it did—merging with another firm, taking on a costly lease—it was too late." As one associate commented, "We came here just because it hadn't woken up to the new world. What I liked about the firm were the very reasons it couldn't last" (Hoffman 1994).

Firms in recent years therefore monitor much more intently the profitability of different practice areas and their trajectories. One partner noted, "The management committee meets [twice a year for several days,] and we look at everybody's practice and we try to talk to people about where their practice is heading or when we see danger signs of a practice slipping off. . . . A practice may ebb and flow, but at a certain point you have to have a performance-based culture in a law firm" (#247).

An especially dramatic example of this occurred in connection with practices related to financial services that were hit hard by the economic downturn in 2008. This same partner described his firm's process of dealing with this:

> [The head of the practice] said, "It will come back, let us keep the most sophisticated cutting edge lawyers who are doing this kind of work, segue them into doing some other types of finance while we wait for it to come back." We gave people a long lead time but we basically said [after] a couple of years, "You ought to look for other opportunities." We downsized about 100 lawyers there. That was probably a market disruption that we won't see again in our lifetimes, but there are things like that practice that recur year after year. (#247)

The Symbolism of Profits per Partner

While termination may be based on financial productivity, what it means to be productive varies from firm to firm. A significant factor in defining this term is the impact of a partner on a firm's profits per partner (PPP). This figure represents the profits of a firm divided by the number of its equity partners. It has become a hugely influential metric by which the success and status of firms are measured. It therefore is not simply a straightforward objective figure, but a highly significant symbol. Understanding this is important to appreciate why firms have moved to a policy where they regard partnership as contingent on performance rather than a permanent status.

Law firm management is concerned not simply with a firm's PPP but with how it compares to other firms'. Not all firms can match the market leaders on this metric, but firms are exquisitely sensitive to how they are doing with respect to firms that they regard as their peers. Peers generally are defined as firms with a similar ranking in the *American Lawyer* ranking of firms by gross revenue, as well as those firms ranked slightly higher. These firms are the ones that a firm tends to consider its closest overall competitors in attempting to obtain business from clients and attract lateral partners.

Considerations of profitability have become especially salient for some firms in light of data suggesting a more pronounced segmentation of the legal market by firms and types of work. Some evidence suggests that the most profitable thirty firms or so are pulling substantially ahead of the others and that they are gaining an increasing proportion of high-end work for business clients that is less price-sensitive than most businesses (Press 2011, 2014; Seal 2019). This group of law firms includes some traditional market leaders as well as newer firms that have been able to adopt successful strategies in the last two to three decades that have greatly enhanced their profitability and visibility. The perception among many observers is that the advantages of being in this top tier will be self-reinforcing, so that it will become increasingly difficult in the future for firms outside of it to move into its ranks. Other firms certainly will be quite profitable, but they will need to compete for work with respect to which clients are more sensitive to price and efficiency.

Many firms outside the top group are eyeing this trend nervously and are determined to be on the right side of the emerging market divide. As one partner observed:

> There is a feeding frenzy among big law firms for the top of the market—big corporations, big private equity firms, big international firms—so how do you continue to distinguish yourself, what are you selling, what are you selling into these markets, who are you, what is your identity and how do you manage that process, and do you do anything out there that destroys

> that identity? You need to understand who you are and what you are trying to sell and you've got to fight for that every day because it's a handful of big players at the top end of that market. (#176)

Improving profitability can be both an effect and a cause in pursuing this goal. Profitability that comes closer to the top firms can serve a signaling function by suggesting to clients that a firm is comparable to these firms in other respects, thus providing a certain halo effect. It also can signal to potential lateral partners who do high-end work that the firm will be able to compensate them handsomely if they move. And yet, the majority of law firm work does not fall into the realm of the top tier. One report suggested that only 20 to 25 percent of legal work required "unique legal experience" while 60 to 70 percent is more related to the day-to-day legal needs of clients (Thomson Reuters and Georgetown Law 2019).

The role of profitability as a symbol reflects that professional services are what economists call credence goods (Wolinsky 1993). This means that their quality can be difficult to assess even after they are consumed. In transactional work, for instance, it can be difficult to say how much value a lawyer or a firm contributed to an acquisition of another company or the sale of a subsidiary. Even in litigation, where outcomes would seem more easily measured, how much of the value of a settlement or a judgment was attributable to the lawyers' skill compared to the importance of the facts, the clarity of the law, the perspective of the judge or fact finder, the bargaining leverage of the parties, and, of course, the skill of the other side?

While clients tend to rely more on individual than firm reputation these days, they still attach some importance to the reputation of the firm. As Burk and McGowan (2011, 65) suggest, the greater focus on individual lawyers "is not to say that a firm's overall brand has become irrelevant." They continue: "We suspect that it is relevant for all firms, although for most it is no more than a relatively weak asset. For example, firm reputation apparently matters to the extent that in-house counsel do not want to be second-guessed for giving an important matter to counsel that no one in senior management or on the board has heard of" (65–66).

This phenomenon reflects the fact that the reputations of elite firms tend to be self-reinforcing, which provides a competitive barrier against other firms that seek to enter their ranks. Their reputations and expertise help them continue to attract business, which in turn enhances their expertise, the credentials of the lawyers whom they are able to recruit, their profitability, and their reputations. These all contribute to their role as market leaders.

Firms that hope to solidify or attain status as major corporate firms attempt to mimic these market leaders in as many respects as possible. The character of legal services as a credence good means that clients and other parties that evaluate firms tend to rely on proxies for quality in doing so. For law firms, these proxies may be the clients whom the firm serves, the extent to which the firm has done work similar to the type that the client needs, the educational background and credentials of the lawyers, the expertise and prominence of particular lawyers in the firm, and PPP. Law firm managers believe that many who assess their firms treat PPP as a concise proxy for these attributes. They therefore place particular emphasis on maintaining PPP that at least approximate, if they do not replicate, this figure for the elite firms.

Another way in which firms tend to mimic market leaders is the compensation for beginning associates. Over the last few decades, many notable increases have been instituted by highly prestigious firms. These increases can be expensive since they tend to produce a ripple effect that results in increases for associates at all levels of seniority. As a matter of pure economic rationality, therefore, it might not be advisable for all law firms in, say, the Am Law 100 to adopt these increases, much less those outside of this group (Bruch 2018). Yet this has generally been the case. Firms have tended not to determine whether their cost structure and revenue base can support these increases. Instead, they have moved swiftly to adopt them, sometimes within hours of the initial firm's announcement. These increases place even greater pressure on PPP, which in turn raises the standard for acceptable partner productivity.[1]

Productivity as a Moving Target

The focus on maintaining PPP and competitive salaries creates pressure for a firm to increase the amount of revenue and profits that are necessary for a partner to retain her position. Firms differ in how they define an acceptable level of productivity. Those who see themselves as inside or within striking distance of the top tier will set it higher, in the course of which they may increasingly limit their work to higher-end services. Even firms with no reasonable aspirations of being in the top tier, however, will periodically assess the profitability of the services they provide and prepare to jettison some of them if the firm's profitability begins to fall below that of their peers. Being a profitable partner thus is not by itself sufficient to ensure job security; a partner must be profitable *enough.*

This instability is accentuated by the fact that volatile financial performance has become a characteristic feature of the law firm sector since the financial crisis. That is, revenues and billable hours may rise or fall in any given year, so that firms "increasingly have to manage unpredictable financial returns from one year to the next." At the same time, "partners generally will live with a decline in billables or revenue, consultants and firm leaders say, just as long as their annual profits don't dip" (Cipriani 2018). When revenues decline, the way to preserve PPP is to cut costs, which means terminating lawyers and practices seen as insufficiently productive. Thus, as the *American Lawyer* notes, fifty of the seventy-eight firms that increased PPP in 2017 did not have revenue increases but used measures such as "equity partner reductions" to maintain PPP (Simons and Bruch 2018).

One partner described how the pruning process at his firm was prompted by the sense that "we were doing just fine as a firm, [but] the gap between our firm and the top tier . . . was getting wider. . . . We weren't keeping up with our so-called peer group." As a result, "we went through a significant blood-letting, a lot of older partners were asked to leave, [the firm suggested to some] practice groups that maybe you would be happier in a different platform" (#228). Another partner said that at his firm:

> For a long time we had way too many clients. Without exception your receivables in the bottom third of your client list are going to be 3X what they are up the chain, so we set out to basically rid ourselves of the third tier. It might have been one-fourth [or] one-third, and we rid ourselves of a lot of lower value work, thinking that would make some big changes. Our realization rate went up from 89 or 90 percent to 96 or 97 percent; that was a lot of money." (#176)

In-demand practices may still fall by the wayside if management does not regard their level of profitability as consistent with the firm's strategic direction. Dechert, for instance, decided in 2006 that its state tax practice did not contribute to the firm's efforts to focus on higher-end work, even though it generated revenues of $10 million "and turned a tidy profit" (Triedman 2007). The firm therefore was not willing to devote resources to its development. As the firm chair wrote in announcing the departure of the partners in this practice, "For a variety of reasons, the development of a nationwide state tax practice is not a strategic priority for Dechert" (Triedman 2007). As a reporter noted:

> In Dechert-speak, that means that the state tax group wasn't going to help build one of the practices the firm sees as having the most profit potential: corporate, hedge and mutual funds, real estate finance, antitrust, securities litigation/white-collar enforcement, product liability, and most recently, IP and arbitration. And if it wasn't serving those practices, it wasn't going to get much in the way of resources from the firm. (Triedman 2007)

Part of the challenge for partners with these expectations is that practice areas are not stable with respect to profitability. As we describe in chapter 4, they tend to go through a cycle in which they begin as innovative services offered by a small number of firms who can charge premium rates for them and eventually become routine work in which profit margins are small. This process appears to be accelerating as a result of factors such as the wider availability and lower cost of information, greater attention to analyzing the workflow involved in legal services, and the increasing ability of clients to identify and parcel out discrete portions of work to low-cost providers.

One partner described how this dynamic has become commonplace in law firm practice:

> The interesting thing is that the low value legal work is not a fixed number of practices. The law work continues to go through an evolution and what was high end, high quality work at some point can become low value. So what that really means is at the back door of your law firm at some point in time somebody that once did high value work who hasn't changed what he's doing is likely to be doing low value work and be asked to move on to a smaller low-value law firm some place. And that happens seamlessly. It used to be a shock in the old days but today people understand it's normal. (#176)

Firms may effectively prune practices without explicitly telling partners that they need to leave by raising rates to levels that less profitable clients can't easily afford. One partner described how "the policies with respect to how billable rates are set have had a significant impact on people like me, who have smaller practices in terms of smaller clients" He elaborated:

PARTNER: [Rates] are generally increased across the board; you are told it's to keep up with whatever the market is, but I'm not sure what market they are talking about. The markets that I'm dealing with are looking for lower rates not higher rates, and that has made it difficult to develop a practice.

INTERVIEWER: So is there the prospect you might lose some clients at some point?

PARTNER: Yes, I think I've already lost work and clients because of that.

INTERVIEWER: Do you have much input into the decision to raise the rates?

PARTNER: In theory, yes; in practice, no.

INTERVIEWER: How is that supposed to work in theory?

PARTNER: In theory there should be some sort of dialogue in how the rate increase might impact the particular practice, but there isn't. I think the decision is that we need to keep up with what the market is for firms of our size so we need to bill accordingly. . . . The firm sees itself as playing in a certain segment of the market, and there are other firms in that segment that they want to not fall behind, because then they might be perceived as instead of a first-tier or second-tier law firm—they would be a third- or fourth-tier law firm. (#19)

This partner admitted that he could foresee that this trend toward rate increases might mean that he would need to leave the firm at some point:

INTERVIEWER: Is there concern among you and the folks you work with that at some point your practice just may not fit where the firm thinks it's going strategically?

PARTNER: Yes. That's certainly an issue for me, yes.

INTERVIEWER: How do you think management would react if you explicitly raised that?

PARTNER: It's hard to say. I think the answer might be that I need to either adjust what practice I want to have or my expectations, or look for other opportunities. (#19)

Sometime after the interview, this partner did leave his firm to join another firm.

Another partner explained that at her firm partners have some flexibility to discount rates for clients who may balk at increases, but that ultimately limits were placed on how far this can go:

> The groups that are saying, "We can't charge these rates and we're going to have to give every client a 25 percent discount," well, over time that has to affect your compensation. Or we may go the way of other firms that have taken a narrower model and have just gotten rid of the less profitable practice areas. . . . You have to decide what practice areas you want to emphasize. You have to live with the realities of the market and where the work is. (#193)

She saw the firm as moving more toward a "practice group profitability model . . . so I think that if you are in a practice over time that is growing and can command high realization or more leverage or whatever drives profit, and this makes your practice area more profitable, then the partners in that group will be recognized over time—and the converse is true also, obviously" (#193).

Pruning and Culture

It is hard to avoid the conclusion that pruning for profitability represents a fairly straightforward expansion of business logic. The traditional large firm that prevailed until the last few decades of the twentieth century generally regarded partnership as a status that continued unabated until retirement or death, rather than being contingent on generating an acceptable level of profits. As one analysis of the traditional firm notes:

> [T]he partnership form of ownership makes the earnings of each partner at least partly dependent on the revenue-generating capacity of all local offices. However, highly professionalized work forces will resist the elaboration of detailed cost structures and financial targets. Furthermore, the complex variety of economic and market circumstances across local offices attributable to their high geographical differentiation creates uncertainty that makes centrally determined, specific targets difficult to achieve and unlikely to be used. (Greenwood, Hinings, and Brown 1990, 735–36)

As a result, "systems of performance appraisal will be tolerant because without specific targets tight accountability is impossible. Moreover, professional organizations have a strong service ethic and a strong concept of community involvement and responsibility. Partnership implies a career commitment, which is inconsistent with financial myopia and tight accountability" (736).

It is clear that firms no longer follow this approach. Increasingly, performance standards are set with an eye on the firm's PPP, not on conditions in local legal markets. Those standards are relative rather than absolute, so that what is a sufficient level of profitability to ensure continued tenure in one year may not suffice two years later. This is characteristic of a greater emphasis on business logic, in which "[t]he degree of tolerance for meeting [financial] targets reduces quite significantly, such that failure to meet individual targets will result in redundancy not only for juniors (where an 'up, or out' policy has been operated for many years) . . . but for partners too" (Cooper et al. 1996).

Partners acknowledge that this development more explicitly relies on business considerations in evaluating themselves and their colleagues. They see this as unavoidable, however, in light of the changing dynamics of the legal market. The risk is that partners may conclude that the firm is concerned only with financial success. This can erode their sense of commitment to it and their willingness to engage in cooperative behavior. The result may be a self-fulfilling prophecy, in which partners act in narrow financially self-interested ways, which reduces trust and willingness to cooperate.

Solving the Prisoner's Dilemma in this instance requires that the firm persuasively communicate that a more stringent termination policy serves the common interest of ensuring that everyone is pulling her weight so that the firm can survive in a competitive market. Some partners, for instance, told us that being more demanding about productivity is the only way to ensure that the firm remains viable enough to preserve its culture. One midcareer partner put it this way:

INTERVIEWER: What do you see as the biggest risks to the firm's culture going forward?

PARTNER: I think that the single biggest risk [is that] there is increasing stratification based on both perceptions of quality and profitability. And if we are not in that top tier by the time I retire it's going to not be as great a place to practice.

INTERVIEWER: In what ways?

PARTNER: Well you won't be able to attract the best work; therefore, you won't be able to attract the best associates, and it's a cycle, and suddenly

> once you are perceived as being a second-tier firm doing second-tier work that's a problem.

> You know, I talked about performance culture, you downsize [a certain] practice not because you don't like those guys, but you can't be running around the country at $500 bucks an hour dealing with [fairly routine matters]. You've got to have the top tier people doing the top tier work in [that field]. You've got to have the top tier people . . . and you've got to be perceived that way, and that perpetuates itself in a positive way, and once that starts slipping it perpetuates itself in a negative way and *the threat to the culture ironically is if you are not competitive in profits per partner*. (#247) (emphasis added)

Several partners we interviewed interpreted their firms' lower tolerance for underperforming partners as contributing to a greater sense of fairness within the firm, and thereby strengthening culture, by holding people more accountable. One partner, for instance, described her firm as one characterized by

> taking pains to emphasize the importance of collegiality, taking pains to emphasize that it's important to share, it's not an eat what you kill type of firm; people are not well regarded if they are, I would say, selfish. . . . I tend to not embrace working with people who are selfish. People who are altruistic tend to want to work with each other, and it seems as though for the most part that they remain in the majority."

At the same time, she observed that "the trend over the last 10–15 years that I've seen [is that] . . . we're getting a little better at letting underperforming partners go." She continued:

> It's not as forgiving a place as it used to be and I don't think that's bad. You can't survive without making any decisions, and also I think there is a benefit to the people who are performing to impose some expectations, and [when] people are asked to leave it's very delicately, privately, gently done, but I've done it, I mean we've done it. (#131)

Not all firms ask underperforming partners to leave. Another option is to "de-equitize" the partner, effectively keeping them a partner in name but removing them from the pool of the lawyers that shares directly in the profitability of the firm. (We discuss the role of partners without equity more in chapter 6.) One consultant described the mindset of firm leaders who de-equitize equity partners: "We don't want to ask [unproductive equity partners] to leave, we don't have a sharp-elbow culture, and we don't take people out back and shoot them, so we're just going to make them nonequity" (Newsham 2019). While firm leaders may believe this preserves culture while also attending to business needs, it may just be delaying the inevitable departure of a partner who can no longer contribute at the level expected by the firm.

Nevertheless, some partners suggested that establishing and enforcing clear expectations can help elicit commitment to the firm. It is worth quoting one partner at some length:

> INTERVIEWER: You mentioned the importance of evaluating on an ongoing basis the productivity of the individual lawyers, as well as practice groups, and making some difficult decisions as you go forward. How can a firm do that and still elicit a sense of loyalty to the firm?
>
> PARTNER: Well, if you don't set up an ongoing process those decisions will be viewed as highly political. If you set up a process and do it for half a dozen years, people will accept the fairness of the process.
>
> INTERVIEWER: So it generates a sense of fairness if everybody knows what the expectations are and feels like they are being applied fairly within the firm? Does that provide assurance that everybody is pulling their own weight or making equal contributions?
>
> PARTNER: Yeah, I think if everybody thinks that compensation is fair they can tolerate one practice area being above the other in profitability and financial contribution and compensation.
>
> INTERVIEWER: Is there a sense that you are enforcing a high standard even if that may mean that you are encouraging some people to find opportunities elsewhere?
>
> PARTNER: Right. (#59)

Another partner echoed this idea:

> PARTNER: If you are successful, you sort of earn your credibility and then nobody really second-guesses what you do.
>
> INTERVIEWER: But you are held accountable because you've got the performance metrics.

PARTNER: And that keeps everybody performing and so that creates the trust. (#76)

From this perspective, knowing that the firm holds other partners accountable creates trust that colleagues are contributing equally to the success of the firm rather than behaving as free riders. This type of accountability furnishes the type of assurance that a few decades ago was provided by small partnerships where partners all knew one another and actively participated in governance. It thus can be seen as a way of solving a Prisoner's Dilemma among partners who may be relative strangers to one another.

One partner made the point this way:

> You have to have a performance-based culture in a law firm. Performance can mean a lot of different things. It can mean that you are a guy who attracts $30 million a year in transactional business. It can also mean that you are an extraordinarily well-respected mentor role model. . . . There are a lot of different ways to contribute to the firm's performance but at the end of the day everybody has to at some level perform. (#247)

Crucial to effectively communicating this message is people's confidence that everyone is subject to the same standards, and that they are fairly applied.

Seen in this light, the demise of Lord, Day can be seen as a product of the firm's failure to take the business steps necessary to save the firm and its culture. At the firm, one article reports, "younger rainmakers—people who attracted lucrative business—felt their efforts propped up the veterans, who were expected to spend their golden years burnishing a firm's reputation by taking on community leadership roles" (Hoffman 1994). In 1986, the firm lost the head of its multimillion-dollar antitrust practice, who took seventeen lawyers and several clients to another firm. "Lord, Day was never able to rebuild its antitrust work. Half the firm's real-estate practice left, as did Richard G. Cohen, its tax chief. In addition to the loss in business, the firm lost prestige: top-flight law school graduates became increasingly difficult to recruit" (Hoffman 1994). The latter development reflects the perceived connection between profitability and status that characterizes the modern law firm world. In this narrative, Lord, Day ultimately collapsed because it could not sustain the profitability that enabled its partners to enjoy the professional rewards of practicing in an elite firm.

Tempering Business Logic

It is difficult to deny that pruning for profitability reflects a significant embrace of business logic. It can be interpreted as generating trust among partners. This trust, however, appears to be the type that results from solving the Prisoner's Dilemma, in that it inspires confidence that it is safe to cooperate because everyone is pulling her fair share. For many firms solving the Assurance Game with respect to terminating partners takes the form of attempting to temper business logic by professional logic, rather than balancing the two in equal measure.

Some firms, for instance, keep a close eye on overall financial performance but opt to provide a broad range of services that vary in their profitability. This allows the firm to define productivity in different ways for different partners. This strategy can mitigate some of the pressure to lay off partners and prune practices and contribute to a more collegial and satisfying culture. Firms 4 and 6 deliberately pursue this approach.

One partner in Firm 6 offered this interpretation of his firm's choice to provide a range of services rather than adopting a "transactional" approach that focuses on high-end matters:

INTERVIEWER: Do you have a sense whether the firm trades off some intangibles for not completely maximizing economic performance, financial performance?

PARTNER: I do have that sense.

INTERVIEWER: And how is that reflected in concrete ways?

PARTNER: I think it's reflected in [the fact] that firms that focus very much on the bottom dollar are very transaction-focused, whereas I think we focus more on making sure that we give clients very good service and that we have almost every practice area represented at the firm. (#245)

He framed this as a choice to eschew top dollar for the sake of allowing lawyers to pursue practices that might be pruned at other firms:

PARTNER: That comes at a cost because not every practice area is that profitable, whereas I think there are certain firms that really prefer to focus on just a few very profitable areas. We are a full service place and there is a lot of value in just helping others and responding to questions that people have. . . . My sense is more that we're more focused on client service even if it means that we do things or we have lawyers who spend their time developing expertise in issues that will not necessarily be that remunerative to the firm.

INTERVIEWER: And that's a deliberate philosophical choice?

PARTNER: It seems to me that way, particularly in light of sort of other firms that I talk to, where the focus is on deal after deal after deal. Those are the high volume, high profit margin practices. . . . If we cared more about profitability we would probably focus more on being more aggressive. (#245)

The firm's approach, in other words, leaves money on the table in the sense that a more selective set of practices could generate higher revenues and profits.

A partner at Firm 4 described his firm's commitment to a range of practices: "[We aim] to have ultimate flexibility to meet each one of our markets and, if we can be, as long as we can be competitive compensation-wise and rate-wise in each one of our markets we can be successful." He recounted the story of one group of partners who came to the firm from another firm because the other firm told them:

> "Your rate next year will be $850 an hour," and that had nothing to with their practice, their client, it was just that was what their rate had to be. And we said, "We can't charge 850 bucks an hour," and they said, "I don't need to make $2 million," and so now they are with us [and] they are charging 650 bucks an hour, and a couple of them are making over a million dollars. They figured, "I'm doing what I want to do, I'm keeping my clients and I'm making a pretty damn good living." But they couldn't fit that into their system, where again [we] preach flexibility and our compensation allows us to do that. . . . It's kind of like a jigsaw puzzle but it all fits together where we can accept people. (#163)

This partner described a practice in her firm in which the partners "don't make as much as the corporate securities lawyers but they love what they do and we love to have them because it's a great full service to offer to our business clients. We don't have to send them to somebody else" (#163). This reflects appreciation of both professional values—"they love what they do"—as well as financial rewards—"great full service" to the firm's business clients. Another partner at Firm 4 interpreted that firm's strategy as serving to temper business by professional logic: "I would also consider us as being less shy about being committed to culture, less given to embracing profits over people, [having a] little bit of caution about going the route of growth and profits, which has been evidenced by the way we've grown. It's slow and steady and cautious, but good and successful" (#131).

As these comments make clear, a full-service strategy can temper business logic for the sake of professional inclusiveness and simultaneously serve a firm's financial interest. One Firm 4 partner described the business benefits of this strategy:

> My view is, I'll take that trade any day to be honest, I mean if I step back and think, "Okay, in terms of stability and longevity would I rather have a bigger product offering that can get my billable number, my origination number higher, versus be at this other firm where I can only sell four things." For me that's a no-brainer, I mean every day of the week I'll [choose the former]. (#165)

Another partner at Firm 6 noted his firm's belief that having a wider range of work helps the firm weather fluctuations in the market: "We think the [narrower] model is tougher in a downturn. . . . We did better in the downturn simply because we had a much broader base" (#238).

Firms that maintain a relatively broad number of practices are able to maintain overall profitability because their partners are willing to accept significant differences in compensation based on the profitability of different practices. The difference between the highest- and lowest-paid equity partners in a firm is known as the "spread." At first blush, a wide spread may seem to reflect an internally competitive firm that proceeds solely on the basis of business logic. This may be the case in some firms. As we discuss in more detail in chapter 9, however, in other firms it may reflect a more inclusive approach that tries to balance business and professional concerns by using differences in compensation to reduce the need to lay off partners. This underscores the point that one cannot simply look at an organizational feature and classify it as expressing business or professional logic. We must understand how people in the organization interpret the meaning of such features.

Not all partners in firms with a large number of practices believe that the firm should take this approach. One partner in Firm 6 acknowledged that

> there are some people [who] say we've got to cut the number of partners because if we got rid of 10 percent of our partners our *American Lawyer* numbers will look better. . . . So there are some people who will say it isn't good enough just to reduce [a partner's compensation] to the point where they're profitable and let him or her decide whether they want to leave, we've got to be more aggressive, get rid of people. (#201)

A firm that offers a narrower range of services is entirely capable of solving the Assurance Game. Management must simply be attuned to other ways of credibly communicating to partners that nonfinancial professional values are important to the firm.

Some firms also temper the pure operation of business logic by being somewhat patient rather than terminating someone on the basis of a single year's dip in performance. From this perspective, ongoing close monitoring of performance can be helpful in identifying potential problems at an early point when there may be opportunities to address them. If those efforts are unsuccessful, a partner at least has an earlier indication that she may have to leave and can plan for that eventuality.

One partner, for instance, said that he believes that regularly keeping an eye on performance enables his firm to be "more humane" by "balancing the business needs with a sense of decency" more than other firms that let problems become serious before they respond. One firm he mentioned, for instance, "didn't change with the times and so when [they] had to they were brutal, they just overnight became brutal." By contrast, his firm did the culling that it thought was necessary, but "did it in a very humane way compared to when people just got shoved out the door overnight with no notice, no nothing" (#228).

Another partner remarked, "We don't cut throats very quickly here and we don't do it very readily. We almost always give people at least two years to retool or rework or rethink their practice" (#237). Firms may also signal the need to leave by phasing out a practice area rather than immediately abandoning it. This involves not devoting new resources to the practice such as entry-level associates, promotions to partner, lateral partners, increases in compensation, and marketing efforts. This provides time for partners in that practice to find another firm in which their work fits.

Another partner noted that his firm adjusts compensation every two years rather than every year. Thus, decisions to let someone go may require a longer process than in some other firms. As he put it,

> There are structural things you need to do to be successful and then there [are] interpersonal [ones]. You can't just do one or the other. We do not do compensation every year. We just don't do it. For equity members of our law firm we do the compensation every two years [because] doing it every year would be like saying to Michael Jordan, "There is an 82-game NBA season but if you have a bad game we're going to bench you." We don't do that. We say we need to look at two years performance before we reset your compensation, the base line. Because one year is too short. You could have had a stepchild who had an illness, right, you could have had your biggest client go out of business, okay. But then what do you do within that two-year window if someone has an extraordinary year? The way we solve that is every year we do bonuses. So we make people whole. (#83)

A partner in another firm made a similar point:

> Everybody goes through cycles and highs and lows and you have a little history. So you can trace the movie and not shoot a freeze frame one time. You have to take into account past accomplishments as well as current and not overrate the current accomplishments to the detriment of people that have made past contributions. (#59)

The extent to which such patience is interpreted as tempering business by professional logic is reflected in the view of one partner that his firm is too forgiving:

> [We] don't fire people as quickly as [we] should. . . . [Y]ou view everyone economically, which is, "What if we cut his comp down to $125,000 and it costs this much to have a portion of a secretary and the utilities and all that, and he only bills X hours at X rate we're still breaking even, we're still making a little bit of money on him." I think it's a terrible way to run a firm. . . . I mean we let people hang on here three, four, five years. You're not doing them any favors. . . . Everyone who knows about law firms who studies them said the same thing: "Don't carry your wounded forever." (#174)

Partners also described ways in which their firms attempted to respect people as professionals amidst the trauma of the financial crisis. One partner noted that his firm made unprecedented layoffs during the bottom of the economic downturn, but "we did it more slowly, we tried to find places for people to go and [did] our best to be as humane about it as you can be in those circumstances." With respect to involuntary departures more generally, "we set deadlines all the time for people to transition out and then extend those deadlines [for] almost endless periods of time [to give them] the maximum chance to find an opportunity" (#165). Another partner said, "where we decided we need to let people go we tried to give them a lot of time to find another home, we tried to help them find a position because not everybody is going to succeed here; in fact, the vast majority of people don't. . . . And so that's just the nature of it, but I think we've always in our group tried to be very humane about it" (#204).

Most partners who spoke of layoffs or instances in which partners were encouraged to leave their firms described these events as occasions for regret, rather than simply as business decisions made by the firm. One partner who described his firm's need to make layoffs during the economic downturn said, "Do I think the firm did the wrong thing? No, I don't. That was the economic reality of the time, but it hurts because you are dealing with people's lives" (#204). Another partner noted that in the firm there is "a slow trend toward what I would call more business discipline, but very much tempered by our disinclination to cut someone off" (#131).

Still another partner said, "We've had practices that just dried up. This firm is pretty good about it; we don't cut someone off at the knees after one or two bad years but over some period of time, after cutting people's compensation we have told people to leave" (#238). Speaking of her firm's layoffs during the worst of the economic downturn, another partner said, "I never want to see that happen again. I don't think the firm wants to see it happen again" (#254).

Many lawyers seemed to be attempting to come to grips with the trend of partner terminations and with its implications for the nature of law practice. This may reflect a desire to continue to distinguish law practice from ordinary business. It also may be based in part on concern for the firm's reputation among potential entry-level and lateral lawyers. One partner suggested:

> Even after the layoffs in 2009 where so many people were doing it, people still got criticized. "How much severance did you give?" The kids these days know it and it has a direct impact on the ability to recruit and it sends market signals too for laterals. So I think also the law firms understand that six months or a year is a very short time frame and someone in a practice group could be slow but the next year you may need them and you're not going

> to be able to attract talent if . . . whenever you are slow you just lay people off. (#253)

One partner contrasted his firm's approach to compensation with what he described as an investment banking mentality. That is, the firm makes an effort to mitigate the frequency and harshness of layoffs. This does seem to distinguish law firms to some degree from other businesses, of which investment banks may be the extreme example.

As Karen Ho (2009, 223) describes in her ethnography of Wall Street investment banking culture, "investment banks, on average, conduct a significant downsizing every year and a half or so, with continual 'purges' in between and along the way." Such layoffs occur in both bull and bear markets, so that "investment banks' up-and-down employment strategy is perhaps their most consistent cultural practice." Banks are hypersensitive to the slightest market movements and to opportunities to profit from them, which means that "Wall Street's approach to downsizing is instantaneous and absolute." The standard practice when layoffs are announced is "forcing downsized employees to pack up and leave within as little as fifteen minutes (or at least that day)." Their belongings are later shipped to them in UPS boxes. As one banker commented:

> I think that every single day you realize that our job could be gone the next day. You have a downturn in the market, and they lay off hundreds of people or you have a downturn in just your desk [your particular area's] performance; all of a sudden they need to lay off people. You know, your company decides they don't want to be in that product anymore; they lay off an entire department. I just think that's part of life here. (Ho 2009, 236)

Ho suggests that this Wall Street model of rapid deployment of resources and personnel in response to market conditions increasingly is presented as the template for the rest of the business world. As she put it, "The workplace practices and approaches to employment that have been cultivated on Wall Street have certainly helped to constitute the brave new workplace in general" (Ho 2009, 243). Investment banks thus tend to be the embodiment of the purely market-driven organization fueled solely by business logic.

By contrast, professional tradition makes law firms unlikely to reach this point in the near future. In this respect, their slower response to downturns in productivity leaves money on the table. At the same time, it is clear that the status of partner in a large law firm is much less secure than a few decades ago.

As one partner put it, "There is no big mother that will support you should things not work. And I think where most of the firms will go at the end of the day is to say, 'We are providing a platform and we will enjoy it if you succeed but there is no net to fall back on'" (#188). Another junior partner who has faced some challenges in getting enough work concluded, "I mean the way I look at it is, look, I'm either going to get appropriately busy and then I'll be happy and they'll be happy with me, or I won't be and neither one of us will be happy and I'll be looking for something else" (#241).

A firm therefore can attempt to honor professional values while meeting business pressures by taking various steps to reduce the need to terminate partners. One is to offer a wide range of practices that differ in profitability, and to compensate partners according to the profitability of each. This may reflect both a business judgment that a diverse set of practices will minimize financial volatility and a willingness to accept somewhat lower profits for the sake of professional values. Another is to ease the impact of terminations by phasing out the resources that a firm allocates to certain practices, and providing partners with a reasonable period of time to find work elsewhere, rather than making rapid adjustments when the profitability of a practice falls. These measures generally do not signal that professional logic has as much weight as business logic with respect to partner terminations. They may, however, help solve the Assurance Game in combination with firm policies on other issues that credibly convey that the firm regards furthering professional values as an intrinsically important part of its culture.

Conclusion

The structural changes in the market since the economic downturn have made partners resigned to the fact that firms may need to let lawyers and practice groups go if they are not meeting financial performance standards. Partners see this as an inevitable feature of law firm life in the "new normal." This undoubtedly strains ties between partners and the firm, especially for partners who may feel vulnerable because of lagging profitability of their individual practices. Furthermore, the dynamism of any given practice area cannot help but prevent most partners from feeling completely secure. While figures are not available, it is also worth noting that the gender dynamics that we describe in chapter 3 with regard to determinations of productivity could make women especially vulnerable to layoffs under these conditions.

There is no denying that pruning for profitability reflects the greater operation of business logic within large law firms. Some partners, however, also interpret it as providing a form of trust that can enhance and help sustain a collegial culture because it provides assurance that every partner is doing her share to make the firm profitable. In addition, management in various ways can provide at least some assurance that a firm is not guided solely by financial considerations. This may involve maintaining a broad range of practices, phasing out certain practice areas, and providing a reasonable period of transition before a partner must leave the firm.

Partners generally seem reconciled to the notion that partnership is no longer forever. To the extent that they regard their own firm as characterized by a deliberate and humane approach to underperforming partners, however, they believe that it stands for values beyond simply profitability. This can be one basis for them to identify with the firm and its culture even in an era in which partnership is more conditional than ever before.

6

The Material Economy of Compensation

Partner compensation is a tremendously important issue in large law firms, especially over the past few decades. Many of the responses to competitive pressures described in previous chapters are implemented in some way through a firm's compensation system. In terms of institutional logics theory, compensation practices are crucial mechanisms for managing demands posed by business and professional logics. As such, they have both material and symbolic significance. For this reason, we devote this chapter and the next to an in-depth examination of law firm partner compensation systems.

The overwhelming trend in large firms is to differentiate compensation based on factors related to perceived productivity. Traditional criteria of merit that reflect the legal profession's internal standards might include the quality of work, collegiality and collaboration, and assumption of nonremunerative firm "citizenship" responsibilities. Modern law firms, however, strongly emphasize considerations such as revenue generation, profitability, hours billed, and obtaining and retaining clients. In this respect, compensation systems reflect the increasing influence of business logic.

A compensation system represents a material dimension of the firm because it both constitutes part of its structure and serves to allocate financial rewards. Compensation also has a symbolic function in that it is an important indication of the value that a firm places on different types of qualities and behavior. For this reason, many partners interpret a firm's compensation system as a message about what it means to be a "good lawyer" in that firm. In this sense, compensation signifies the relative weight of business and professional logics in the overall value system of the firm.

One way to express the dual significance of compensation is that it constitutes a material economy that distributes financial rewards and a symbolic economy that allocates respect. It therefore has a powerful effect on partners' understandings of the character of their firms, their roles within them, and what it means to be a professional. The discussion in this chapter focuses on the material economy and how it operates, while the next chapter examines the symbolic economy. We spend time in this chapter describing compensation systems in some detail to provide a foundation for appreciating how intricate features of these systems can have powerful symbolic meanings.

Overview

The key role of compensation in the modern large firm is reflected in comments by several partners. One partner describes the significance of compensation this way:

> At the end of the day, after all of these things, the barometer is compensation, okay? Compensation sends incentives, it sends signals, it conveys culture. This is the language that we speak, it's the way we know how we're valued. [W]e know everything by how we are compensated, by whatever the metrics are for compensation. (#79)

Similarly, when asked what is most important in differentiating law firm cultures from one another, another partner responded,

> I would say that one of the big things is their compensation system. . . . That is one of the things that I would look at—not so much the executive committee, the management committee, but the comp committee. [H]ow does the comp committee work? (#16)

When asked what features indicate the culture of a potential law firm merger partner, another partner emphasized,

> Well, one of the things for example is . . . how do you do compensation and how are you rewarding people because that tells you a lot right there. What are your views on pro bono and community service? Those are the ques-

tions you really ask. To what extent do you [reward] cross selling and team approaches and those kinds of things?" (#111)

When market pressures were less fierce and large firms had greater assurance of steady work from regular clients, a firm had less need explicitly to use compensation to encourage entrepreneurial behavior. Rather, firms used a pure "lockstep" system that based lawyers' compensation solely on seniority: those who made partner in a particular year advanced in "lockstep" up the compensation scale. This practice was designed to encourage the collaboration that was necessary to serve the firm's clients, while fostering a sense of collegiality and equality among partners.

The fact that compensation was rarely a source of conflict, or even the subject of much explicit attention, within law firms was ostensibly an indication that nonfinancial professional values as well as financial rewards were important to a firm. As noted in our discussion of Gilson and Mnookin in chapter 1, lockstep served a business purpose by providing incentives that were appropriate for an oligarchic market in legal services. Its formal equality, however, allowed firms to downplay their status as business enterprises. Under such circumstances, partners did not interpret compensation as a signal of what it meant to be a good lawyer in the firm.

As we have discussed, firms today generally do not have the stable client relationships that provide firm-specific capital. They instead must rely on their lawyers to ensure a steady stream of work. Most firms see the incentives ostensibly resulting from lockstep compensation as ill suited for this market since partners of the same seniority receive the same rewards regardless of their efforts to obtain clients. A firm's compensation system therefore becomes a crucial instrument of its business strategy because it creates incentives for partners to bring in the work on which the firm relies. It also helps firms respond to the competitive lateral partner market. A firm needs to be able to pay enough both to keep its key partners from defecting and to attract profitable ones from other firms.

Compensation policy includes decisions about whether to promote a lawyer from a salaried employee to an equity partner who is entitled to a share of profits from the firm, as well as decisions about the share of income to which each equity partner is entitled. In recent years firms have based both decisions more explicitly on determinations of economic productivity than on other dimensions of a lawyer's work.

Economic productivity typically is measured on a spectrum from obtaining and maintaining relationships with clients, known as origination, on one end, to the number of hours that a lawyer bills on the other end. Those who originate business are known as rainmakers, and those who generate revenues by doing work for clients are known as service partners. Some service partners may receive additional credit for assuming responsibility for managing client matters. With respect to promotions to equity partner, a salaried lawyer must be able to make a "business case" that he is likely to develop relationships with a significant number of clients or to manage a substantial amount of work for a rainmaker's clients. This requirement has resulted in the promotion of a shrinking percentage of lawyers to equity partner. With respect to compensation of equity partners, the trend is to treat origination as a more important factor.

The sections that follow describe the structure of the modern large law firm partnership, the system for promoting people to partner, the process of determining compensation for equity partners, and the ways in which the latter process reflects both formal decisions by firm management and informal bargaining among partners.

Partnership Structure and Promotion

Understanding the material economy of compensation requires an appreciation of how evolving competitive pressures on law firms have changed career opportunities and the meaning of partnership. Junior lawyers traditionally entered a firm as associates and were considered for promotion to equity partner after seven to nine years, although that period has moved closer to ten to fourteen years since the financial crisis (Galanter and Henderson 2008). Equity partners are the working owners of law firms and have some voice in the governance of the firm, as well as a share in the financial profits. Upon entering the equity partner ranks, a new partner must also contribute capital, for which the firm typically makes financing available.

Criteria for promotion to partner traditionally included production of high-quality work, ability to relate to clients, and some potential to attract business (Galanter and Palay 1991, 30). Due to the long-term nature of client relationships in the first part of the twentieth century (Pollock 1990), business generation, or origination, ability was less important. As the relationships between law firms and clients became more attenuated and short-term, however, the role of origination began to loom larger in law firm promotion decisions (Regan 2004, 15–49).

Although law firms historically followed an "up or out" model under which lawyers who were not promoted to partnership were asked to leave the firm, most firms in the last few decades have departed from this "one-tier" partnership model. When law firms encountered financial difficulty in the 1990s, they began to look for new ways to increase profitability. This led to growth in what are called income or nonequity partners (Galanter and Henderson 2008, 1867). These partners do not share in the firm's profits but are paid a salary and are eligible for annual bonuses. They are sometimes given voting rights, but the distinction between income and equity partners is primarily that the majority of the income partner's salary is fixed rather than variable with the firm's profitability.

The introduction of this tier of partners enables firms to elevate associates to partner-level positions without diluting the value of equity partners' shares in the firm, and the firm's profits per equity partner (PPP), by giving additional lawyers a claim on the firm's profits. Some income partners may eventually rise to equity status, but many do not. One consultant estimated that firms can increase their profits per equity partner by as much as 20 percent by extending the length of time before a partner can become an equity partner. *American Lawyer* confirms that 175 of the top 200 firms have "two-tier" partnerships that consist of both income and equity partners (Newsham 2019).

A tier of income partners is attractive to firms because it can lessen the risk of making poor promotion decisions. This can be particularly important when a firm is facing economic uncertainty. According to one partner:

> [W]e're oftentimes sitting there with two people [of] seemingly equal quality and we're guessing who is going to be the business generator ten years down the road. Why not make them both income partners so that they can have the title to the outside world as partner and let's see? And you may be surprised. I mean, there are people who blossom much to your surprise, [and] there are people you think they've got everything going for them but somehow they are not able to generate business. (#111)

Designation as income partner therefore reflects an intermediate status between associate and equity partner. In some firms, income partners have a certain number of years to develop enough relationships with clients to establish a business case for their promotion. If they do not establish such a case, they may be asked to leave the firm. In other firms, income partners may remain in the position indefinitely even if they do not generate their

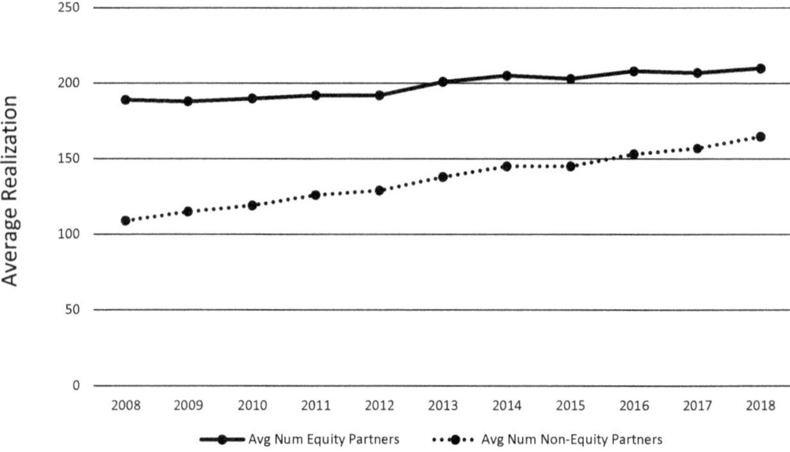

Figure 3. Growth in equity and nonequity partnership ranks in AmLaw 100 firms, 2008–18.

own clients, especially if they have specialties that are valuable to the firm (Altonji 2009).

A pronounced trend that emerged shortly after the financial downturn of 2008 has been (1) little or no increase in equity partners combined with significant growth in compensation for such partners, along with (2) a substantial increase in income partners, whose compensation has been relatively flat (Simons 2019). In 2000, 78 percent of partners held equity in their firms, but by 2018 the figure had declined to 56 percent (Randazzo 2019).

As we describe in chapter 5, firms are highly sensitive to their PPP ranking. Because that figure is calculated based on the number of equity partners who have a claim on profits, a prospective new equity partner generally is expected to generate profits at least equal to, and ideally greater than, a firm's PPP. This is known as the "business case" for promotion. As a result, nonequity partner ranks have increased in recent years while equity partnership numbers have remained relatively flat (see fig. 3).

Partners interviewed for this study confirm this observation. According to one respondent, "[w]hen I made partner it was easier, right, it was work hard, be a good lawyer and you'll probably make partner. Now it's more of a business case. Is this person going to be a business generator?" (#111).

As another partner observed:

> [I]n the pressure world of keeping numbers up . . . so that the market thinks the firm is doing well, the firm can only make so many equity partners every

> year—whereas before they used to make them just because you were here three years [and] you did a great job as an income partner. . . .
>
> . . . [I]t's more than ever a function of room within the equity ranks and the firm taking a hard line on not wanting to issue more shares, trying to keep the per share value high to keep the people who are here. . . . And then they want obviously to have a share value that is high to attract people from the lateral market. (#103)

Increased partner mobility also has served to reduce the rate of promotion to equity partner. Firms tend increasingly to look to laterals from other firms with large books of business to fill their equity partner ranks (Hildebrandt Consulting and Citi Private Bank 2013). This development means fewer equity partner promotion opportunities from within the firm. As one partner remarked, "There [are] probably on an annual basis more equity laterals brought in than equity promotions from within. That sends a signal to your income partners that makes them wonder, '[W]ell, how am I ever going to get paid, I guess I've got to go somewhere else'" (#103).

One income partner lamented:

> I think for a lot of us who are in the income partner bracket, we're just not sure how we can make equity unless we have . . . access to a client who will bring in at least a couple million dollars a year. You know, if [I had] a best friend who is a general counsel of a multi-million dollar company or something like that . . . I would have brought that in already. That's the case for a lot of people. So given the contracting demand for legal services out there and . . . the situation internally where it's very difficult to make equity, I think there are . . . a lot of people saying, "How am I going to get there? It's just impossible to get there because you can't make equity by working hard." That's just not in the cards anymore, whereas it used to be. (#101)

Some associates or income partners may also be promoted to equity partner because they provide important services for clients that other partners bring to the firm. A tax lawyer, for instance, can be integral to business transactions in which a corporate partner's clients are involved. A regulatory lawyer can be a valuable resource for that same partner's clients who operate in a heavily regulated industry. Lawyers such as these may not have an opportunity to develop ongoing close relationships with major clients. The business case for their promotion is that they have specialized expertise that the firm's important clients need on an ongoing basis. Even if they become equity partners, however, they will be paid substantially less than rainmakers.

Finally, it is worth noting that some firms may increase their PPP by reducing the number of partners whose compensation is based more than 50 percent on a share of profits, which is the criterion that the *American Lawyer* uses to determine who is an equity partner in its calculation of PPP. In 2018, Morrison & Foerster was one such firm. The number of partners whose compensation served to characterize them as equity partners fell from 224 to 167, which resulted in an increase in income partners from 86 to 129 (Strom 2019). As a result, PPP increased from $1.74 million to just under $2 million even though revenues declined by 1.9 percent. The adjustment reflected the sixth year in a row that the firm reduced the number of equity partners. The firm is by no means the only one that has adopted this approach in recent years.

Equity Partner Compensation

One of the classic categorizations of attorneys in law firms is Finders, Minders, and Grinders (Stein 2010). Finders are those lawyers who find, or bring in, new clients. Minders are those who mind, or manage, matters for colleagues' clients. And Grinders are those who toil away at the work required to provide services to clients. While these categories typically apply to all lawyers in a firm, from associates (the Grinders) to senior partners (the Finders), the partnership can also be classified into roughly the same three categories.

Rather than viewing these distinctions as discrete categories, one might think of them as a spectrum on which one can locate any particular partner. At the Finder end of the spectrum are those partners who spend virtually all their time developing new and existing client relationships and little if any on legal work. Further down the spectrum are Finders who bring clients to the firm but also work on matters for those clients.

The next location on the spectrum is partners who are a combination of Finders and Minders. They bring clients to the firm, do some work for them, but also assume some responsibility for managing matters for other partners' clients based on referrals from their colleagues. A pure Minder may work only on managing matters for colleagues' clients. Next, some partners are a combination of Minders and Grinders. Their work for others' clients consists of some management responsibility and some contribution of more specialized expertise. Finally, pure Grinders play supporting roles by solely providing technical assistance, such as analyzing the tax treatment of a transaction.

The closer a partner is to the Finder end of the spectrum, the more one can characterize him as a rainmaker whose contribution to the firm consists of origination of business. The closer a partner is to a pure Grinder, the more one can think of him as a service partner who does work for other partners' clients. As we discuss below, compensation generally increases the closer a partner is to the Finder end of the spectrum.

The Building Blocks of Compensation

Compensation for equity partners is largely determined by the percentage of the profit pool that is allocated to each partner. The profit pool is comprised of units or shares allocated across the equity partnership. Unlike a corporation, where the number of equity shares remains relatively steady over time, the number of units in a partnership pool is periodically reset—often on an annual or biennial basis—based on the number and performance of equity partners.

Most large US firms rely on a combination of numerical metrics and subjective assessment as the basis for compensation. As one study puts it, the numerical metrics are meant to reflect "the extent to which a partner functions as an individual cash flow generator within the firm" (Williams and Richardson 2010, 623).

Origination. One key factor in determining compensation in most law firms is origination, which is based on the dollar value of revenue from clients and/or matters the partners have brought into the firm.[1] Many firms in the past provided origination credit only to someone who brought a client into the firm, regardless of whether that person originated new matters for that client. In recent years, many firms have added credit for persons who originate new matters for existing clients.

Origination credit entitles a partner to a certain amount of revenue from work for clients he brought to the firm or from new matters done for existing clients. In the latter case, both the partner who obtained the client and the one who generated the new matter will receive credit. This is the case regardless of who does the work for the client. One report indicated that origination credit based on bringing a client to the firm ranges from 20 to 25 percent of billings for that client, and is as high as 33 percent in some firms (Rose 2010, 5). The credit sometimes ends after a certain period of time but can continue indefinitely as long as the client continues to send work to the law firm. One early theory on why origination first entered the compensation calculation is that by providing origination credits, firms would encourage lawyers to share work instead of hoarding it to maximize the amount of hours they billed (Smith 1940, 650).

Management Credit. Some firms provide credit for managing a client matter, even if the partner did not bring the client in the door and therefore does not qualify for origination credits. In this way, the firm rewards partners who play a large role in ensuring that a client's needs are being met on an ongoing basis. Another version of this approach is to give a partner some credit for hours billed by lawyers who are actively under her supervision.

Personal Production. Since law firms' business models are largely based on billable hours, a key aspect of compensation is the amount of time a lawyer bills over the course of the evaluation period. A firm may also take into account collection realization, which is the percentage of bills sent to clients that clients actually pay, to arrive at a figure representing personal revenue generation.

Realization. Rate realization rate is the percentage of standard billing rates that is collected. It reflects discounts from standard billing rates that reflect negotiations with clients and any fee reductions made before billing the client.

One survey of partners, 75 percent of whom were in firms with more than 250 lawyers, found that the top three factors that their firms considered "very important" or "important" were revenue collection, origination, and billable hours, in that order (Williams and Richardson 2010, 623). Consistent with this finding, one law firm consultant explains, "[T]he two most important partner compensation criteria in law firms remain the ability to bring in new clients to the firm and to be personally productive, as measured by fees collected as a working lawyer" (Cotterman 2009, 10). As we discuss below, there is reason to believe that origination has taken on even greater significance in recent years.

Subjective Assessment. Most firms provide an opportunity for subjective considerations to affect compensation to some extent, to enable firms to reward behavior that is not easily measured. Firms employing these systems have discretion to take into account factors related to firm citizenship activity, such as serving on committees, undertaking projects for the firm, and general cooperative behavior that may not be directly related to generating revenues.

The Compensation Process

Compensation for equity partners in systems that incorporate subjective factors is generally decided by a group of partners on the compensation committee. A recent survey of AmLaw 200 firms indicates that just under half of the firms rely on the executive committee to determine compensation, while the remainder use a designated compensation committee (Peery 2018, 15). In conducting its deliberations, the committee gathers data from the firm's operational and financial systems. Typically, these data are augmented by interviews with partners and practice leaders in the firm. Some firms encourage partners to write a memo to the committee detailing their accomplishments that might not otherwise appear obvious from the data. The compensation decisions are then discussed in what is often painstaking detail and can require hundreds of hours of work by the committee (Nanda and Rohrer 2012a; Nanda and Rohrer 2012b).

Compensation is typically a prospective process. That is, the compensation committee decides at the beginning of the year how many shares are allocated to each equity partner for that year based on performance in the past year, or sometimes two. The ultimate annual value of each share therefore depends on the financial performance of the firm over the course of the coming year.

Many firms allocate shares every year, but some firms attempt to smooth out the peaks and valleys in individual performance by basing compensation decisions on averages for two or three prior years. Our research, however, suggests that competitive pressures may be prompting firms to focus on briefer periods so that compensation can be adjusted more quickly to reflect recent performance. As one partner reflected:

> It has always been that people didn't move up very fast but they didn't move down very fast, that was our mantra. The last three or four years have changed that. . . . We used to look at five-year data, now we look more at three-year data because . . . what happened five years ago, pre-2008, is not very relevant. We're looking at what's happening now right [*sic*]. It's not exactly what have you done for me lately but . . . you don't want to artificially keep [someone who is increasing in value to the firm] down because three years ago they hadn't been doing much. . . . [Y]ou've got to be responsive to that or they're walking out the door. (#10)

This shift in approach reflects a broader trend whereby firms respond more quickly to changes in the market to stay competitive for both clients and partners.

Many firms also reserve some portion of partner profits for a bonus pool, which can be used to reward stellar performance during the year that was not foreseen in the unit allocation process (for example, landing a very large client in the middle of the year).

Transparency in Compensation

In the majority of US firms, equity partner compensation is an "open" system in which data are shared openly among the members of the partnership (Wesemann and Jarrett-Kerr 2012, 8–9). In these firms, partners generally know the amount of each partner's compensation, and data such as hours billed, realization, business originated, and time spent on management of matters, but they do not know the precise weight of each factor in arriving at the ultimate compensation figure.

Keeping partners satisfied with compensation in such firms can be especially difficult. Research indicates that people's satisfaction with their financial condition is based not on the amount of money that they have but on how much they have compared to other people they regard as peers (Chen, Choi, and Chi 2002, 808). Firms therefore spend a considerable amount of time and energy in determining partner compensation so that partners regard the decisions as fair and legitimate. One partner on the compensation committee of his firm described the process:

> We spend a lot of time on compensation. We do partner compensation every year . . . and that takes a lot of time. It's three days of meetings just as a committee plus all the meetings with individual partners. . . . There is an initial meeting with each partner just to say, "Well, tell us whatever you want to tell us," and everyone does a little report about their own performance, and then there is a follow-up meeting where we say, here is what we are going to recommend that you go up, you go down, you stay the same. . . . I'm on the committee, so I may be a little biased in my views, but I think it's a very transparent process. Everybody knows what every other partner makes. Everybody gets a week or two weeks to comment on either their own or other people's compensation before it's finalized. . . . [E]verybody knows what you are making and everybody has a chance to be heard, which I think all [provides] due process. . . . (#48)

The firm also pays a lot of attention to the composition of the committee:

> [T]he compensation committee is in part . . . management but it's . . . voted on, so it's not as if it's purely [a] management decision. And so to me it's actually pretty transparent; it's got representatives of all the departments plus at-large people, so I feel like all the different interests are represented on the committee, and I think the committee has pretty good information. (#48)

While firms may be transparent about the amount of partners' compensation, they are less so with respect to the weight assigned to each financial metric and the impact of any subjective assessment in making compensation decisions. As we discuss in the next chapter, this can affect partners' perception of the fairness of compensation.

Weighting Origination

Since the compensation committee meets in private, partners not on the committee do not know how decisions are made in individual instances. This creates some ambiguity about what type of behavior the firm is rewarding. Research on law firm compensation, however, indicates that origination credit plays an increasingly important role in many firms' compensation systems (Lowe 2013). According to a recent survey of over 2,000 law firm partners by legal search consultants Major, Lindsey & Africa, 69 percent of all respondents reported that origination credit was the most important factor driving compensation (Lowe 2018, 41).

The *American Lawyer* reports that 83 percent of firms track origination credit, and "[i]n the vast majority of those who do, according to Bruce MacEwen, president of consultant Adam Smith, Esq., it dwarfs collections, profitability metrics and billable hours in its impact on compensation." Similarly, the publication notes, "It's 'the single most important determinative factor in partners compensation' in law firms, Altman Weil principal Jim Cotterman says." The rationale, Cotterman says, is that "the metric tracks lawyers' ability to generate a financially profitable book of business that provides work for themselves, their team, and others across the firm. 'Without that,' he adds, 'there is no firm'" (Packel 2019).

When asked about the factors that go into calculating equity partner compensation, one partner in our study replied:

> As far as I understand it, it's basically how much money did you get credited for as an originator. Everybody wants origination credit and that is where

> the money comes from. If you have a lot of origination credit you get paid more, which is why people run around fighting to get origination credit and are jealous in regard to their clients. (#21)

When originations play a large role in compensation, the stakes can be high. As one partner noted, "[Y]ou just can't work enough hours to make the big money . . . at any law firm. You have to have the originations or you're the billing partner [because] those are the numbers that really drive the compensation of various different partners . . ." (#101).

This fact creates challenges for female partners in light of the fact that, as we mention in chapter 3, the value of their originations is only 43 percent of the value of men's. Furthermore, as we also note in that chapter, women often are asked to serve on committees that benefit the firm but may not enhance their compensation. As the Major Lindsey survey reports, "Only 3% felt nonbillable hours were viewed as being Very Important (with 29% saying they felt they were Not at all Important to their firm), and the majority of respondents believed that good citizenship also [was] not viewed as important" (Lowe 2018, 40).

Firms regard giving substantial weight to origination as crucial to avoid losing highly profitable partners to other firms in the lateral market and to lure such partners to them. As one partner remarked:

> [T]oday, to attract top talent, you are in a bidding war situation that you may not have been in ten years ago. It's a different world because getting work from big multinational companies is a ticket to generating revenues in a way that may not be the case with smaller companies. . . . [I]f our business model now is that we're competing with global firms for partners, we have to pay partners these big amounts of money. (#71)

Virtually every large firm's PPP figure is available in the legal press. This gives partners at a firm at least a general idea of how much they might be able to make elsewhere. While partners making less than the market rate may stay at a firm for a while out of a sense of loyalty or for other nonfinancial reasons, if the gap becomes too large they may choose to go. As one partner observed:

> [S]ome partners who generate a lot of the income here don't make what they could in the marketplace, and a lot of them stay in part because they love the culture, they love the environment, but at a certain point the

> amount of delta between what they make here and what they could make elsewhere is just too large for them to stay. (#12)

The result of this dynamic is effectively a two-tiered equity partner compensation system. Rainmakers (the "Finders") with a large number of origination credits generally earn substantially more than service partners ("the Minders" and "the Grinders"), whose compensation is based mainly on the number of hours that they bill. As firms compete for top rainmakers, they are increasingly likely to reward their most important rainmakers more highly than the average partner and to pay them significantly more than the lowest-paid one. As introduced in chapter 5, the difference between the equity partners with the highest and lowest compensation is known as the spread. Many firms traditionally had a relatively small spread of 3:1 or perhaps 4:1. Recent research suggests that spreads have moved considerably further apart. Kirkland & Ellis, for instance, is reported to have a spread of 43:1 between its highest- and lowest-paid partners, and close to 9:1 between highest- and lowest- paid equity partners (Randazzo 2019). These greater spreads generally reflect increasingly more weight given to origination in the calculation of compensation. As we discuss in the next chapter, however, in some firms a large spread may be the result of a firm that chooses to provide a wide range of practices with varying levels of revenues and profits. Such firms may attempt to use adjustment of compensation according to financial productivity to further both business and professional values.

Nonetheless, as the *American Lawyer* notes, "Given the damage caused by losing commercially strong partners, it's not surprising to see firm leaders moving systematically to tighten economics-to-compensation linkages" (Simons 2019). Measures to implement this include

> comp[ensation] ladders that vary sharply by country; different comp trajectories for partners in inherently low-leverage practices; introduction of a new lower-tier comp level; moves down the scale for those no longer performing commensurately with their comp level; greater distance from top to bottom of bands; and glide paths for partners in the later stages of their careers. (Simons 2019)

Compensation in the modern law firm therefore constitutes a material economy whose distribution of financial rewards is significantly shaped by the desire to satisfy rainmakers in the firm and to attract them from other firms. Firms see themselves as having no choice but to operate compensation systems with these features. As one income partner acknowledges:

> [W]e try to balance [it with] preserving our culture . . . but the reality is that we have to adapt to the way that the economics of the law firm industry are moving. . . . [Y]ou can't just put your head in the sand and plug your ears and say, "No, no, we're just going to keep doing it the way that we did it ten years ago because that is how we like to do it, we don't change." You do that, then eventually you'll just be a dinosaur. So you have no choice but to adapt. (#71)

At least some firms have begun to rethink the heavy emphasis on origination or how it is distributed. One concern is that this emphasis may lead partners to hoard a client and do work for which a partner is not best qualified, rather than bringing in a colleague with more expertise. Another is that it may lead partners to bring in clients that do not fit the firm's strategic direction (Packel 2019).

Mintz Levin, for instance, in 2015 adopted a system in which no partner receives more than 75 percent of an origination credit. The remainder is credited to a colleague who helped obtain the client in question or to the firm. In addition, partners who develop new business for existing clients may now receive origination credit. The limit on credit is intended to "reinforce a spirit of collaboration and ensure the right attorneys are brought to the client." The credit for new matters "is intended to benefit rising lawyers, who . . . are less likely to be white men." The chair of the firm notes that the change in policy resulted in a reduction in credit for some partners from $8 million to $6 million. "The trick," he said, "is to make that $8 million into $10 million by building up the clients more because you have the right incentives in place" (Packel 2019).

King & Spaulding has a system under which origination credits last for only three years, after which they revert to the firm. In addition, several partners are entitled to claim such credit, based on making the initial connection with the client, helping obtain a matter, or performing the work. This is designed to encourage partners to "go out and sell as a team." Other firms have adopted additional categories of credits beyond origination, which reflects appreciation that "clients come to a firm in different ways and stay for different reasons" (Packel 2019).

It remains to be seen how many firms will move in the direction of revising the current emphasis on origination. As one law firm consultant says, "'The biggest trend is that firms are increasingly recognizing that it is a problem more than you actually see any action to correct it'" (Packel 2019).

The Internal Market of the Firm

Dynamics of an Unregulated Market

Origination credits and personal production based on billable hours are the two main inputs that determine partner compensation in modern firms. While each factor appears relatively objective, a closer examination reveals that each is the product of a set of complex interactions among partners in the firm. Our interviews indicate that many firms feel fairly constrained in attempting to direct the outcome of these negotiations. These interactions therefore constitute a relatively unregulated market in which partners negotiate, and sometimes compete for, origination credit, relationships with clients, and a steady stream of work. The value of a partner's services affects his bargaining power in requesting a share of origination credits and obtaining work from other partners that increases billable hours. While firms make some attempt to regulate this internal market, most partners regard it as being ultimately dominated by informal bargaining.

The simplest instance of origination credit is when a partner alone brings in a matter that involves a new client to the firm. The partner receives all origination credit for that matter, and this credit is then factored into compensation decisions. If additional matters arise for which the client needs assistance from other lawyers in the firm, the partner who brought in the first matter will continue to receive origination credits in the form of some percentage of the value of those additional matters.

Whether a partner will share any of that credit with the partners doing the work on these other matters will depend on informal discussion, and perhaps negotiation, between the rainmaker and his other other partners. One partner's description captures the ambiguity and personal judgment that is involved in origination sharing as she described someone she spoke to from a newly acquired foreign office:

> [S]he said, "I just got something for someone in the US to do for one of my clients; I think I'll just maybe take . . . five percent of the origination [credit] because I'm not going to do any of the work." And I said, "No, you have to

take at least 50 [percent] . . . because it's your client [and] that's what people do here." (#92)

A partner in another firm commented:

> It's constantly negotiated. Only in the last few years have I started really dealing with this origination mess, it's a mess. Everybody is fighting for a piece of this and "I deserve this." There are legacy people who do have origination credit even though they don't do anything, it's just their old client. (#21)

A team comprised of different partners from the firm may also make a presentation, or "pitch," in an effort to win business from a new client. If the work involves a corporate matter, for example, the effort may be led by a partner with an especially strong reputation for work on mergers and acquisitions. Other partners on the team might be those who have expertise in a particular area that relates to the matter, such as a specific regulatory regime, treatment under the tax law, or a form of financing. The lead partners may select for the presentation those legal experts with whom they have worked in the past.

If the firm wins the business, origination credit ordinarily will go to the corporate partner who was seen as leading the pitch because of the view that his reputation was the most important reason that the client chose the firm. This partner may be regarded as having the best chance of developing an ongoing relationship with the client, or it may be that the firm wants to ensure that this partner is satisfied with his compensation. To the extent that the firm grows relationships with existing clients, the partners who already have the most origination credits are in the best position to accumulate more of them. If the firm does not revise this allocation, and if other partners on the pitch team are unable to negotiate for a share of credits, the perception of some partners may be, as one partner put it, "The rich get richer" (#98).

Some firms attempt to lessen the need for negotiation over origination credits by awarding management credit to the main partners working on or managing matters for major clients. While this type of credit may enhance the recipients' compensation, it typically has a less substantial impact on compensation calculations than do origination credits. Other firms may impose a "sunset" provision, which places a time limit on the period in which the firm grants origination credits, while some may require a minimum amount of rainmaker involvement with a client's matter to be eligible for credits derived from it.

For several reasons, however, most firms tend to be fairly deferential to partners with respect to the allocation of origination credits between lawyers already in the firm. First, it is impossible to specify in advance an appropriate division of origination credits, given the myriad kinds of situations and forms of partner collaborations that arise. A firm that actively monitored the division of credits would therefore need to spend substantial time analyzing the facts of each particular situation.

Second, in a firm comprised of professionals accustomed to a large measure of independence, law firm leaders generally assume that informal agreements by partners involved are likely to be regarded as more legitimate bases for the distribution of credits than an edict by management. Third, firms encourage partners to seek out new clients and want to avoid adopting any policy that may create a disincentive for them to do so.

Finally, firms are quite sensitive to the risk that a rainmaker who generates significant business may bristle at what he regards as interference with his judgment about origination credits, and that the rainmaker may respond by leaving the firm. As Robert Nelson's (1988) seminal work of the late 1980s illuminated, partners who have close relationships with clients constitute centers of power that exist outside of the formal authority structure of the firm.

Law firm management may exhibit similar restraint in attempting to ensure that service partners have enough billable hours. Firms generally take the view that a partner who has a relationship with a client is the best judge of who will be most helpful in performing the work that needs to be done. As one partner commented:

> [W]e want to keep people busy. . . . [M]any of our people are quite versatile and they can do lots of things. But I never, ever say to a practice leader or substantial person who has a case, "I want you to use X. I know you don't want to use X but damn it, you use X." That is not the way we operate here. It's persuasion sometimes, cajolery sometimes, but I'm not saying to a substantial person, "Use X." (#10)

This tendency toward deference leads most service partners to regard the internal market of the firm as largely unregulated, dependent on informal negotiations and bargaining power. One income partner described it this way:

> [W]hat's interesting . . . as an associate, you are in a regulated world. As a partner, you're in a completely deregulated world. . . . It's a completely free

market system. . . . I spend more time trying to gather up work internally than I do externally because obviously it's just better; the odds are better. [T]he problem with it is that I am competing against fellow partners, and the thing is—and this is not just the junior partners saying this; I think senior partners say this—is that you're not worried about competition outside of this building; you're worried about competition inside the building. (#101)

Belief that the process is unregulated gives rise to some partners' sense that the allocation of origination credits in particular can be quite unpredictable. When asked how much sharing of origination credits there is in his firm, one income partner replied:

> Well, it depends on the person. . . . There is sort of a guideline of what it should be, but how it actually is, really is—it depends on who you are, which group you're in, which other partner you're dealing with, etc., etc. And there are so many different factors. [I] would like to be able to say if you are doing this amount of work on this project then you are going to get this cut of originations but that's not the case. . . . It is completely unpredictable. It's the Wild, Wild West. (#101)

Another partner described his different experiences when working as part of two teams attempting to win new business from an existing client:

> [I]f I'm an originator, it means somehow I was important to the decision to select us. So it may have been the relationship partner doing the pitch, but he had me front and center in the pitch book. [He's saying], "Here is the reason you should choose us over somebody else because we've got the corporate team and then we've got [this partner] on the regulatory team to support it." And you know, that relationship partner happens to be generous and he does things right.
>
> [On the other hand, there was] this transaction I was not involved in originating the matter, but I was instrumental to getting it done. Now if I was that other partner, I would revise origination to reflect [my] role, but he chose not to do that. So, you know, it's a crapshoot. . . . (#103)

The bargaining leverage of partners seeking origination credit from rainmakers will depend on the size of a new matter, its significance to the firm's business strategy, how crucial the services of the non-rainmaker are, whether this partner is in a position to refer work in the future to the first partner, and the personal relationship between the two partners. It may also depend on the importance of the role one partner plays in the ongoing work of the partner who is entitled to the origination credit. A partner who regularly serves as a key lieutenant is more likely to receive some credit than a partner who works occasionally on a narrow technical aspect of a matter.

The bargaining leverage of a service partner will also depend on the availability of other partners who are available to do work for a rainmaker. The most significant component of a service partner's compensation is the amount of revenues that he generates from the hours billed. A service partner therefore needs a steady flow of work from rainmakers. This need may inhibit him from pushing too hard for origination credit with a rainmaker, for fear that he will develop a reputation that leads such partners to turn to someone less demanding when they need help.

Service partners generally do not have the leverage within the firm to bargain if they are unhappy, particularly if they work primarily with one or two rainmakers who "feed" them work on a regular basis. Should these rainmakers decide to leave, a service partner realistically needs to follow them or find himself without a source of work in the firm. Likewise, a service partner without his own book of business is not terribly attractive on the lateral market. He therefore has limited ability to leave for another firm.

Women and the Internal Market

Women may be especially disadvantaged by the informal internal market for credits. One study indicated that 84 percent of nonminority female equity partners and 82 percent of nonminority female income partners reported being denied their fair share of origination credit in the last three years (Williams and Richardson 2010, 634). Some 86 percent of female minority partners overall reported the same.

Such outcomes may reflect the challenges that women face in bargaining and negotiating situations. Research on corporate managers indicates that women are less likely than men to initiate negotiations, are less likely to see situations as negotiable, and have more anxiety than men about negotiating (Babcock et al. 2006; Babcock and Laschever 2003). This tendency also is apparent among graduates entering the workforce. One study found that while 57 percent of male students attempted to negotiate their initial compensation offers, only 7 percent of female students did so (Babcock and Laschever 2003). As one group of scholars notes, "Women's reluctance as compared to men to initiate negotiations may be an important and underexplored explanation for the asymmetric distribution of resources, such as compensation, within organizations" (Bowles, Babcock, and Lai 2007, 85).

Research suggests that such reluctance is not simply because of timidity or lack of skill, but may reflect sensitivity to the potential penalties that women suffer by initiating negotiation and bargaining assertively. As one group of scholars observes, studies show that

> women tend to present themselves more modestly than do men, and that a modest self-presentation style tends to undermine perceived competence, particularly as compared to those who self-promote in a stereotypically masculine way. However, if women attempt to overcome this "deficiency" by behaving in a more masculine self-promoting manner, they are perceived as technically skilled but lacking in social competence. (Bowles, Babcock, and Lai 2007, 85)

Research confirms and illustrates the operation of this phenomenon. One study, for instance, found that male evaluators penalized women more than men for attempting to negotiate higher compensation. As the authors describe:

> Men were significantly more inclined to work with nicer and less demanding women who accepted their compensation offers without comment than they were with those who attempted to negotiate for higher compensation, even though they perceived women who spoke up to be just as competent as women who demurred. (Bowles, Babcock, and Lai 2007, 99)

In the law firm setting, this penalty can be especially significant, in light of the fact that many partners—service partners in particular—must cultivate good relationships with rainmakers to receive a sufficiently steady flow of business to be regarded as productive.

Research also indicates that women's reluctance to negotiate is affected by "situational ambiguity" (Bowles, Babcock, and McGinn 2005, 952). This reflects the extent to which a situation has features that provide clear guidance to parties in their interaction with one another. Such ambiguity is greater the less that parties understand about the limitations of the bargaining range and the appropriate standards for agreement. In this case, "[l]ack of clear standards for agreement (e.g., benchmarks or focal points), or the presence of multiple possible standards, creates uncertainty about the range of likely agreement" (953). Such ambiguity characterizes bargaining over credits in a firm's internal market, which generally is unregulated by the firm and depends on interpersonal dynamics. Thus women may be especially unwilling to initiate negotiation over origination credits in this market. Given the prominence of these credits, such reluctance can exacerbate any other sources of inequality that may affect women's compensation.

One prominent scholar suggests that organizations can reduce the influence of gender dynamics by "making more transparent what career opportunities, resources, or rewards are negotiable and what the standards are for attaining them" (Bowles 2012, 28). This would require firms to set limits on rainmaker autonomy by providing more guidance on how credits should be shared. One can imagine that firms may have some reluctance to do this in light of the potential of rainmakers to depart for other firms if they are dissatisfied with their current situation.

The degree of transparency in a firm's compensation system also could have some effect on women's perception of fairness. One female partner described her understanding of how a closed compensation system in some firms might create suspicion about decisions:

> [I can see how people could support] a closed compensation system because . . . you don't have this in-fighting amongst partners fighting for credit. [But I imagine] that when you have a closed compensation system . . . it can perpetuate some issues. One of the big issues for women lawyers has been how you attribute billing partner and [managing] partner credit. When there is a black box compensation system and not necessarily a lot of communication coming out of the committee about how they made their decisions it leaves a lot of open questions. (#239)

She also suggested that insufficient transparency about compensation in any firm, whether or not it uses a closed system, can be a source of concern:

> [Our firm also] hasn't been as great about communicating what really is going on behind the curtain to people. . . . And I think part of it is who gets to make those decisions: that at the end of the day the billing partner is the one that has the authority to decide who gets [managing] credit and who

> doesn't. You know you can kind of rage against the machine all you want but if you are not the decision maker there is of no check on the decision makers [and] you'll just get yourself frustrated. (#239)

Ambiguity about compensation decisions thus can disadvantage women, particularly if they are reluctant to advocate for themselves for fear of triggering a backlash that could impair their ability to obtain work in the firm's internal market. This ambiguity may exacerbate the extent to which ostensible objective compensation metrics can subtly be the product of less visible gender dynamics (Rhode 2011, 2014; Ridgeway 2011; Wald 2010, 2015).

Summary

The internal market of the firm thus has an important influence on the most important numbers that the firm uses to set partner compensation. Unlike the firm's formal determination of compensation, however, this internal market is regarded by most partners as largely unregulated. Many firms attempt to encourage partners to share origination credit, but firms generally are uneasy about explicitly overriding a partner's decision about the division of credits. Most outcomes in the internal market therefore reflect individual personalities and informal negotiation. Our research does not provide a systematic assessment of how this situation affects women, but other scholarship suggests that this unregulated market may be especially problematic for them.

Conclusion

From a perspective that sees business and professional concerns as inherently antagonistic, compensation decisions in large law firms now appear to be dominated by business considerations at the expense of professional values. The role of compensation as a crucial instrument of business strategy, greater emphasis on financial metrics, and the increasing importance of business generation in determining compensation all suggest that how firms reward partners is now driven strictly by the bottom line.

The reality, however, is more complicated than this. Business concerns clearly do play a more important role than a few decades ago in decisions regarding both promotion to equity partner and compensation of such partners. At the same time, partners' interpretation of compensations systems can be more subtle, reflecting perceptions that systems combine business concerns and professional values to varying degrees.

Assuming that recent trends in compensation represent the triumph of business over professional logic within large law firms thus oversimplifies a more complex reality. The meaning of policies and practices depend in large measure on how lawyers in these firms interpret them. That is, the compatibility or antagonism between business and professional logics within a firm is not simply an objective material feature of a firm, but a matter of how partners perceive the relationship between these two logics within it.

This reflects the fact that compensation within a firm represents not simply a material economy that distributes financial rewards, but a symbolic economy that allocates professional respect. As we discuss in the next chapter, perceptions of the ways in which this economy allocates the latter good can have a profound impact on the culture of a firm, lawyers' understanding of themselves as professionals, and their perception of the relative influence of business and professional logics in their firms.

7

The Symbolic Economy of Compensation

Both the amount of compensation and the way that it is determined can shape organizational culture in important ways. In particular, the compensation system can affect the extent to which a partner regards herself as a relatively self-sufficient free agent or as a member of a larger interdependent community within the firm. As one partner suggested:

> [I]f [the compensation system] is eat what you kill and you're paid for working for your client in your own silo, then it's much easier for you to pull up and leave. You don't have those sort of roots that are expanding out of your own insular group because you don't depend on anybody else for your own revenues and therefore your own compensation. (#16)

The previous chapter describes how large law firms now use compensation more explicitly as a crucial instrument of business strategy, and how they place greater emphasis on revenue generation as the basis for both promotion and compensation of equity partners. It also suggests that these policies do not necessarily signify that business logic dominates such firms. A firm still may seek to create an environment that also provides the nonfinancial rewards that we identify with professionalism.

The extent to which a firm can effectively use its compensation system to create such an environment depends substantially on the meanings that partners assign to that system. Understanding the meaning of compensation practices for law firm partners requires that we appreciate that such practices represent more than simply a process for distributing financial rewards. When partners talk about compensation, they tend to refer to sources and criteria of value other than money that provide meaning in their lives as professionals. This reflects the more general phenomenon that money has powerful symbolic meanings beyond its material significance (Zelizer 1994).

It is striking how many lawyers in our study referred to the amount of their compensation as far more than they could reasonably expect or deserve to make. One lawyer, for instance, said, "I talked to my kids and my wife about it. . . . [I]t is a ridiculous amount of money. I almost feel guilty about it and I'm not kidding you" (#79). Another mused, "When I look outside of the window I wonder why in the world I'm being compensated anywhere near what I'm being compensated when there are other people who are very talented and very educated that aren't earning nearly as much" (#72). Another partner said, "I'm always shocked when I hear that somebody thinks that they should be making more money than what we are already paid. . . . We are all overpaid" (#53).

Even allowing for a certain amount of self-serving modesty, these unprompted comments suggest that concern with compensation is not animated simply by the pursuit of financial gain. Rather, it reflects the fact that compensation is simultaneously a part of two different economies in the modern law firm. The material economy of compensation allocates financial rewards, while the symbolic economy of compensation allocates the nonfinancial good of respect that can shape a sense of professional identity. The implicit criteria by which the firm distributes respect can have profound significance for its ability to create the kind of firm-specific capital that can help sustain a culture that nurtures professional values.

The fact that compensation has this dual character should not be surprising. As one scholar observes, "Money is probably the most emotionally meaningful object in contemporary life: only food and sex are its close competitors as common carriers of such strong and diverse feelings, significance, and strivings" (Krueger 1986, 3; see also Furnham and Argyle 1998; Mitchell and Mickel 1999). Furthermore, those meanings are not merely the product of idiosyncratic individual interpretations. They arise as a result of one's location in social relationships. Two other scholars observe, "Like all other social objects, money has meaning that depends on its use and context" (Carruthers and Espeland 1998, 1386). As a result, "it is misguided to try and identify universally representational properties of money and link these to its meaning. The meaning of money does not depend on some characteristic that is common to all money. Instead, its meaning depends on what people in a particular context do with it" (1387).

In the context of law firm compensation, decisions and negotiations are not simply about money but about the extent to which business skills and more traditional professional skills form the bases on which respect is allocated in a given law firm. They thus represent efforts to define the boundaries of the potentially all-encompassing influence of business logic in the modern law firm.

Overview

A symbolic economy in a law firm communicates the extent to which each partner is valued and respected within the firm. This economy serves to allocate two forms of respect: impersonal and personal. It allocates *impersonal* respect to the extent that partners believe that compensation is awarded fairly. A partner who concludes that she has been compensated fairly believes that she has been treated consistently with how comparable partners in the firm are treated. This belief gives her confidence that each person's contributions are evaluated by a common standard that is impartially applied. This means that the firm's compensation process reflects the value of formal equality: the firm does not play favorites or base compensation on criteria unrelated to the merits (Lowe 2012, 7).[1] This communicates a sense of impersonal respect. One partner put it this way:

> If [compensation] seems to play favorites or if people don't feel that as individuals they are respected within the system or that some people are playing politics or entrenched positions for their own benefit rather than the firm's benefit, then I think that becomes very divisive for the firm. (#122)

The symbolic economy allocates *personal* respect to the extent that a partner believes that her compensation reflects the particular ways in which she contributes to the success of the firm. This form of contribution may not be fully captured in the numerical metrics that serve as inputs into the compensation decision. It involves less easily measured behavior such as demonstrating generosity toward colleagues, effectively collaborating with others, mentoring junior lawyers, doing high-quality legal work, assuming responsibilities on behalf of the firm, and participating in community and pro bono activities. A firm that recognizes the importance of these traditional professional sources of esteem affords a partner personal respect by providing assurance that hers compensation will not be determined solely by metrics that focus solely on economic productivity.

To the extent that partners' satisfaction with compensation reflects satisfaction with their place in the symbolic economy, they may develop deeper ties to a firm than those based solely on financial benefits. These ties can provide them with intrinsic motivation to act for the benefit of the firm. Such loyalty often translates into a form of firm-specific capital that serves as a buffer against the many centrifugal forces to which law firms are subject. This stability can enable a firm to nurture a distinctive culture that is not driven solely by market forces.

While the formal law firm compensation decision is an important part of the symbolic economy of compensation, it is not the only one. As we describe in chapter 6, much of the activity that affects partner compensation occurs on the individual partner level in the internal market for origination credits and billable hours. Partners have wide latitude in how they behave in this market. Many partners are skeptical that firms' exhortations to share credit and work do much to create any widespread ethos of generosity. There are, however, limits to how far firms can push partners to behave magnanimously in this market, given the ever-present risk that a rainmaker may decide to leave for another firm with less demanding management. This can present a challenge to firms that seek to convey professional respect to partners through the compensation process.

The symbolic economy of compensation, in other words, operates on two levels. The first is the firm's formal process for determining compensation. The second is informal bargaining over origination credits and billable hours. The first level is regulated by a central authority, which means that the firm has the ability directly to determine outcomes. The latter level, however, is largely deregulated, meaning that the firm must rely more on attempts to inculcate informal norms and organizational culture to affect behavior. The extent to which a firm is successful in this endeavor can have a substantial impact on the perceived fairness of the symbolic economy.

Money and Respect

Conceptualizing compensation as part of a symbolic economy reflects appreciation that a partner may regard compensation as not simply the amount of financial reward that she receives, but as a judgment about her value as a lawyer. Within this economy, a partner's concern with compensation reflects sensitivity to the professional respect she enjoys within the firm. This respect can be the basis for what researchers call "organization-based self-esteem" (Gardner, Van Dyne, and Pierce 2004). This reflects "an assessment of personal adequacy and worthiness as an organizational member. . . . [E]mployees with high organization-based self-esteem believe that they are important, meaningful and worthwhile within their employing organization" (310).

Law firm partners may be especially inclined to interpret compensation as indicative of their value in the firm. Most firms lack a robust system for providing the kind of meaningful, timely feedback on partner performance that is more common in other professional service firms such as accounting and management consulting organizations (DeLong, Gabarro, and Lees 2007). Firms instead tend to assume that the amount of compensation received communicates messages about performance.

Thus, in many firms, compensation is an important, if not the sole, indicator of performance. "I think of compensation as your review," remarks one income partner. "[A]s a partner, no one tells you how you are doing or how you are doing compared to other people. . . . So when you get your compensation you find out . . . do you value me, do you think I am doing a good job" (DeLong, Gabarro, and Lees 2007, 164).

Another reason that compensation carries such importance in law firms is that firms generally lack other ways of signaling recognition for partners. Corporate enterprises, for instance, can often rely on special awards, selective training opportunities, promotions, or new titles to convey respect for accomplishment. Law firms, however, are relatively flat organizations without the highly differentiated organizational positions and titles that characterize the corporate world.

Some partners therefore may lack any clear sense of how well they're doing other than by how well they are compensated. As one partner put it, "We suffer from an imposter complex; we fear that someday we are all going to be found out for the frauds that we are. We are all insecure, we all seek validation, and the way we measure our validation is by the way we are compensated" (#179). One partner recounted how he would have reacted had the firm paid him less than the amount that he calculated he was due:

> [I]f I had gotten less than I had asked for in that example I gave you, I'm sure I would have felt like they are not valuing my work at the level they should. I tend to think, based on my life experience, that people are heavily motivated by a sense of self-worth and wanting to be liked by people. I think it's very

> deeply seated stuff that goes on, and compensation is kind of an objective measure of that. (#94)

Differences in compensation thus create the risk that those who earn less may interpret their compensation as reflecting a lack of respect from the firm. A partner may believe, for instance, that she has been loyal to the firm and has engaged in firm citizenship activities for many years. She may feel that the firm does not value her loyalty, however, because she receives less compensation than an incoming lateral with a big book of business. As one partner observed:

> You see many people who come in laterally; you have enticed them with higher compensation, and so you have people who have worked here for a long time say, "You know, I've been working here for twenty years and now this other person who has contributed nothing to this firm to date comes in and is making more money than I am." . . . And so people say, "Well, they are taking loyalty for granted and putting a premium on trading on your values in the market, so what I should do is threaten to leave [unless] they'll pay me more money—or I should leave and then I'll come back as a lateral!" (#52)

Similarly, a partner may believe that she is working just as hard as a colleague who receives higher compensation, but that her lower compensation signals that the firm does not value her work as highly as it does the work of her colleague. Rainmakers and service partners exemplify differing ways in which lawyers can be valued. The former represent the emergent business and marketing orientation that has become a necessity in law firms. By contrast, service partners exemplify the values involved in the traditional professional ideal of doing good work, which these partners sometimes feel is not given enough respect. As one service partner put it, the differences in compensation between rainmakers and service partners "[reflect] just your relative importance in the firm" (#72).

A firm's compensation system allocates respect on two levels: (1) the firm promotion and compensation decision and (2) negotiation among partners in an internal market for credit and billable hours.

Respect and Promotion

As we describe in the previous chapter, the rate of promotion to equity partners in large firms has declined in recent years, as firms have placed increasing emphasis on a "business case" for promotion. In some firms promotion is from associate to equity partner, while in most it is from income to equity status. Such advancement is an important dimension of the compensation process because it changes the basis for compensation from salary to entitlement to a share of the firm's profits. In this respect, the promotion process is part of the material economy of the firm.

Income partners, however, also interpret a firm's promotion process as a signal about respect. This signal depends in particular on the extent to which a firm keeps them fully apprised of their individual prospects for advancement to equity partner. Consider one income partner's description of why he would not want to have that status indefinitely:

> I wouldn't [be interested in that] because there [are] certainly first class and second class citizens. . . . Certain partners have more at stake and have more of a voice, and as I continue on my career I want to continue on that trajectory and have a voice and be able to be on par with my partners, so that we can talk about the challenges that face us and choose a path to steer. (#23)

A firm providing guidance on how to proceed to obtain a promotion to equity partner therefore can signal respect for an income partner, while a failure to do so leaves a partner with a sense that she is not valued and that her career is at a dead end. One income partner suggested how firms might address this issue:

> I would like to think, especially in the early years of partnership, there would be a formal process, and not just the good graces of the people who have always looked out for you, whereby firm management would sit down and say where are we, what are you trying to do, how are you doing and how can the firm help. . . . It's really a matter of simply making [people] feel like they have a future and giving them evidence of it, which ties into the sense of being respected and cared for. (#98)

Another partner who is involved in compensation decisions acknowledges the potential for service partners to feel that their lack of many opportunities elsewhere makes them vulnerable to being short-changed in compensation compared to rainmakers:

> You try to explain why you do what you do, and that the market is what the market is, and indeed most of them, although they don't like it, are very

> smart people. They get that if they were to walk out the door tomorrow they are more valuable to us and better compensated here than they would be anywhere else. Now I don't throw that in their face, I don't think that's constructive, but it's the facts and it's a sad fact.
>
> This economy and the constant struggle to keep people from being poached have required that more of the compensation dollars go to the producers, away from the service people. That has happened over the last five or six years, and it's become more acute in the last three. That does present morale challenges—no question about it. (#10)

Firm 3 attempts to address concerns about limited opportunity for income partner advancement by using compensation to provide temporary financial rewards to balance the inability to achieve a promotion. An income partner described the process:

> I do know that with folks who are not making the next step to equity, and are being told the second year in a row [that] they are not making it, the firm is using compensation mechanisms to make somebody who gets basically turned down from the equity ranks . . . feel whole. The idea is to try to give them a compensation level that is equivalent to a first-year equity partner. . . . [The firm has] got to find a way to keep them happy, even if they don't have room for them in the equity ranks. (#103)

Compensation in this instance is meant to signify not simply an increase in material rewards, but recognition that lawyers will feel disappointed that they have not been able to move up into the equity ranks. In this sense, the additional compensation allocates respect in the symbolic economy.

The promotion process thus can play a role in communicating respect within the firm. As the remainder of the chapter discusses, the equity partner compensation process can play an even more significant role in the symbolic economy.

The Firm Compensation Decision

Distributive Justice

Considerable research indicates that people's satisfaction with their compensation implicitly focuses not on the absolute amount that they receive but on comparison between that amount and the amount they believe they deserve (Gerhart and Rynes 2003, 61). Satisfaction with compensation therefore "is a function of the *discrepancy* between perceived pay level and what an employee believes his or her pay 'should' be" (60–61) (emphasis in original).

How do people determine the amount they think they deserve? Much social science research confirms what most of us know intuitively: how satisfied we are with our compensation depends on how it compares with what others receive whom we regard as our peers (Adams 1963; Festinger 1954; Kulik and Ambrose 1992; Lee and Martin 1991).

Law firm partners indicate that dissatisfaction with compensation based on comparison with others is a pervasive feature of law firm life. One partner described how preoccupied a colleague can become with how much someone else makes compared to him: "People can get ridiculously consumed. Why did that person make 50 cents more than I did? [T]he person who makes 50 cents more cares not at all; the person who made 50 cents less goes crazy" (#14). Another partner observed:

> We used to always have this conversation every time someone would come in and bitch about their compensation. They would start by saying, "First of all, let me just say I'm making more money than I ever thought I could—but why is he making five dollars more than I am?" Lawyers always want to win the gold star. (#10)

Still another partner commented:

> What happens with a lot of lawyers is, you know, you look and you go, "Wow, I'm making $600,000. That's a lot of money; I never thought I would make that much money—but wait a minute, I think that guy next door is making $650,000. Now you know I'm smarter than he is because I got better grades in law school." You know how lawyers are. (#111)

One income partner described his dissatisfaction with his compensation compared to that of equity partners with whom he works:

> PARTNER: I'm losing my enthusiasm because I feel like I'm being taken advantage of.
>
> INTERVIEWER: Taken advantage of in what way?
>
> PARTNER: You are paid a lot less as a nonequity partner than an equity

> partner, that's the way. As much as I like a lot of my colleagues and as much as I very much appreciate how a couple of them have played a large role in making me who I am today, nonetheless this isn't a charity and I work very hard and I work as hard as many others who get paid a lot more than I do. (#98)

For this partner, the relevant input is how hard someone works; his unhappiness with compensation rests on the belief that people who work no harder than he receive significantly more financial reward.

A partner might also use a lateral partner entering the firm as a standard for assessing her own compensation, to the extent that information about this person is available. One partner noted:

> One of the things that I have become attuned to, and it has been an area of friction in compensation and in the firm in general, is what I call the "Everyone loves a lateral" phenomenon, where the lateral market takes over and you have laterals come over. And [when] you impose them into the comp structure, they are getting paid at levels well above what they could command if they were home grown. There is natural friction . . . and what comes out is the idea that I may be better off on the open market than I am at my own firm. (#23)

A partner's sense of unfairness may be intensified by a conviction that she has made important contributions to the firm over the years that the incoming partner has not. One partner echoed this sentiment about the arrival of high-paid laterals: "They are probably right that it is important to bring in that new group, [but] then you are diluting the value of the shares of other people who have been here for a while and have been dedicated to the firm" (#72).

A partner might also use as a compensation benchmark people in other firms whom they think make a similar contribution to their firms, such as people in the same practice area or who work with similar types of clients. Professionals are especially likely to use people outside their organization as peers (Kulik and Ambrose 1992, 224–25). Information about these people is often less available than information about people inside the organization. For law firm partners, however, there is considerable information about what partners at other firms make. The legal press is one source of such information, but search firms, or "headhunters," play probably the most significant role in furnishing information about compensation in other firms.

Even a partner not actively seeking opportunities at other firms is likely to receive enough information through calls from headhunters in the course of her daily practice to have an idea of what other firms are prepared to pay if she were to go on the market. In these ways, a partner can select someone at another firm as a benchmark that guides an assessment of her current compensation.

Most firms identify the factors used in determining compensation, and many provide extensive information about all partners' originations, hours billed, realization, and other factors taken into account in determining contributions to the firm. The availability of this information increases the likelihood that an individual will look to a fellow partner with similar inputs as her basis for comparison.

Most firms do not specify in detail how the compensation committee weighs factors in a particular case. Many also give the compensation committee discretion to subjectively assess a partner's contribution beyond financial metrics, reflecting the view that it is impossible to specify in advance all the ways that someone may contribute to the success of the firm. By taking into account individual circumstances that affect performance, the firm encourages and rewards organizational citizenship and increases firm-specific capital by establishing what partners perceive as a fair compensation system.

Relying in part on subjective assessments theoretically pays respect to a partner as a unique individual by valuing the particular ways in which she contributes to the firm and by acknowledging any difficulties encountered in doing so. This can help solve the Assurance Game by communicating that individual financial productivity is not the only value to which the firm is committed.

One partner contrasted his firm's compensation system with an approach that he called "eat what you kill":

> Eat what you kill is at the end of the year you hit the print button on the computer and it generates all the numbers, and whatever the numbers say goes to compensation—there would be no point for management. We spend three months [reviewing data] until we announce bonuses and base compensation. Why do we do that? Because it's not eat what you kill; it's qualitative merit contribution based. We go through every single partner and we say, "Okay, the numbers suggest this, is there anything else we need to know?" (#83)

A partner may, for instance, agree to refrain from representing a client on a certain matter to avoid a conflict that would otherwise require the firm to forgo representing a new, potentially valuable, client. Or she may spend time on an important pro bono case or on producing high-quality work for a client on a matter that does not generate large revenues. Recognizing these contributions in compensation signals that the firm values contributions that reflect both business and professional values. To the extent that it rewards activity that does not directly generate revenue, the firm can be seen as leaving some money on the table.

Similarly, as we describe in chapter 4, for instance, a firm may hold a partner's compensation relatively constant even though she is building a new practice area that is not generating immediate revenues. This reflects business logic in that the firm is investing in the partner, but partners indicate that the firm's willingness to pay more than current metrics dictate, and to assume the risk that the investment may not pay off, also conveys respect for a partner's desire for professional growth.

One income partner suggested that a firm might use the discretion furnished by subjective assessment to do more to reward those who have been loyal to it:

> [T]here is something to be said about people who are home grown and who have institutional knowledge and who know the people here and who actually do have a certain affinity for the firm, as opposed to someone who is coming in just for the paycheck. So I think that provides some value and it doesn't take very much to keep those guys happy. . . . If you throw just a small amount like $50,000 here, $30,000 here, I think people would be very happy in this economy and stay and try to do what they need to do. (#101)

Those who receive more compensation than numerical metrics warrant based on subjective considerations are likely to feel that the firm respects them by not basing their compensation solely on "the numbers." This can be taken as a signal that the firm is not concerned simply with short-term financial reward and the behaviors that produce it. Rather, the firm recognizes that people make contributions by acting cooperatively in way that express professional values.

The firm also has an opportunity to affirm the importance of considerations beyond objective financial metrics by penalizing partners who violate norms of collegiality and acceptable behavior. As one partner described this process:

> We see all the numbers. And then we'll say, "Well, this suggests this partner should make $600,000," and then the practice group lead will say, "Oh, no she should not because"—and I've seen this happen—"this individual has been so rude to her secretary and we need to send a message, so this individual knows that on the numbers she should get $600,000, but let's pay her $525,000." As soon as she sees her compensation number, she'll insist on a meeting, and we're prepared for the meeting. And we say, "We mean business. We don't yell at this law firm, we don't demean, and we don't belittle. It's not our culture." Now, some laterals are not accustomed to that, so we have to help them. (#83)

At the extreme, a firm may not only penalize a partner who acts unacceptably, even if she generates significant revenues, but also ask her to leave. This can send a powerful signal that a firm is willing to leave money on the table for the sake of nonfinancial values.

A system with a subjective compensation component thus can create the expectation that a firm values some things more than the numbers, such as organizational citizenship or the quality of a partner's work. When this expectation is met, it can provide a partner with the sense that she is valued for a broad range of contributions to the firm. This can help solve the Assurance Game by conveying a sense of at least some balance between reliance on business and professional logics. When this expectation is not met, however, it can result in disillusionment and the perception that compensation is really just about narrow financial metrics—in other words, that business logic is dominant and professional logic is marginal.

A firm that provides room in the compensation process for subjective assessments may thus find that the discretion it offers can be a double-edged sword. On the one hand, it can enhance partners' sense of being personally respected. On the other, it can increase the risk that people will construe relatively low compensation as an indication of personal disrespect. Providing discretion to make subjective judgments also creates the risk that people will regard the compensation process as unpredictable and opaque rather than transparent. This can create concern about favoritism, especially toward management and its friends.

The tension in many firms is that management may believe that business pressures limit its ability to give significant weight to factors that are not directly related to profitability. One compensation committee partner, for instance, described some partners' belief that the intellectual quality of their work should be a major factor in determining compensation:

> I've had a discussion with one of my partners . . . who always says we should reward people on how smart they are, and I say, "You know what, here's the problem: the clients vote on that. And you may be really smart, but if people aren't hiring you, that's an issue. And you may think you're smarter than this guy next door, but clients love him and they keep hiring him." (#111)

It is important to appreciate that perceptions of distributive justice may be more complex than a simple comparison of compensation figures might suggest. One example of this is the meaning of the "spread." As we discuss in chapter 4, this is the difference in a firm between the compensation of the highest and lowest equity partners. One might assume that the larger the spread, the more a firm is driven by business logic and the greater the dissatisfaction of those at the low end of the scale. This is not necessarily true, however. First, many partners who are not rainmakers regard it as appropriate to provide high compensation to those who are. With the decline in long-term client relationships, all partners understand how essential it is for colleagues to bring in clients, and service partners appreciate the flow of work that rainmakers provide. As one partner declared, "I've said for however long I'm a partner that I don't care if Joe over there makes a huge amount of money. I'm so grateful that he creates work for me to do that it doesn't bother me. . . . [We should] pay whatever we can to keep him" (#119).

Similarly, another self-described service partner stated:

> I think the appropriate level of compensation and recognition is given to people who bring in the business. I mean, I think maybe in past years . . . when clients were more loyal, rainmaking wasn't that big a deal, but in today's legal marketplace it's extremely competitive, there are a lot of smart people out there at a lot of different law firms so if someone has the skill and talent to bring in and maintain client relations I don't have a problem with them being well compensated and treated well. (#154)

In addition, the meaning of a substantial spread to many partners in a firm may be that it reflects the firm's choice to include partners who make a wide range of contributions in practices that generate varying levels of revenue. We mentioned in chapter 4 that Firms 4 and 6 have adopted this philosophy in providing a wide range of services. The result is that Firm 4 has an especially large spread. As one partner in the firm put it, "we have a broad definition of the partnership. The reason the spread is acceptable is because people understand that you are compensated based on your contribution, and contributions vary" (#151). Those variations may reflect different rate structures in different geographical markets, differences in the extent to which a service is more complex or routine, and individuals' choices about their practices.

Another partner in Firm 4 explained the firm's spread in this way: "We have some people who just bring in huge amounts of work and work all the time and are tremendously valuable from an economic [standpoint]. . . . On the other hand, we have [other] partners who [don't do this] who we still want to keep as partners in the firm." Differences in compensation in the firm thus serve to "keep people together and build a culture" that is "kinder and gentler" than in some other firms (#119).

Another Firm 4 partner described his firm's spread as reflecting "individual choices about productivity, and that's okay within [our] culture, whereas in [another firm's] culture I think that would result in some pressure on you" (#144). Another partner in this firm said that the firm needs to make sure that persons in the lower compensation tiers have a chance to move up. Those "who can't or don't really care to can still remain part of the firm and enjoy what they are doing, and still contribute, and we're all better off as a result" (#137). Yet another Firm 4 partner explained that, compared to other firms, "we are definitely a big tent and we're definitely much more tolerant of different people's choices" (#145). In these ways, substantial differences in compensation among equity partners may reflect a firm's desire to establish an inclusive collegial culture instead of one driven solely by financial considerations.

Consistent with a desire for inclusiveness, some firms may use differences in compensation to deal with what in other firms would be regarded as levels of productivity that warrant termination. As we have described, some firms establish minimum levels of revenue generation for partners to remain with the firm or decide to jettison areas of practice that they regard as insufficiently profitable. Firms that prefer to avoid these approaches can use compensation adjustments as an alternative to termination.

As one Firm 4 partner described her firm's philosophy, "Rather than fire partners who aren't producing or cut our partners by 10 percent, there tends to be a sense that we'll deal with it in the compensation process" (#128). Another partner in Firm 4 confirmed that "as opposed to asking people to leave we'll deal with it through compensation [so] those people may not make as much as everybody else" (#119). Still another partner in the firm reinforced this idea: "[W]e don't need to terminate people when they have a couple of bad years because we have a compensation system that can accommodate that" (#121).

One partner in Firm 6 explained how a relatively low spread among partners can indicate a firm that focuses only on high-profitability matters and is intolerant of work that fails to meet this standard. He noted that some firms "are not very flexible with their rate structures," so that "if there is business that has a low realization rate they would rather not have it than to cut their realization because that cuts into their profits per partner" (#214). As we describe in chapter 5, firms also may attempt to protect profits per partner through the process of pruning partners whose clients cannot afford rates as high as many other partners in the firm.

Thus, as one partner said, it may be misleading to say that in a firm with a large spread, "that's just a have and have-not system." He continued, "Well, you could also take the view that we could have [a lower spread] if we just get rid of everybody below [a certain productivity level]. We don't want to do that" (#214). As a partner in Firm 4 put it, "if you are okay with not being compensated as much as some of your peers who are being more productive, that's your choice" (#144).

A partner in Firm 4 acknowledged that some people in her firm "look at that *American Lawyer* [profits per partner] number and say to themselves, 'We could improve that number if we got rid of some of these practice areas.'" Most people in the firm, however, "think that focusing [solely] on that number is absolutely ridiculous" (#136). The firm's relatively large spread in compensation allows it the flexibility to attract laterals with large books of business without the need to cut partners.

Firms thus may take various steps to enhance perceptions of distributive justice in ways that communicate respect for a range of contributions. Some steps help solve the Prisoner's Dilemma by signaling that cooperative behavior will be financially rewarded and narrow self-interested behavior will not. Others help solve the Assurance Game by recognizing contributions beyond those that contribute to financial profitability. As the next section describes, it is also important, however, that partners regard the compensation process itself as a fair one.

Procedural Justice

Belief in fair process can enhance satisfaction with compensation, even if someone is not completely happy with how much she receives (Tyler and Blader 2002). What contributes to belief that a process is fair? One thing is reliance on factors that are known to everyone:

> INTERVIEWER: Would you say that overall people trust the compensation committee to get it right?
>
> PARTNER: I do. . . . Each time I go into [the compensation] process thinking I'm getting ready to get mad, and then when I analyze it I realize, "Well, I think actually it's about where it should be." To give you an example, every two years your share allocation gets readjusted, and theoretically it can go up or down. The one before [when] I asked for a pretty substantial increase, and I did it based on my calculation of the amount of revenue, overhead, and all the rest of it. I said, "This is how much I think I should get," and that is what I got. . . . That's gone a long way in terms of building my confidence in the system. . . . Given my understanding of how the system is supposed to work, I got what I was supposed to get. (#94)

Another important component of a fair process is an opportunity to be heard. One partner noted:

> Each partner has an opportunity to write a memo . . . about who has been helpful, who has been maybe difficult for you. What are you doing in the community? What are your pro bono activities? Tell us all of that or tell us if you've had a serious illness in the family, because that is something we take into account, too. Has somebody had a tough year because, you know, kid's been sick, wife's been sick, husband's been sick. We take that into account and normally that would mean that there is unlikely to be any movement in their comp even if there was a bad year. (#111)

Another partner echoed the importance of giving colleagues an opportunity to tell their story:

> Every year at the end of the year we do compensation review. Now I'm talking about partners who are making a million dollars a year, they are making a

> lot of money, but we don't know their full story. A partner making a million dollars a year may be supporting his mother-in-law, his cousin, her best friend, whatever, and so in compensation I will sit down and talk to partners about what their hopes and expectations are and how it's relevant to their life, rather than just imposing their compensation on them. (#83)

Such opportunities can serve to provide assurance that the firm is not guided solely by business logic but respects partners as unique individuals with distinctive aspirations and responsibilities. This is, of course, a humane policy in any organization. In a law firm, however, it also is consistent with a traditional professional ethos of the partnership as a group of individuals who have responsibilities to one another that go beyond financial considerations.

The fact that firms tend not to disclose the weight that various factors have in the compensation decision can create some concerns about whether the process is fair. As one partner put it:

> [T]he factors that are in compensation are sort of enumerated now, and many of them are amorphous factors, but you don't really know how they are applied. There is really no sense of how they are applied. It's basically just in the mind of the beholder. And you don't really have any sense of how it's applied. (#72)

As another partner articulated, this can give rise to suspicion that compensation reflects partiality or favoritism rather than the consistent application of uniform standards: "I think the problem is . . . that we're not really sure how our compensation is driven. [Y]ou have certain people given big compensation when they don't necessarily have the big numbers, but maybe they have the right relationship to certain people in management" (#101).

Uncertainty about the bases for compensation decisions can lead partners to suspect that decisions either reflect personal favoritism or, notwithstanding what the firm says, are based strictly on financial metrics. The first can result in a lack of impersonal trust, the second a lack of personal trust. Either can lead to a sense that one is not respected by the firm.

Even if law firm management appreciates that the substantive and procedural aspects of its compensation system comprise a symbolic economy that sends important messages about respect, it faces a potentially formidable obstacle in conveying such respect. This is that the factors on which a firm relies in determining compensation are often subject to bargaining among partners over credits. The operation of this market can strongly affect partners' sense of the extent to which they are valued because decisions about whether and how much to share credit are made by colleagues with whom a partner directly works. Firms attempt, to varying degrees, to encourage partners to share credits in this market. The ability of rainmakers to go elsewhere, however, often imposes a practical limit on how much firms can do. The result is that firm management cannot completely control perceptions within the firm about the relative significance of business and professional logics.

The Internal Market of the Firm

The most psychologically salient symbolic outcomes in firms' internal markets usually involve origination credits. A partner's skill set and need for billable work affect her bargaining power in obtaining such credits. While firms make some effort to prevent egregiously unfair outcomes in this market, many partners regard it as largely unregulated. As a result, outcomes tend to reflect the personalities of individual partners and the dynamics of ad hoc negotiation.

Bargaining in the Market

A partner's satisfaction with the allocation of origination credits in the internal market depends on the same considerations as those that affect her satisfaction with the firm's decision about her compensation. First, does a partner believe that another partner has given her the credits she deserves in light of her contribution on a matter? Second, does a partner believe that another partner has relied on a fair process to determine whether to share credits or how many to share? Finally, what has another partner's decision about origination credits communicated about the respect that partner has for her?

The respect that is allocated in these interactions can be even more vivid and personally significant than what the firm conveys in its compensation decision because it occurs through the personal interaction of partners. A partner interacts with a firm about her compensation once a year for a limited period of time. The conversation focuses on her particular compensation, but part of it may well touch on general factors affecting her compensation for which she is not responsible, such as the firm's business strategy, general economic conditions, and the amount of demand in the partner's practice area.

A firm's determination of compensation is thus likely to be based at least in part on considerations that do not reflect personally on her. In addition, it reflects a judgment by "the firm," which may be an abstract entity to a partner in a large firm notwithstanding the personal importance of the compensation decision.

By contrast, decisions about the division of origination credits allocate respect through direct personal interactions between individual partners. They reflect a particular colleague's judgment about the value of another partner's contributions. This judgment is more intensely personal than a firm's determination of a partner's compensation. The respect or disrespect it communicates therefore can be especially meaningful. One service partner elaborated on this point:

> [There are cases where] I am confident that I've been a part of helping us land some of our largest corporate work, confident. But when it comes time to reward people, it's the corporate guy who landed the deal who gets all the gravy. What we do often isn't even given its own matter in the sense that we might be given some of the credit for that piece of the deal. It's just you are expected to contribute, but frankly it just means I'm billing my hours so at that point I might as well be a second year associate. (#98)

Another service partner described the conflict that can arise over sharing origination credits:

> [There was an] individual who left a year ago who did not act fairly, and people got very upset. An existing client of someone else's would be brought in and he would want to take the full origination credit or one of his clients would have a new matter that actually was the kind of work he didn't do and so he would bring in someone else to do the work but he wanted to keep all the origination credit. Those are the kind of things people remember and then that does increase resentment. (#6)

These psychological dynamics of the firm's internal market influence a partner's satisfaction with the outcomes of that market. A partner's conclusions about whether she has received what she deserves will be sensitive to whether she believes the internal market has appropriately recognized her contributions. That market tends to substantially weight the development of personal relationships with clients as a measure of contributions.

By contrast, a service partner's definition of his contribution may focus on the quality of his legal work. The latter, however, may not represent currency in the market for origination credits. This can trigger a sense of unfairness. Even more disconcerting, a service partner may believe that he contributes by interacting with and responding to a client far more regularly than the partner who brought the client to the firm. The failure of the latter partner to acknowledge this by sharing origination credits may provoke an especially acute sense that a partner is not receiving what he deserves.

If partners also regard the process as unfair, this will only accentuate their belief that substantive outcomes are unfair. A service partner's receipt of origination credits depends on the generosity of a rainmaker and whatever bargain the service partner is able to strike. In most cases, in other words, the process involves an informal personal interaction rather than the uniform application of any general rules. Therefore, most partners are unlikely to regard the internal market as operating on neutral principles.

The fact that discretionary personal decisions are perceived to drive the market for origination credit makes it more likely, then, that a service partner will question the fairness of the process that produces those outcomes. As one service partner put it, "I think that because of the way the compensation is structured, it just makes sense for you to keep all the originations and really try to monopolize the client relationship so that the younger guy can't be a threat to you" (#101).

Personal respect in the internal market is shaped in important ways by service partners' dependence on rainmakers. This inequality stems from the close relationships rainmakers form with clients, not on the quality of their legal work. Those who do not have many such relationships rely for work on those who do. In other words, service partners who contribute by providing good work determined by professional standards depend on rainmakers who are seen as contributing by using business skills to obtain clients. A service partner therefore may regard his status as a reflection of the priority of business over professional logic in the firm.

Furthermore, all partners are members of a profession with traditional aspirations to individual independence and control over one's practice. Rainmakers, however, come much closer to realizing these aspirations than do service partners. Even though partners ostensibly have equal formal status, the relationship between a rainmaker and a service partner can effectively approach that of an employer and an employee. If a service partner is unhappy with a rainmaker's decision about origination credits, he may well feel constrained in asserting any claim because of his need to obtain a regular flow of work from a rainmaker. One income partner described her experience:

> I will go to one of my mentors here and I'll say, "Okay, what do I do now? I really developed this relationship—maybe the partner originally had a relationship with the general counsel, but let's say that general counsel is no longer there and now I am . . . best friends with the new general counsel, [and I've] been doing work for them." So the question is, "Shouldn't I be originating partner?" Sometimes I'll get the advice, "Don't bite the hand that feeds you." (#64)

This dynamic can make interactions between partners in the firm's internal market especially fraught with the potential for resentment. Notwithstanding a service partner's acknowledgment of his substantive dependence, he may take offense at any behavior by a rainmaker that underscores it and makes it more explicit. As one service partner put it, "[T]he partner-associate thing isn't all that different from the equity partner-income partner thing, and I feel a lot more like a well-paid associate sometimes" (#98).

Furthermore, both partners know that the rainmaker is not wholly self-sufficient. She must rely on service partners to do the work for the clients that she brings in and to do whatever it takes to keep them happy. There is, in other words, some degree of mutual dependence between a rainmaker and service partner, even if one party to the relationship is less dependent than the other. A service partner may thus resent a rainmaker who hoards origination credits not simply because it has a financial impact but also because a rainmaker is effectively denying the contributions of her colleague and is asserting a self-sufficiency that they both know is false. A service partner described the sense of unfairness that can result from this denial of mutual dependence:

> Our compensation structure is based in part on the idea of originations and I don't think enough people play fair. . . . The same guy who brought client X in 30 years ago is still getting 50 percent of everything everybody else does, and, hey man, if I get 50 percent from everybody, I would be thrilled. . . . Someone brings the work in and I do 98 percent of the work with my team of associates, and I feel like he's getting compensated and I'm not. (#98)

A service partner with whom a rainmaker refuses to share origination credit may regard the refusal as a personal devaluation of his work and his status within the firm. More broadly, the refusal may communicate that the service partner is not so much an independent professional as someone whose work life is subject to the demands of more powerful colleagues. This feeling may be exacerbated by the feeling that rainmakers "get away with murder here just because they are viewed as money-makers" (#21). As one partner observed of these types of partners:

> If they don't feel like helping out on getting more work for the firm because it's just inconsistent with their self-interest, they don't. There is some of that, and I don't know how you resolve it because those are folks who say, "Look, if I don't get my way, I'm out of here." I guess you have to be prepared to say "Okay, good-bye," but that takes some guts. (#21)

Interactions in the internal market thus may lead a partner to conclude that the firm is a place in which most people are likely to pursue their own interest, and that she needs to protect herself by doing the same. This generally means eschewing cooperative behavior that would benefit the firm and is valued under traditional professional ideals. Or interaction may lead a partner to conclude that the firm is a place in which people have some commitment to shared values and are willing to temper self-interest for the sake of the larger good.

A partner who reaches the latter conclusion is more likely to feel that she can do the same, trusting that others will not take advantage of her if she does. That does not mean that considerations of self-interest are never salient; there inevitably are occasions when they are. What it means is that a partner has enough confidence in her colleagues that she does not feel the need to relentlessly pursue only personal rewards without regard for others.

The sense of trust that can emerge from interactions in the internal market can be fragile; trust is more easily destroyed than created. It can, however, generate a virtuous cycle, in which trust leads to a willingness to behave generously, which signals to others that it is safe to trust, which in turn leads them to be generous. As more people trust and behave accordingly, the message can become stronger and more widely communicated.

Given their portable book of business, why would rainmakers be interested in helping create a more cooperative firm culture to which members would have some allegiance? First, most narrowly, this type of culture might increase the origination credits that a partner receives from fellow rainmakers. Many rainmakers are not just Finders. To differing degrees they also are

Minders who do work for other rainmakers' clients. An ethos of sharing origination credits could enhance the compensation that they receive from playing the latter role.

More broadly, even if a rainmaker's concern is mainly obtaining financial rewards, a firm in which people are committed and engaged is also one that is more productive. People who do not feel respected or safe to look beyond their own interest are less willing to share ideas or to go the extra mile to get the job done. This is especially true in organizations in the knowledge industry, which compete by generating innovative solutions for their clients and customers (Kim and Mauborgne 2003, 127).

If a firm's internal market tends to communicate disrespect for service partners, this may lead to disengagement by partners who are essential to serving clients and keeping them satisfied. Some research also suggests that employees in professional service firms who occupy such positions are especially important sources of innovation (Smets et al. 2009). Enlightened self-interest can therefore motivate a rainmaker to act in the internal market in a way that allocates respect to service partners. In this regard, a firm that can encourage rainmakers to be generous can help solve the Prisoner's Dilemma.

Finally, one should not assume that all rainmakers are interested only in financial rewards. Our interviews indicate that many partners value the opportunity to be of service to clients, to work in a collegial atmosphere, to do high-quality work, to participate in intrinsically meaningful work, and to serve society in some way. Others also value being part of a firm that has a historical legacy that exemplifies these values. We are social animals, and being involved with others in pursuing a common purpose is a powerful source of satisfaction (Amabile and Kramer 2011). A rainmaker therefore may value cooperation as a good in itself, not simply as a means to maximize long-term self-interest. A firm that can provide this as well as financial rewards can create strong firm-specific capital. This may induce rainmakers to stay at the firm even if they could obtain higher compensation elsewhere.

The symbolic importance of generosity by rainmakers also can help a firm solve the Assurance Game by allocating respect to fellow partners as professionals that is not based simply on financial metrics. It can serve to downplay a service partner's dependence, acknowledge the rainmaker's own dependence on her colleagues, and recognize the quality of a service partner's work. It can communicate that someone who may be a service partner is a valued professional colleague rather than an underling.

Such generosity is especially meaningful because it is not required. A service partner knows that a rainmaker who shares origination credit has chosen to do so. The rainmaker, in other words, has acted fairly not to fulfill an obligation but because she wants to acknowledge the value of the service partner's assistance. This can deliver a powerful message to the latter about his value as a lawyer and forge strong personal and institutional ties.

Perhaps the most powerful way to influence the internal market is for major rainmakers to forgo taking as many credits, and as much compensation, as they could. Modeling the kind of behavior that the firm wants to see can have a powerful effect on partners. We heard several stories of how the willingness of partners with large books of business to do this has shaped the culture of a firm. One partner related the philosophy of a colleague who is a major rainmaker in the firm:

> [H]e could probably demand five times the compensation he makes, but what he does is that he will take less compensation for himself and say, "Compensate these other people who are really important to my practice well." And so that simultaneously binds them to him and keeps them happy and keeps them here. He's always made a point of saying that it's a point of pride that he leaves money on the table; he doesn't extract out of the firm all the money he could and that's an example for other people too. (#52)

Such generosity can serve the practical financial purpose of creating a cadre of loyal colleagues who are willing to pitch in to help the rainmaker. At the same time, the rainmaker is making a smaller claim on the financial rewards of obtaining such assistance than she could. In that respect, she is tempering business logic by professional logic. She is communicating that she values collaboration not simply for its instrumental benefits but for its intrinsically valuable camaraderie and sense of shared purpose. Lawyers who have benefited from this practice and who themselves have become major rainmakers tend to feel a strong obligation to follow this example in dealing with junior lawyers. In this way, a rainmaker's acts of generosity can have a powerful ripple effect that shapes the atmosphere and culture of a firm.

Firm Influence on the Internal Market

For all these reasons, a law firm has a substantial interest in ensuring that partner interactions in its internal market allocate the respect from colleagues that is so crucial to a partner's sense of connection to the firm. As we discuss below, firms attempt in various ways to influence behavior in the internal market by tempering the operation of business logic with measures that reflect professional logic.

First, a firm may limit the period during which origination credit is available or require that a partner have substantial ongoing involvement in a matter. Second, a firm may award management credits to partners for managing matters for the clients of their colleagues. This practice attempts to reduce the extent to which compensation reflects partners' dependence on rainmakers' willingness to share origination credits.

Management credits typically do not boost compensation as much as origination credits do. They do, however, recognize the importance and value of high-quality work and client service in addition to the business development skills that are reflected in origination credits. By sending this message, the award of management credits underscores that rainmakers are not self-sufficient. They must necessarily rely on the contributions of their colleagues who possess traditional professional skills to ensure that clients remain satisfied and continue to turn to the rainmaker when they have legal needs.

Third, firms may attempt to encourage rainmakers to share credits with others. Some provide guidelines that indicate how origination credit should be divided in certain situations (Nanda and Rohrer 2012b), while others rely on more general exhortations to be fair. On occasion, a compensation committee may adjust a partner's compensation because it believes that she has been unfairly hoarding origination credits. One committee member reports, "[W]e talk to people about being hogs and we tell them that they get punished when they are hogs. . . . [We tell them], '[Y]ou might have made this but you're making this because you're not a team player.'" The partner went on to give an example:

> [T]his person thinks they are the billing attorney, but they really don't have much responsibility anymore, so we look at that. We get the self-evaluations and we look at that, but in addition to the numbers we get all of the backup behind the numbers. So that if somebody claims to be billing attorney for X Corp we know if they really are or if they aren't. So somebody will say, "Well, geez, my numbers are so spectacular." And we'll say, "Well, yeah, but you don't even know who the general counsel is anymore at the client and it's really so and so who should get credit." (#111)

As we mention in chapter 3, Firm 3's willingness to adjust partner compensation contributes to what partners regard as an especially collaborative culture. A Firm 3 partner familiar with the compensation process described one instance in which the firm refused to credit a partner for all the origination credit that he claimed because the committee felt the lawyers around the partner deserved more compensation:

> One partner . . . had two younger partners and his practice overall was down and he did as much as he could himself and took all the origination credit for himself. His younger partners had about 1400 billable hours each [and] he had like 3200; he had six million dollars of originated business [and] they had $450,000 each, and they were in a team. At first, if you just looked at the numbers, the guy would have gotten a very high six-figure bonus based on his base compensation. And they would have got nothing and they would have gotten dinged because they were non-equity partners. Over the course of the two months that reviews for compensation took place he lost what I think was about $600,000. (#105)

Another example in which a firm may have no choice but to be involved in the allocation of origination credits is when a lateral partner enters the firm. The same Firm 3 partner described a common scenario:

> [T]he hardest areas are where the firm represents a company, has a set of relationships, and a [new] partner comes into the firm who has a different relationship with the same company. . . . [T]his partner starts selling his [client] contact about his relationship [with the new firm] and says, "We already represent you, so you should give us some work," and then a new piece of work comes in.
>
> There is no formula for that but . . . there is also the right way to behave. I mean you are a team. . . . [I]f you were doing things right you just would split it. . . . What I try to do is get people here to recognize there are these rules and to call me when they have questions or somebody is treating them badly. (#105)

Our research suggests, however, that most firms adjust origination credits infrequently, reserving it for especially egregious instances. One partner described the delicacy of adjusting the compensation of rainmakers for being insufficiently generous:

INTERVIEWER: To what extent can the firm use compensation to try to drive some of the cooperative behavior?

PARTNER: You can. The issue is this: it's easy to give the carrot and say, "I'm going to give you extra money because you did what we want you to do." We do that and we make it known that we do it. What we don't do enough is use it as a stick. We don't say, "Hey, asshole, we don't like what you've done. You would have made X but you're going to make X less something because of the way you acted," because right now that asshole probably is producing $5 million of business. He says, "Okay, [if] you don't want me, I'll go down the street and they'll pay me double what you're paying me." It really does handcuff [you] from using compensation as much as you like. (#10)

Even Firm 3's willingness to be more assertive than most firms in adjusting origination credits has its limits. As the Firm 3 partner who described his firm's efforts acknowledged, "Now again life isn't perfect. You try sending those messages to people who don't receive them well and who are very valuable to the firm, and this is where you get into the underbelly of law firms and lawyers" (#105).

An additional limitation of adjusting compensation to penalize failures to share credit is that firms generally do not publicize the fact when they do it. The rainmaker will know about it, as will any partners whose compensation is increased as a result of the adjustment. Other partners, however, likely will not. This can limit the extent to which the penalty communicates that the firm takes its sharing guidelines seriously. Law firms' limited use of punishment thus deprives them of what can be a powerful way of communicating values in other organizations.

Firm 3 addresses this situation by distributing information about the extent to which individual partners share credits. The effectiveness of this, of course, depends on how much concern a partner has about being seen as stingy in sharing credits. One pragmatic reason may be that a partner could find it more difficult to convince service partners to work on her projects because of such a reputation. Another may be a desire to avoid losing esteem from peers in the firm, who may acknowledge her business skills but think less of her as a colleague. Even a partner concerned about reputational damage for purely instrumental reasons nonetheless may eventually internalize those norms.

A law firm's internal market therefore plays a crucial role in the symbolic economy of compensation. Because decisions about sharing credit are made by colleagues with whom a partner works, they can send especially vivid messages about respect. Those messages, of course, have intensely personal significance. In addition, they serve more broadly to communicate to partners the extent to which the firm is shaped mainly by its members' self-interested behavior or by a more expansive sense of common purpose.

Compensation Transparency

Given that individuals tend to base satisfaction with their rewards on comparison with what others receive, one plausible way of minimizing dissatisfaction might be simply not to provide information to partners about the compensation of their colleagues. A few firms (approximately 14 percent by one recent account) take this approach by adopting what is called a "black box" or closed compensation system. Closed systems can give the leadership team latitude to compensate certain partners in line with the market, regardless of the opinions of other partners in the firm. Richard Rosenbaum, executive chair of Greenberg Traurig, prefers his firm's closed system: "This allows us to run what is a large business in many disparate locations and practices without politics and without visible competition between our shareholders. This has been a major plus in our culture. It allows us to make decisions that make sense to the market" (Kay 2012).

There were some differences among the six firms in our study in how widely they circulate compensation information. Firm 6 is somewhat less expansive than the other firms. It does not disseminate individual partner compensation figures among the entire partnership, but does to partners in firm and various practice managing positions. Other partners also can arrange to view such information. Interviewees said that their impression is that few partners elect to do this, however, since there is an unspoken ethos that discourages it. Partners in the firm indicated that this policy creates a collegial atmosphere in which compensation simply is not a topic of everyday conversation, much less debate. We regard Firm 6 as having an especially strong culture, which might lead an observer to conclude that limiting the availability of compensation information among partners can be an effective way to build such a culture.

On the other hand, Firm 4 also has a particularly strong culture in which compensation is openly discussed among partners. Its partners, however, regard the firm's complete transparency about individual partner compensation as an important factor in sustaining this culture. They emphasized how this establishes confidence in the fairness of compensation decisions, and how lack of transparency could lead to concerns about favoritism.

We note in the previous chapter, for instance, how female partners might be concerned that a "black box" system could conceal unjustified inequalities in compensation between men and women. A recent class action filed by female associates against Jones, Day cited to the firm's black box system as one way in which the firm systematically disadvantaged women. The complaint quoted a statement on the firm's website describing this system and its rationale:

> The financial relationship of a lawyer to Jones Day is confidential. Other than the very small number of people who advise the Managing Partner on these issues, no partner at Jones Day knows anything about the amount of income allocated to any other partner. Similarly, associate compensation is also confidential, for the same reasons: Jones Day compensates its associates individually, not by lockstep and certainly not based on some billable hours formula, and thus every associate's compensation is the product of his or her individual contributions, and cannot be fairly compared to any other individual. What is sometimes critically referred to by those outside Jones Day as a "lack of transparency" is almost universally viewed inside Jones Day as one of its great strengths. This confidentiality removes any temptation to try to compare apples and oranges; it eliminates the chance of creating inappropriate comparisons and jealousies; and most importantly, it does not allow even the possibility of creating barriers to the effective interaction of all Jones Day lawyers.[2]

Plaintiffs contended, however, that "Jones Day's system of 'black box' compensation results in the systematic underpayment of women," that "subjective factors are a mere pretext to underpay women," and that "Jones Day maintains a discriminatory pay system, which it facilitates by keeping compensation confidential."[3]

At the same time, lawyers at other firms with black box systems maintain that the lack of information helps produce a collegial culture. Indeed, some partners in open systems have told us informally that they would prefer a closed system because of the competition that widespread knowledge of all partners' compensation generates. One firm not in our study, Baker McKenzie, moved in summer 2018 from an open system for its North American equity partners to one in which compensation information is not automatically provided to partners. "The firm no longer distributes the information and instead makes it available upon request," the firm said in a statement. "This change was well-received by many partners and has promoted more collaboration among our partnership" (Tribe 2019).

Our interviews suggest that the fundamental value that produces comfort with a compensation system is not transparency but trust. A strong culture may not only be the product of a closed system but what makes it acceptable in the first place. Through a variety of measures, management in such firms has inspired trust in partners that it makes compensation and other partnership decisions fairly. Partners therefore accept limited availability of compensation information because they believe that management will make equitable decisions. As the Jones Day lawsuit may suggest, if lawyers lack confidence that management acts fairly toward all lawyers in the firm, a black box system can become instead an object of suspicion.

Some firms have never had a closed compensation system, or they moved to an open system a long time ago. For these firms, compensation transparency is a long-standing practice. Transparency may not be enough by itself to establish trust in management, but reducing it is likely to diminish such trust. Notwithstanding Baker McKenzie's change, several partners told us that moving from closed to an open system typically has been a one-way ratchet. Moving in the opposite direction creates the risk that management will be seen as acting in bad faith by being unwilling to act openly.

In sum, firms in which partners are comfortable with the firm not automatically circulating individual compensation figures to all lawyers likely are those that have taken meaningful steps to solve the Prisoner's Dilemma and the Assurance Game. To the extent this enables them to establish a strong culture, limited compensation transparency may help reinforce it by removing one source of possible dissension.

Firms with fully transparent systems must deal with potential dissatisfaction with compensation as an additional challenge in creating a strong culture. To the extent that they can inspire confidence that compensation decisions are made fairly, this can reinforce other measures that the firm adopts in attempting to solve the Prisoner's Dilemma and the Assurance Game.

Conclusion

Intensifying competitive pressures in recent years have led law firms to attach more importance to skills commonly associated with operating a successful business and to contributions more readily identified as directly contributing to revenue generation. The increasing importance of these skills means that a good law firm lawyer is now not simply someone who does excellent legal work or helps to create a collegial atmosphere within the firm. The greater importance of more commercial attributes is reflected in increasing emphasis on them in determining partner compensation.

The result is that the compensation process has taken on significance as an occasion for considering—and sometimes contesting—the relative value of those qualities that characterize a good lawyer. In this way, the process of determining compensation invokes interpretive schemes associated with different institutional logics.

A firm that hopes to nurture a distinctive culture will need to persuade its partners that its compensation system balances business necessities and professional values. In other words, it must define what it means to be a good lawyer in ways that will elicit partner commitment to the firm. This reflects the fact that interpretations of the material features of an organization are "part of an historical process by which firms and the people who work in them not only accumulate wealth, but also obtain their identity" (Cooper et al. 1996, 643). This perspective underscores that compensation is part of both a material and a symbolic economy within the firm.

Different firms manage this tension between logics and interpretive schemes in different ways. A firm's compensation process can provide one source of insight into how it attempts to do so. Firms' perceived need in recent years to weigh business skills more heavily because of competitive pressures means that compensation decisions may present, in especially stark relief, contests over the relative value of business skills and more traditional professional capabilities. Such contests shape each firm's culture and the meaning of professionalism for the lawyers that practice within it. The cumulative effect of these conversations and decisions will shape how lawyers understand their roles in an emerging, more commercial, version of the modern law firm.

8

Luring Laterals

A long shadow looms over every law firm that wants to sustain the kind of distinctive culture described in earlier chapters: an active lateral market in which substantial numbers of partners jump from one firm for another. Regardless of how well a firm balances business and professional logics, its efforts are vulnerable to unraveling because of the instability caused by frequent departures and arrivals in the lateral market. The departure of partners can drain the firm of lawyers who understand its norms and expectations, while the arrival of new ones may bring lawyers with very different understandings of appropriate behavior. Solving the Prisoner's Dilemma and the Assurance Game requires close attention to this dynamic, along with deliberate strategies to respond to it.

Lateral hiring is now institutionalized among large firms—a taken-for-granted feature of the large firm market. One 2019 survey reported that over half of the nation's largest 200 firms average more than one lateral hire every two months (Bruch, Ellenhorn, and Rosenberg 2019). The *American Lawyer* has documented data on lateral moves since 2000. By 2000, the trend was already well established, with 70 percent of the top 200 law firms hiring at least one lateral partner; by 2011, the figure was 89 percent (Henderson and Zorn 2013). The *American Lawyer* reported that 92.5 percent of the respondents to its survey of new partners in AmLaw 200 firms in November 2015 had already been approached by legal recruiters (McQueen 2016). A 2018 survey of law firm leaders in firms of over 250 lawyers indicated that over 79 percent had acquired laterals or other law firms "specifically to improve profitability" (Clay and Seeger 2018, 38). Furthermore, more than 72 percent of leaders of firms of all sizes said that "increased lateral movement" is a permanent trend (1).

One commentator describes the lateral market this way:

> [T]he concept of luring laterals away with money isn't new—it's been going on for decades—and of course firms have always sought to backfill those positions. But, it's never been this aggressive, the profile of the moves has never been this high, and the current market represents an escalation in "capillary action"—the movement of high-powered, apex partners upward in the hierarchy—that is creating a tit-for-tat scenario and is changing the way that the business of law is being done. (Parnell 2018, quoted in Thomson Reuters and Georgetown Law 2019)

The increase in lateral movement is also reflected in data for different geographic markets. As the 2019 Annual Report on the Legal Market by Georgetown Law's Center on Ethics and the Legal Profession and Thomson Reuters reports:

> ALM Intelligence recently tallied the total number of lateral partner moves in key geographic markets for the period from 2010 through 2017, and the results—taken as reported—are astonishing. In New York, for example, there were 4,445 lateral partner moves, representing 35 percent of all partners in the market. In Washington, the number of moves was 3,759, or 43 percent of all partners. And in two jurisdictions—Chicago and Atlanta—lateral moves exceeded 50 percent of all partners in the market. (Thomson Reuters and Georgetown Law 2019, 14)

One partner attributed the intense competition for lateral partners to the pursuit of major global clients:

> Today, to attract top talent, you are in a bidding war situation that you may not have been in ten years ago. It's a different world in that sense, because getting work from big multinational . . . companies is a ticket to generating revenues in a way that may not be the case with smaller companies. . . . If our business model now is that we're competing with global firms for partners, we have to pay partners these big amounts of money. (#71)

While there has been no empirical research comparing lateral movement in law firms with other professional service organizations, accounting and consulting firms appear to rely on lateral hiring much less than law firms do (Koltin Consulting Group 2014). Law firm expert Richard Rapp has suggested that this reflects the fact that the reputations of individual lawyers tend to be more significant than those of law firms, in contrast to the importance of organizational reputations for other professional service firms. In addition, Rapp notes, partner compensation varies more across law firms than is the case in other business organizations. "Each law firm with its own often-opaque private pay arrangements is distinct," and "no single plan dominates." For individual partners, lateral movement thus represents "arbitrage—reducing the imbalances between the pay and perquisites of partnership offered by different firms" (Rapp 2016).

Another factor contributing to an active lateral market is that, unlike other organizations, law firms are precluded from enforcing noncompete covenants against partners who leave the firm. They also are significantly constrained in imposing any financial penalties on such partners (Regan 1999). As a result, partners are able to take clients with them when they move from one firm to another. Ironically, this reinforcement of a free market in partners is based on the view that enforcing such restrictions would represent an unwelcome intrusion of business logic into what should be an arena of professionalism. As one prominent judicial opinion rejecting enforcement of a penalty stated, "[T]he practice of law must be carefully governed by ethical considerations rather than by the economic concerns that guide strictly commercial enterprises."[1]

In any event, Rapp (2016) predicts that "the lateral hiring 'frenzy' will be long-lived." As law firms prune partners who threaten to bring down profitability, they will also seek to hire partners who can increase it. The sections that follow discuss the prominent role of the lateral market in the competition among law firms. While regular reliance on this market reflects the greater influence of business logic within large law firms, some firms adopt approaches that attempt to preserve a role for professional values in this process.

Dynamics of the Lateral Market

Lateral versus Organic Growth

Although lateral hiring is an accepted practice among large law firms, it is not the only path to expanding the partnership. Increasing partner ranks through the "organic" means of promoting associates is one alternative. Law firms, however, are increasingly eschewing this alternative in favor of lateral hires and mergers.

Law firms traditionally relied on an apprenticeship model in which junior lawyers learned from interaction with senior ones (Galanter and Palay 1991). The most valuable training for associates was to learn from senior lawyers who evaluated associates' work and explained the ways in which it fell short or could be improved. This feature was seen as integral to law practice as a profession.

Training and developing junior lawyers are expensive and time consuming activities, however. In addition, with some partner rates at $1,000 an hour and more, such mentorship can involve significant opportunity costs. Furthermore, determining which associates have future business development ability is difficult, so the payoff from any investment is highly uncertain. Investing in lateral hires may therefore seem to be a "safer" risk since the incoming attorneys have already proved themselves in other firms and are theoretically able to bring their clients with them and/or attract new clients immediately upon arrival.

In addition, the partnership structure tends to discourage long-term investments by firms. Profits are distributed among the partners at the end of each year, with an eye on ensuring PPP rates that compare to peer firms'. When partners leave, they take their capital with them and receive retirement payments, but no longer have a financial interest in the firm and its long-term trajectory. Reinforcing a short-term perspective is the perception that an intensely competitive legal market can produce rapid changes in a firm's fortunes, which can have adverse effects on its reputation and the willingness of profitable partners to stay. Firms believe that they need to seize opportunities to expand their practices as quickly as possible, with no time to be patient while the firm gradually builds its expertise. One study reports that the most frequently cited reason for hiring lateral partners is to strengthen existing practice areas (Bruch, Ellenhorn, and Rosenberg 2019).

The Book of Business

The currency in the lateral market is a partner's "book of business," or the clients with whom a partner maintains the primary relationship. For some firms, the dollar value of a partner's book of business represents a quantitative threshold below which firms will not seriously consider a potential lateral.

One partner described the approach of his firm: "They won't even look at you any more for a lateral unless you've got a book of business that can support the compensation you would like to get" (#66). Several partners told us that a lawyer needs a book worth $3–4 million in revenues even to attract interest from any large firm. One study estimated that about $17.1 billion in business moved between firms in the lateral market between 2014 and 2018 (Bruch, Ellenhorn, and Rosenberg 2019).

One interviewee observed, "Since the advent of the *American Lawyer* and the explosion of the headhunting or recruiting profession it's very easy if you know your metrics to pick up the phone and ask a recruiter what kind of money you could be making at another law firm" (#247). One partner aptly described the reaction of recruiters when she tells them she does not have a substantial book of business: "[The recruiters say,] 'Hey you have a great background, great resume, blah, blah, blah,' and then the moment I say I don't have any portable book of business [they say] 'oh nice knowing you,' click" (#101). Another partner coming out of government explained the challenges of finding a position without having clients:

> [People had previously] left the US Attorney's office and [had become] partners at firms despite the fact that presumably they were walking in without a book of business. By the latter half of '09 when I started looking . . . the legal market was a completely different world. I put out a lot of feelers both personally and through friends and through using recruiting firms and pretty much across the board the answer back was, "No matter how great you are, and we've heard of you, and you have a great reputation and your credentials are great, you seem great, we don't bring people in as partner unless they are walking in with $2 million worth of business." (#42)

We describe in chapter 5 the particular challenges that women face in building books of business and becoming rainmakers. One female partner explained why there are so few women in senior leadership roles in firms; the same dynamic can apply to attractiveness as a lateral hire.

> Once you then get into business generation then you don't see the women doing it. I mean a little bit, there are a couple of women who have a decent . . . amount of business. But by and large the women just don't bring in as much business so they don't excel as much as the men. (#24)

Without a portable book of business, women have fewer options in the lateral market. This means fewer opportunities to gain the significant increases in compensation that can be available in that market. It also can mean less bargaining leverage with their firms.

Lateral Hiring as Signaling

Because firms regard client and competitor perceptions of a firm's stature and aspirations as crucial, lateral hiring can be rich with signaling. The signaling is even more important given the opacity of the lateral hiring market (Connelly et al. 2011). The ethics rules add to this lack of transparency. Not only do the rules prohibit firms from talking to a potential lateral's clients about whether they would follow a partner to another firm, they also forbid seeking information about a partner's work for those clients. Here is how one partner explained the challenge:

> You can talk about your deal history or your case history and a lot of it is public record, so the nature of the deals or cases you've worked on is known, the types of transactions, the types of skills that come into it. Then you can talk to them about what you did on that deal or how you think about this particular area of the law or this type of practice. But you never really know how they do it until you actually see them draft an agreement or negotiate a deal or supervise an associate or, you know, reel in the fish. (#34)

The unknowns, however, go beyond technical expertise or client portability:

> I think that the person you don't know sometimes looks better than the person you know. . . . A lot of laterals were not successful in their prior lives for a reason, some of them had real skeletons in the closet. So we do a lot more due diligence now, but I think we've bought a lot of clunkers. I think that to some degree we fooled ourselves into thinking that we could develop practices by acquiring [the] right people. (#31)

The lateral market's opacity leaves considerable room for firms to attempt to send signals about its market position through its lateral hiring strategy, both to the public and to partners in other firms. The legal press reports regularly on lateral hires (the *American Lawyer* has a regular column called "Comings and Goings"), and firms typically issue press releases when they hire a new partner.

Before Dewey & LeBoeuf famously imploded in 2013, for example, it had an explicit strategy of moving into the upper tier of law firms. Stephen Davis, chair of the predecessor firm LeBoeuf Lamb, followed an aggressive lateral hiring strategy. His first big coup was hiring prominent securities lawyer Ralph Ferrera in 2004, a move that was widely seen as a signal of the firm's lofty aspirations. In 2007, Davis engineered a merger with Dewey Ballantine, a firm widely believed to be a "fading beauty" among elite New York firms. From this platform, Davis doubled down on his quest to lure big-name laterals using huge compensation guarantees. Davis predicted that the firm would be a "premier New York law firm with global reach" (Longstreth and Raymond 2012). Little indicates that Davis drew on many other tools besides lateral hiring and mergers to pursue these goals.

Henderson and Zorn's (2013) analysis of lateral hiring data shows that a shift has taken place since the 2008 financial crisis. Before the financial crisis, the average lateral move was to a firm with higher revenues per lawyer, indicating that partners were moving from less profitable to more profitable firms. By 2011, however, the average lateral move was to a firm with lower revenues per lawyer. One explanation for this shift, as chapter 7 describes, is that law firms have been trying to pare down their partnership ranks to improve profitability. As some of these less productive partners are asked to leave, they find new homes in firms that are a few rungs down on the prestige ladder. Even though the incoming partner was viewed as insufficiently productive at his old firm, the new firm can signal that it is able to attract partners from premier firms.

Despite the large number of firms engaged in lateral hiring, data suggest that it can be a hit-or-miss proposition. For instance, while Altman Weil's 2018 survey of law firm leaders indicated that more than 77 percent in recent years had acquired lateral partners or law firms specifically to increase profitability, only slightly under 56 percent of the leaders said that such activity had significantly furthered this objective (Clay and Seeger 2018, 39). Another survey of the 1,130 laterals hired in 2011 by the 100 firms with the highest profits per partner found that 47 percent of laterals do not stay more than five years. "Given that it takes two or three years for a lateral to come up to speed at a new firm," the survey reports, "and that two-to-three years of strong performance are needed to recoup recruiting costs and compensation-above-contribution[,] not staying 5 years is a loss-making proposition" (Simons 2017). Those who do stay often do not meet expectations; one study found that only 38 percent brought their expected book of business with them successfully and 30 percent either underperformed or significantly underperformed based on the business they were expected to bring with them (Bruch, Ellenhorn, and Rosenberg 2019).

Despite these cautionary notes, most firms see little choice but to actively participate in the lateral market. Growth is necessary to remain competitive, and most firms believe that lateral hiring is the best way to achieve this. Furthermore, even firms that place less emphasis on growth are vulnerable to partner departures, and regard lateral hiring as necessary to replace the partners who leave.

Cultural Risks

While an active lateral market can benefit firms and lawyers, it also can have destabilizing effects on both. As one leader of a large US firm lamented, the dominance of the lateral market represents "the death of loyalty in the practice of law" (#40). A partner at another firm described the instability that an active lateral market can cause:

> The market is starting to look [like] sports teams; you know, we trade some stars, stars keep leaving and going and the whole game if you are the coach is to temporarily get together a team and then it moves on. That's the huge external pressure that law firms are facing and [the question is] how much do they succumb to that. . . . At the end of the day it probably doesn't make that much sense for clients. Clients are probably deluded if they think there is some . . . great individual and it's not the firm as a whole that is delivering to them. (#179)

Another impact of lateral hiring is its effect on the compensation structure of the firm. On the one hand:

> There are firms throwing crazy amounts of money around these days and I do think . . . more so than ever [the] mentality is get [it] while you can . . . because who knows what tomorrow is going to hold. And that's a challenge. More so than ever you've got to pay your performers. (#203)

On the other hand:

> [Y]ou typically expand by cherry picking your people from other law firms and . . . if we're cherry picking these people, then we've got to pay these people a premium to bring those people in. So that means we can give a short shrift to people who have been here for a long time. (#72).

Law firm expert David Parnell (2018) suggests that increasingly aggressive recruiting of highly profitable partners by a small group of wealthy firms is beginning to have highly destabilizing effects for the entire legal market. "Left behind the vacating partners," he comments, "are voids that the firms are aggressively trying to backfill with, of course, rainmakers from other firms, which creates a self-perpetuating cycle." The result is that the leadership of firms that lose high-profile partners must

> offer bigger payouts for new laterals that can fill the huge empty shoes. As you might imagine, this pisses off existing partners—"Why is the new person with $9M in business getting paid $1.5M more than me when I have $9M in business AND I've been here 20 years; where the hell is the loyalty?" and further destabilizes the firm's partnership. In the end, this "life cycle" of sorts weakens the firm's appeal to current and potential partners and clients and otherwise leaves the firms vulnerable. (Parnell 2018)

Finally, several partners noted the basic difficulty of maintaining a stable firm culture in the face of frequent departures and arrivals of partners. As one partner said about his firm: "We've grown fast by the addition of laterals. Like in chemistry, every time you add a drop of something new, the composition of the entire solution changes" (Nanda and Rohrer 2012a, 11). Another partner observed:

> I don't think there is time spent thinking as much about the culture of a small group [of laterals] rather than their book of business and how their expertise adds to our resume. When that happens, you get powerful individuals often who end up on the executive committee that are heads of these groups that may have a different way of doing business and they don't get the [traditional firm culture] because that is not them. And I've seen it erode our culture. (#254)

This risk is especially pronounced when a firm brings in a relatively large group of laterals:

> They have their culture. We have our culture, it's very hard to integrate them. So if you have a firm where you bring associates up . . . the ladder, they get integrated into the culture [and] every once in a while you [may] bring in some laterals. When you bring in a whole group, that says to me nobody is really concerned about the culture. Of course, if somebody has two horns maybe you're not going to bring them in. But if they've got a book of business, that's our culture. (#189)

Notwithstanding this risk to culture, many firms seem willing to take it. The vice chair of AmLaw 100 firm Winston & Strawn, for instance, has said, "The clear preference of the firm is to grow through larger groups of lawyers. It's not to say we won't make additions for individuals. But, where we have excelled in terms of the lateral market over the past say five years or more is when we brought in large groups of lawyers." Similarly, the CEO of Cozen O'Connor says, "[G]roups are more likely to bring their clients without battle from their prior firm than one-offs are." In addition, he says, groups can provide operational efficiencies: "If a firm does not need to increase overhead in costs, such as real estate and IT, then the group's revenue, less their direct costs," for items such as compensation and administrative secretarial support, "should fall to your bottom line." By adding a group, "I can now spread my overhead costs over more lawyers. In a sense, I'm getting additional revenue without increasing my costs" (Strom and Simmons 2018).

Our interviews indicate that firms may attempt to take firm culture into account in the lateral hiring process mainly in three ways. The first is to use the lateral hiring process as a means of "expanding the firm's platform" rather than simply "buying a revenue stream." The second is to include into the hiring decision an assessment of whether a prospective lateral will fit comfortably within the firm's culture. The third is to devote significant time and resources to ensuring that laterals are integrated into the firm both financially and culturally. As we discuss, each of these can solve the Prisoner's Dilemma by emphasizing collaboration as a key element of a firm's business strategy. To the extent that management can credibly communicate in this process that collaboration is an intrinsically valuable feature of a firm's culture, it also may help solve the Assurance Game.

Lateral Hiring and Professional Values

"Expanding the Platform"

Partners consistently used two terms to describe different philosophies with respect to lateral hiring. One approach, which can further both business and professional values, is to use such hiring to "expand the platform" of the firm. The metaphor of the platform describes the strategic fit between a lateral's practice and the firm's geographic and practice orientation. Thus: "The move really came because I felt for me personally, for my practice personally, it was a stronger platform; we had more practices to offer nationally and internationally" (#36). Another partner noted, "We are never going to attract the people that do [a certain type of practice] because . . . that's not part of our strategic plan. So we're not the right platform for them, so we're wasting our time" (#11).

Expanding the platform thus seeks to identify partners in other firms whose practices would complement the services that the firm currently offers. Ideally, existing clients will have a demand for the services that the new partners will provide, and the new partners' clients will find the firm's existing practices appealing. New and existing partners, in other words, will be able to cross-sell services to clients, as well as to collaborate in offering expanded services to them.

Here is how one partner described lateral hiring as an effort to expand the firm's platform:

> We did a strategic assessment several years ago of one of our [specialty] practices and . . . through market research we felt we were losing business because we didn't have a West Coast office. Even though we had a brand name [in the] market . . . we were having trouble on the West Coast. So part of gaining market share was to increase our presence [there]. Then we said, "Okay, who can do that for us?" And we identified different people that we thought could do that. [Partner A] was one of them because he's the brand in California, so we had a strategy to go after him and thank God it was successful. (#11)

A platform in theory provides the potential for synergies and ties with other partners. It thus implies that there is a certain coherence to the firm's acquisition of practices and office locations:

> Presumably the reason that you bring on a new group is for the synergy . . . so that you know it works well with your existing platform so that two and two can be five as opposed to four. I mean, that's what your goal is. (#16)

One partner who had recently moved from another firm discussed the importance of coming to a firm that would be collaborative:

> [The firm] convinced us that the firm truly has a culture of working across department lines and office lines because we said to them another problem we had at [our old firm] was [that] our practice was one where we have to have very significant, very sophisticated help from [a variety of practices]. . . . So the firm just totally lived up to its commitment to give us the support that we needed and enabled us to grow a practice that we couldn't have done in our old shop no matter how lucky we got with new cases from clients. (#228)

An alternative approach to lateral hiring is to use it to "buy a revenue stream." This approach seeks to identify prospective laterals whose book of business will increase the profitability of the firm, without regard to whether new partners will be collaborating with existing partners in doing so. The new partners simply add their profit stream to that of the firm, and will not necessarily expand opportunities for their colleagues. Such partners theoretically could work in their own silos, with minimal interaction with others in the firm, especially if they bring along an entire practice group from another firm.

Such behavior can be less profitable for a firm than collaboration. In this respect, a strategy of expanding the platform can solve the Prisoner's Dilemma. Many partners also tend to criticize buying a revenue stream, however, as a narrow focus on business objectives without regard for other values. One partner described how a policy of buying a revenue stream could endanger a firm's culture:

> The real risk would be [that] they start hiring people just for the money, so it boils down to "we're hiring this person for the money, that's the reason, and we're not looking at other considerations." If you are hiring people just for the money then people will start to catch on and say, "Oh, if they are hiring people only for the money then maybe what I'm doing is only for the money, these other things don't really count." You could see how that would break down a culture. People catch on and at the end of the day they are acting as if money is the only thing that matters." (#179)

These comments indicate that a lateral hiring strategy of expanding the platform can be important not simply because of the financial benefits it provides but as an affirmation that the firm is not guided solely by business considerations. As such, the strategy reflects an effort to ensure that partners enjoy both financial and professional rewards from practicing in the firm. It thus has the potential to solve both the Prisoner's Dilemma and the Assurance Game.

One partner's comparison of his firm and another firm vividly illustrates the difference between seeking to expand a firm's platform and buying a revenue stream:

> It took five minutes to figure it out, in the process of interviewing at [Firm A], I was asked a thousand questions about [Company B], who was the client that was coming with me, and what they could do for them and how much business there was and how certain I was I could bring that business, millions of questions about how they were all going to do all these great things for [the client], not one question in three weeks' worth of back and forth with them about where we might fit into something they already did, not one, not one. Because that is not what they were interested in.

By contrast, at his current firm:

> The first time I ever sat down here with a bunch of senior partners and the chairman, every one of them was like, "Oh my God there are so many places where you guys would fit in to what we do and we could see bringing you out to see this one and that one." Some of that has happened and frankly more than I think [would happen] at your average firm. It was a dramatically different approach. (#150)

Another partner compared his current firm with his previous one. "[We] won't buy a practice, [we] won't buy a revenue stream, that's just not who we are here. We don't need another guy with $10 million bucks, what's the point? There's got to be a lot more on the table that makes sense for a variety of other reasons." At his prior firm, however, "We would buy a revenue stream tomorrow, if you showed me the numbers" (#76).

While many respondents hastened to reassure us that their firm did not attempt to buy revenue streams, they suggested that it happens at "other" firms.

This distinction perhaps signals an underlying discomfort with hiring lateral partners, one that is allayed by the belief that the firm is making decisions about laterals that will help the firm succeed:

> I am highly confident that nobody [says] we're just trying to buy a stream of revenue, buy a book of business. Mathematically it [may] work but culturally it doesn't work—otherwise you become a law firm of a bunch of people that share offices and silos. It's only if it really fits with what we're trying to accomplish, what we are strategically trying to do. . . . Lateral partners need to work within our global plan. And our global plan isn't just to add more people; it's to be consistent with our practice. (#69)

The complementarity of practices that reflects expansion of a firm's platform increases the likelihood of collaboration between new and existing partners, which in turn helps integrate laterals into the firm. This can provide more substantial financial benefits than simply buying a revenue stream. It also can help partners develop personal ties that are an important source of professional satisfaction. Partners note that the existence of such ties affects their receptivity to calls from recruiters. As one said, "I get a lot of calls by headhunters, but if I [were] to go to someplace else, there is the possibility of me earning a bit more money, yet [here] I really enjoy the work, I really enjoy the clients, I enjoy the people that I work with, so those are important aspects and I'm sure it's driven differently by every individual" (#72).

Another partner remarked:

> I could never imagine going to another firm and having a better situation in the sense that I would lose the relationships that I developed over eight years, both in terms of other practice groups, people that I know how to call on and have rapport with, people that have had a relationship where I know they can help out or we have a good way of allocating work, or I know that I can get certain types of questions answered where it's not my specialty, and we have a team that works [well]. (#71)

This is consistent with research that indicates that a key predictor of whether an individual will leave a job is whether they have a "best friend" at work (Harter, Schmidt, and Keyes 2003). For law firm partners, the existence of such relationships can provide a form of firm-specific capital that tempers the potentially destabilizing effects of active lateral hiring. Such ties thus help partners serve their clients better, but also are professionally and personally rewarding.

Screening for Cultural Fit

Most firms profess to screen prospective laterals to ensure that they will fit culturally within the firm. At the same time, the notion of cultural fit is hard for partners. Many partners expressed it in terms of not hiring "jerks." They often invoked this notion as a way to emphasize their own firm's culture:

> Excuse the French, but the low asshole quotient was a high factor. We weren't always successful in that, but that was . . . definitely the watchword— we're good guys and girls and we want to keep that. (#76)
>
> I remember a couple of years ago we had a guy . . . who wanted to come here and he had worked at the SEC. I knew him a little bit at the SEC, but I heard a lot about him, about how this guy was a really difficult guy to work with, and so when he was interviewed and we were sitting around a table talking about him, I said, "Look, I just have to tell you that this is this guy's reputation. It was at the SEC and I understand it's the same way in private practice." They looked around and said, "That's enough for us. He's not coming." (#66)
>
> Traditionally there has been what I would refer to as a no asshole rule, and I am familiar with at least one example of someone who had a big book of business where a decision was made not to pursue them because he was viewed as a jerk. That rule is still at least somewhat in effect. (#82)

Identifying cultural fit tends to rely on intuitive assessments more than rigorous analysis:

> When I interview laterals I kind of have to go with my gut . . . because I find it's very hard in a 30-minute setting or an hour to really get a feel for a person, so you feel out what you can. Obviously you want to get a sense of whether this person is the kind of person who has red flags in their past, [who] is going to be somebody who isn't really a team player or is going to be difficult or is really out for themselves. Or is this a person who is going to be the kind of person who, if you have a problem on Friday at 5:00, they want to help you as opposed to just want[ing] to find a way to punt it to

somebody else. That's a valuable thing, and you want people around who . . . [want] to help you. (#71)

Another partner emphasized the importance of reputation:

INTERVIEWER: What are the main considerations that your group looks for when considering hiring a lateral partner?

PARTNER: I think they really have to be people who work with us well. I mean they have to be good lawyers and all that, but I think there [are] people everyone has said there is no way we want that person no matter what book of business they have.

INTERVIEWER: And what types of people [are] that?

PARTNER: Obviously people who are just difficult, just obnoxious. It doesn't mean you have to be socially friendly with everybody, but you are looking for decent people. That's been a pretty high priority. (#73)

Refusing to hire profitable but unpleasant people can send a message about the importance of professional values by leaving money on the table. One partner, for instance, described his firm's decision not to pursue certain people who otherwise had sterling credentials:

When we were looking for an antitrust lawyer we spoke to several of the very top tier prestigious antitrust lawyers in town, you know, guys who had been assistant attorney general, counsel to the FTC. We took a pass on a number of practices because we said, you know, that person is just going to be oil and water with this law firm, they are too demanding, they are too difficult and it's just not worth it. (#247)

Partners varied, sometimes within the same firm, in their views of whether a big book of business might lead a firm to overlook a potentially difficult personality. One partner noted that who is considered a "jerk" can be in the eye of the beholder:

What do you mean by no jerks? It's completely different from what I mean about no jerks. What they mean about no jerks [is] you can't throw the vase through the window. What I mean about no jerks is don't turn your back on me . . . those words . . . only give you just the most superficial insight into what's really going on. (#131)

In addition, the larger the group of laterals brought in from another firm at one time, the less credible is the firm's claim that cultural fit is an important criterion in hiring. One partner, for instance, noted that the firm recently hired more than thirty lawyers in a particular practice group from another firm:

> In terms of the culture, I would say when a firm brings in a group of 35 lawyers from another firm, what's the difference what the culture is? You are a corporate entity, it doesn't matter whether they are part of your culture or not, it's a business, you've made it clear this is just a business, we're looking at the bottom line. . . . So what is the importance of firm culture if you're bringing in that many lawyers who were not brought up within the firm culture?

As he said, "I wonder if [our firm] interviewed [people at the other firm] and said, 'Well, we would like to know about the culture of your firm before we bring in 35 people.' I don't think that happened" (#189).

Partners suggested that a good indication of whether a firm takes cultural fit seriously in hiring laterals is whether the firm ensures that several people interview a prospective partner. One report describes Sheppard Mullin's approach (a firm that was not part of our study). Prospective laterals visit "almost all of the firm's domestic offices, plus [participate in] video conferences," meeting what may be as many as 200 partners in the process. The chair of the firm says that this process benefits the firm by

> ensuring that partners have a chance to meet the prospective candidate before a partnership-wide vote on whether to bring the person on board—something that happens for all laterals. All those meetings also help Sheppard Mullin spot potential red flags, such as a sharp-elbowed personality or a siloed practice that doesn't offer as many synergies as the firm would hope. The idea, from the firm's perspective, is to give each candidate a very close look to determine their potential fit from both a cultural and business perspective. (Flaherty 2018)

Involving this many partners in the process is another way of leaving money on the table. As the *American Lawyer* noted, this can be a successful approach "[i]f you have a billable hour (or dozens) to spare." The strategy appears to work for Sheppard Mullin, which reportedly has retained 70 percent of the laterals it has hired since 2001, compared to the roughly 50 percent average within the industry. Another lateral partner describes how the process of being hired at Munger Tolles involved meeting about 100 lawyers, or about half the firm. "It was a tremendous amount of time," he said, "a tremendous amount of otherwise billable hours. I think that shows how seriously Munger takes it" (Flaherty 2018). The forgone revenues from engaging in such a process can help solve the Assurance Game by communicating a firm's commitment to a culture guided at least in part by professional values.

Integrating Laterals

Even if a firm's lateral hiring is guided by the goal of expanding its platform and the desire to achieve cultural fit, there is no guarantee that it will be successful. Simply putting people together does not mean that they will actually collaborate. One partner described the challenges with trying to form the ties that would lead to synergies between practices upon arriving at a new firm:

> When you first get there you think . . . all the . . . 1,800 lawyers or at least 700 partners [will] see [the] notice come up on their screen that we have this group of [Specialty A] lawyers now in [City A] and they all [will] immediately . . . focus on it and wake up every morning think[ing], how can I take advantage of the fact that we now have this team? Whereas the truth is everyone is focusing on their own thing and it's amazing how many people . . . to this day . . . don't even know that we have such resources in [City A]. . . .
>
> Even after I had been at [the firm] for three years I remember . . . one time being really annoyed because there was this partner in [City B] [who] had a matter right up my alley . . . and he gave it to this other partner in [my office] because he didn't know of my existence. . . . I don't blame anybody, [but] the point is you have to be going to [other] offices—I've been to [another office] at least six or seven times—you go to those offices, you walk around the halls, and you just have to stay top of mind with people so they remember that you are here. (#244)

An effort to expand the platform thus may end up as nothing more than the purchase of a revenue stream unless a firm takes active steps to nurture and support collaboration after lateral partners arrive. These steps can be interpreted as a means to ensure that lateral hiring will generate financial benefits. The amount of time and resources a firm devotes to this, however, also can represent money left on the table that signals the intrinsic value of collaboration.

Legal recruiter Major, Lindsey & Africa (MLA) emphasizes the importance of deliberate integration programs in expanding opportunities for other partners and the firm. Its surveys on lateral satisfaction include a section on "how effectively firms integrate laterals into the culture and business" of the firm. The inclusion of this section, the firm reports,

> found its genesis in our experience that often the most unhappy laterals were those whose firms failed to make them true partners with a stake in the enterprise other than a purely financial one. Without common ties of some kind, and lacking a long common history of "thick and thin" that once helped to bind partners together, it can otherwise be tempting to abandon ship at the first sign of stormy weather. (Lindsey and Lowe 2014, 28)

MLA's 2014 lateral satisfaction report indicates that partners whose new firms make the most effective efforts to integrate them into the firm and its culture, "including the non-business aspects of making a newcomer feel 'part of the family,'" are most likely to be satisfied with their moves, while partners whose firms failed to do so are less satisfied (Lindsey and Lowe 2014, 28). While firms are doing better at integrating lateral partners than they did a decade ago, they still "seem to do a better job at the relatively short-term and focused task of recruiting lateral partners than at the on-going and more diffuse challenge of fully integrating these new partners into the firm" (47).

One consultant notes that "[r]eal integration requires much more than providing current firm partners and clients information about a lateral partner's practice skills and value proposition" because, "despite the enthusiasm of partners invested in recruiting a lateral lawyer, there are always others who perceive their new colleague as an opportunity to lose far more than gain. After all, a lateral partner has just divorced his old firm and taken valuable assets with him. Who's to say that won't happen again?" These concerns "have only intensified during the economic slowdown. Partners worried about filling their own plates are even more reluctant to share their client contacts with someone they have no particular reason to trust" (Ostrow 2010). In other words, a firm must persuade its partners that it is safe to cooperate.

Genuine integration thus requires sensitivity to both business and interpersonal considerations. One partner noted that his firm created a formal role for him as the full-time head of lateral integration, which is a rarity among large firms. "When I started the function," he says,

> I thought it was as simple as, "Let's have a written integration plan that we come up with in connection with our decision to recruit someone," and we do it collaboratively, it's an actual written document. When people join in the first 30 days we sit down with buddies who are going to work on that and we set out some goals and everybody goes off and does their thing. If life worked like that it would be great, but it didn't work. (#105)

Over time, he found, integration efforts need to be tailored to the particular situations of individuals, in collaboration with people in the relevant practice group. In general, this involves

> introducing the [laterals] to lawyers who practice in areas where they need expertise. Not just having a cup of coffee but trying to actually broker meetings to talk about opportunities that they have for their clients with the new platform they have. Then there are meetings where we go over our client list after a couple of months. The key thing is to get them settled with their clients. That's the first thing you do. . . . [O]nce they are comfortable and they get set, in a couple of months it's stage two, which is, "[W]hat can you do that we haven't been able to do with our existing client base and which clients would you like to meet?' Then we contact the relationship partners and we try to put them together.

Aside from initiating this process, a crucial function that the partner serves is to provide laterals a meaningful sense of connection to the firm. Part of this involves helping them meet their business objectives: "I'm always in touch with the lateral candidates, look at their financial performance, sit down with them, talk about what they are doing right, what they are doing wrong, and provide the senior management in the firm with a short table that basically subjectively describes whether someone is meeting expectations, exceeding them or is below or below but improving and with a short note about why" (#105). Beyond this, however, "It's my job to stayed connected, it's my job to know when somebody is feeling disconnected." As the partner elaborates, it's important that

> there is somebody who actually is advocating for them, whom they can call and complain to who knows the firm, who will tell them when they are full of it or tell them that they've got a good point, and here is how we are going to solve this, or here is what I am going to do and work out a plan. [It's] that feeling that this person has a connection to the management of the firm and they have easy access no matter how large the firm. (#105)

This partner emphasized that playing this role can be important to reinforce the nonfinancial aspects of the firm's culture: "I think the key to keeping the glue is to have enough touch points in the law firm that people feel like it's their home, they like coming to work, they like seeing the person, they are going to hear from that person or those people all the time" (#105).

A firm that devotes attention to lateral integration thus can further both business and professional values. Integration enhances the ability of other partners to generate business from the arrival of a lateral, while building ties that provide a source of professional satisfaction. It also helps ensure that laterals will come to a genuine understanding of the cultural values of the firm through interaction with and exposure to colleagues. In addition, the firm signals to partners that it is willing to devote resources to integration, including otherwise billable time, for the sake of longer-term collaborative goals. This is another way of providing assurance of commitment to professional values by leaving money on the table.

Conclusion

The prominent role of the lateral market poses a significant challenge for firms that desire to sustain a distinctive culture that does not simply reflect business imperatives. A firm has no assurance that partners with major client relationships will remain with it if they receive more attractive offers from other firms. Recognition of this vulnerability, as well as the desire to grow to stay competitive, means that firms are actively recruiting in the lateral market on an ongoing basis.

This creates the risk that partners will perceive the firm as emphasizing business values at the expense of other concerns. Even if a firm attempts to maintain a culture that gives weight to professional values, the regular departures and arrivals associated with the lateral market can make it difficult for partners to have a common understanding of what those values mean in the firm. The result may be reversion to the least common denominator of financial performance as the unifying value.

Firms may attempt to mitigate the potential cultural risks of active involvement in the lateral market. They may seek to screen laterals according to cultural fit, hire them with the goal of expanding the firm's platform rather than simply buying a revenue stream, and work on genuinely integrating laterals into the firm. These measures may simultaneously serve both business and professional values, especially by promoting collaboration that furthers financial goals and provides intrinsic rewards for partners. These practices can take time, however, and forgoing them may offer greater short-term rewards in a market in which patience is not always seen as a virtue.

9

Trusted Advisors and Service Providers

The preceding chapters describe how increasing business demands on law firms can pose challenges in ensuring due regard for what traditionally were considered nonfinancial professional values. Some of those values include practicing in a collaborative environment in which people help colleagues without expecting financial rewards, working together to solve intellectually challenging problems, treating one another fairly, being willing when necessary to subordinate one's own interest to those of colleagues or the firm, helping to strengthen the firm, and being valued for the quality of legal work as defined by internal professional standards.

Any analysis of professionalism under current market conditions would be incomplete, however, if it did not discuss an important component of the concept of a profession—that professionals in general, and lawyers in particular, are assumed to play a distinctive social role that involves adhering to ethical obligations that distinguish them from members of other occupations.

Some commentators suggest that intensifying market pressures are eroding lawyers' willingness and opportunity to play a social role that involves ethical obligations beyond furthering clients' interests. With respect to lawyers' willingness to play this role, some argue that it is diminishing because of the increasing pressures to meet individual financial goals and the greater influence that clients now wield over lawyers. On this view, lawyers are less likely than previously to exercise professional independence in questioning or seeking to temper client demands. Marc Galanter and William Henderson (2008), for instance, suggest that the trend is that "large law firm lawyers will be less independent of their clients and thus less reliable exemplars of professional ethics" (1872). They conclude, "In this highly atomized economic climate, it is likely that ethical gray zones will get resolved in the client's favor, and insecure lawyers will be less likely to acknowledge any black or white" (1913).

Other critics argue that the changing nature of law firm work means that lawyers simply have less opportunity to play a distinctive social role. Anthony Kronman (1993) suggests that the attenuation of long-term relationships between firms and clients means that clients now are more inclined to turn to a firm for a discrete matter on which they need specialized expertise. The result, he argues, is that lawyers are less familiar with the overall affairs of clients and tend to be called upon for work that requires a relatively narrow focus. These conditions, he argues, are inimical to the ability to exercise the deliberative wisdom that characterizes the lawyer-statesman. Unlike a generation ago, a lawyer is in less of a position to "synthesize, to integrate from a single point of view all the considerations that the client's case presents" (289).

Others echo this claim by pointing to the fact that many companies now treat law firms akin to other vendors from whom they purchase goods and services by giving authority to procurement offices to determine the terms on which they engage firms (Habte 2017). One report on the increasingly demanding obligations imposed by such terms concludes that they have "the potential to reduce the distinctiveness of . . . lawyers as legal professionals, such that they are seen as, perceive themselves to be, and begin to behave like, mere 'service providers'" (Vaughan and Coe 2015, 1; see also Terry 2008). A service provider ostensibly adopts the approach that "the customer is always right," thus neglecting the obligation of a professional to provide independent advice.

This chapter assesses the claim that modern law firm lawyers have diminishing willingness and opportunity to act as independent professionals with unique ethical obligations. For obvious reasons, receiving candid answers from partners about the first part of this claim—willingness—can be difficult. Fear of anticipated social disapproval may make them reluctant to acknowledge that greater insecurity in obtaining and keeping clients has led them to be more tolerant of client demands than they would be in more of a seller's market. They may be sensitive to the perception that they are not living up to a professional ideal, especially because of ostensibly crass commercial reasons.

In addition, some lawyers may be experiencing cognitive dissonance. A lawyer may acquiesce in client demands more readily than she knows she should, but the discomfort caused by admitting this can lead her to rationalize that her behavior is consistent with professional obligations. In doing so, she can draw on the resonance of the professional ethos of service to the client and emphasize this ideal in articulating her professional role. In this way, she can implicitly redefine her role in a way that is consistent with her behavior, and thus report that market conditions have not appreciably affected her ability to act in accordance with professional responsibilities.

In our first few interviews at the outset of our project, we asked partners whether they thought the claim is accurate that business demands are placing greater pressure on lawyers' willingness to act as independent professionals for whom the customer is not automatically right. Partners acknowledged how an observer might think that the shift to a buyer's market could create this risk. They all said, however, that they did not see this happening with either themselves or their colleagues. They said that they did not see greater pressure from clients to assist with questionable behavior, nor less willingness on the part of partners to challenge clients when appropriate because of fear of losing clients. Instances of clients trying to enlist lawyers in improper behavior, they said, actually are fairly rare, and most lawyers have sufficient commitment to their ethical obligations, as well as awareness of the risk of violating them, to resist such attempts.

The dynamics we have described, however, suggest that we should not automatically take all such declarations at face value. We then shifted our approach in a way that tended to elicit more illuminating answers. Rather than directly asking questions about the impact of business pressures, we began simply to ask partners how they conceived of their professional role. This was not preceded by any suggestion of what that role should be, nor by any suggestion that market conditions are changing how lawyers understand it.

Partners tended to characterize their role ideally as serving as a "trusted advisor" to a client. As we elaborate in this chapter, the trusted advisor differs both from a lawyer who sees her role as only to further the client's desires and one who regards her role as ensuring either that the client acts in accordance with broad moral principles or the demands of justice. Partners said they find serving as a trusted advisor rewarding because it can provide an opportunity to counsel a client on the spirit as well as the letter of the law, and on considerations that go beyond legal compliance. We then asked partners whether there is less occasion than before to play the role of trusted advisor because clients now seek narrower technical assistance from outside counsel or because clients are less receptive than before to expansive advice. While some lawyers acknowledged some movement in this direction, most said that their work continues to offer opportunities to play this role. Their responses provided a subtler account of the relationship between inside and outside counsel than a zero-sum game in which the assumption of greater responsibility by the former automatically means a narrower scope of work for the latter.

The Trusted Advisor

When asked how they conceive of their professional role, a striking number of partners referred to their aspiration to serve as a "trusted advisor" to clients. Thus, one partner said that his "goal as a lawyer is to be viewed as a counselor to your client, a trusted advisor" (#266). "I think the ideal relationship with your client," another lawyer said, "would be to understand your client's business and strategy and be able to broadly recommend in the legal area things that they could do or not do, and you would have more of a sense of the overall strategy of the company" (#262).

One lawyer described the professional rewards she receives from this role:

> I do really think whether you are advising a public interest client or a pro bono client or a corporate client, what you are doing is advising them on the best course of action, you are advocating for them, and really the skills are the same. . . . [T]he core emotional satisfaction of helping someone solve a problem is, I think the same, and [it's what] I really like. That is what I went to law school for, and I do feel like I get to do that on a daily basis.

She then described how her work on regulatory compliance can do this:

> That happens a lot with compliance clients. . . . It can range from working with a very sophisticated client that is a federal government contractor who really has a very sophisticated compliance system and you are helping them with the gray areas, and then sometimes it's helping new companies or start-ups, or companies that have just suddenly grown, put in place their compliance policy procedures. That's also fun, too, because you have to really customize it [in terms of] what's really appropriate for a small company and how can they do this is in a very nimble easy way. (#260)

In a similar vein, another lawyer said:

> In a law firm context, obviously sophisticated clients come to you with complex problems that they can't solve and they are looking to you to help them

> solve it and there is a lot of satisfaction with that. There is also satisfaction with helping the unsophisticated client and basically telling them everything they should do and saying, "Don't worry about it" . . . and there is a lot of satisfaction [telling someone] that you've got their back, and even though this legal system is complex and seems overwhelming that you are not going to let them drown in that. (#95)

What considerations do outside counsel discuss when clients turn to them for their judgment as trusted advisors? Counsel take into account a wide range of concerns, but one common language for describing them is in terms of risks. Thus, for instance, one partner was asked what kinds of considerations are included in advice that involves professional judgment. He responded, "It's kind of, 'Okay here are the three options—high, medium, low risk—what do you think we should do,' that kind of a question." He continued:

> Or [a client may ask], "We decided we really want to pursue that option; given how you think this will play out, what else should we do or what other resources should we line up internally?" It's kind of like, "You've been through the war, you can see how this could play out, what else do you think we should be doing to try to handle that risk or mitigate that risk or alert our organization?" (#139)

One such risk is legal risk: the strength of the argument that what the client chooses to do is legally permitted. A lawyer may tell the client:

> "If this is what you want to do, we can't tell you for sure that you are going to be on totally safe ground. We think in our experience that what the FTC has focused on over the last several years and what they really care about doesn't fall within this, but as a technical matter we can't point to some safe harbor that says the way you are doing it is totally fine." [S]o you help them assess the risk, because usually when it is black and white it's easy enough that they don't need to call you. So when you . . . craft a solution you try to craft [one] that works but that is the least risky possible or involves the least gray area possible.
>
> [Acting as a trusted advisor means dealing with] more and more of the [issues] that are in the gray area and so you present the risk. Ultimately it's the client's decision, but in most cases they will ask us, "Well what do you

think?" Or they don't have to ask, we just say, "Well this is what I think when you balance all the risks and the consequences." They very much appreciate when we provide that level of judgment and advice. (#160)

Another lawyer observes:

> Most situations in my experience when you are giving advice, you are giving advice to somebody who does not want to be anywhere near the edge and so your advice is embedded in: here is my advice, here is why it's my advice, here is where the risk spectrum is by policy. Most people will simply stay away from this whole category of the gray zone. If you want me to analyze a gray zone in a more nuanced way I can do that, but it's a dangerous place to be and most people just don't want to go there. (#121)

A common focus in advising clients is "what's the regulatory risk?" One lawyer spoke for many when she said that her role is to "lay out what the options are. I always like to give them, 'This is your range of options: the most prudent is this, the most risky is that,' and we'll talk about what is in the middle and I'll ask, 'How risk averse are you on this'" (#74)?

Most partners we asked said that they see their role in advising on legal risk as including discussion not only of the letter but the spirit of the law:

> INTERVIEWER: If something would be within the letter of the law but you feel like maybe it's not consistent with the purpose or spirit, would you feel any sort of professional responsibility to say something?
>
> PARTNER: Yes, definitely. I mean, I think it's very much advising both on the letter and saying, "Look, there are no cases here that say you can't do that, it could be this way, it could be that way, strictly speaking it's okay but it is not a best practice. It's not the kind of thing that you should be moving towards, it's the kind of thing you should be moving away from." I do think that's right. (#37)

Another partner echoed this view:

> INTERVIEWER: [E]ven beyond the technical letter of the law, to what extent does the spirit or purpose of the law enter into your assessment of what a client wants to do?

PARTNER: That's a good question. We actually had that happen yesterday. A situation where a client was contemplating doing something that, while under the technical reading of a regulation we could not say that that would trigger any negative consequences, but that sort of action was going to potentially violate the spirit of the law. We could not predict what the agency would do if they were to view the facts as they might have played out so we told them, "We don't see it's a direct violation but it's against the spirit of the law." They actually decided to do something different. (#103)

Lawyers see the trusted advisor as responsible for discussing not only the risk of action by a regulator but a wide range of other concerns based on the reaction of a number of constituencies. One partner was asked whether he advises the client on the likely reaction of parties such as "creditors or investors or suppliers or other parties like that." His response was, "Definitely. So a question we might get is, 'Does our customer have a valid indemnification claim against us?' I think sometimes we just know that there is a bigger issue involved, and that they have to think about the relationship with the customer. [T]hey really just want our answer not only to whether they have a basis to say yes or no, but on the bigger picture. . . . [T]hey almost always want our thoughts on the bigger question" (#48).

Another partner described how this may occur in the context of helping form private equity funds:

PARTNER: The sponsor wants to do something and they ask, "Am I permitted to do it under the legal documents?" If we give answers like, "Yes you are technically permitted to do it," or, "You are probably able to do it," the question then becomes, "If you do it are you going to really tick off your investors?" So it's not just legal advice but it's also in our experience investor relations advice and guiding them or at least flagging that, "Hey, this is one of those moments when you also need to be thinking with your investor relations hat on."

INTERVIEWER: So you have to look at the set of relationships in which they are embedded, so to speak.

PARTNER: Right. (#160)

One lawyer working on real estate and construction law elaborated on how such concerns are relevant in providing advice. The interviewer asked,

"So when you talk about broad advice, you mentioned saying, 'Yeah, you can do this technically, but . . .' What follows the 'but?'" He replied:

> The professional judgment. I'll give you an example of something I'm dealing with for a handful of clients right now, which is projects that aren't being finished on time. I'll say, "Here are the tools that the contract has to address this, let's talk about the potential negative things that are going to happen if you exercise those tools. Maybe instead let's think about what the other side is going through right now and what their concerns are. What buttons can we push, what communications could we have to get it to where you want to be?" [That] isn't necessarily a legal process. So that's the kind of thing, it's the experience in the industry. (#136)

In other cases, this lawyer may say, "This is very likely going to be in your local newspaper because it's a big project in your locality, let's talk about what that's going to look like and what your actions are going to do to do that. And again that is absolutely broader professional judgment, not, you know, technical legal stuff." He noted that "in some ways the biggest problems that we can run into is lawyers on the other side who are just providing technical [advice], you know, 'Raise this clause and raise that clause and dah, dah dah,' instead of stepping back from the whole thing and saying, 'Let's all talk about how we can collectively turn this in a better direction'" (#136).

Similarly, one lawyer was asked whether she considers the interests of stakeholders such as "customers, suppliers, investors, employees, and the community" when acting as a trusted advisor. She responded, "Yeah, I think you have to keep in mind all those constituencies and interests to truly be a good lawyer to the situation" (#59).

More broadly, companies are increasingly sensitive to the reputational consequences of different courses of action. When asked about this, one partner said of his clients, "I mean nobody wants to get in trouble with the FDA, particularly with some of the issues that have been coming out lately and how they seem to spill over into the press, and then from there spill over into the plaintiff's bar. So reputational risk is a big part" of the advice that he gives (#74).

This lawyer elaborated on how his clients that provide medical devices approach the question of product risks:

> I can't say there is any client that we deal with which really doesn't pay attention to what the health risk is related to an event. I mean, they know that if

your device is failing, or your device is hurting people, or God forbid killing people, you know they don't want that reputation. They don't want those products out in the market doing that, they are going to do everything in their power to make sure that doesn't happen.

He explained how he advises these clients on the risks that their products might pose:

> Hypothetically any device could kill any day if it is used incorrectly. We know that, but what we always counsel our clients is, "Well, what's the reasonable worst case and that's the theme that the FDA really relies on as well. . . . What's the reasonable worst case of this event occurring and what's the reasonable worst injury that could occur if it were to happen. And so as long as we're dealing with a reasonableness standard I think that we always get to the right decision at the end of the day. (#74)

One lawyer noted that in providing broad advice on an issue:

> It may be something that is perfectly legal but could lead to a bad outcome in an area where there is a high risk of reputational damage. If somebody wants to invest in a country where there is a relatively high risk of bribery, we just want to make sure the client is aware of that and that they don't go into that with their eyes closed. We might say, "Well, you can do that, but you should be aware that's an area of constant scrutiny by the SEC with regard to non-GAAP financial measures that are changed on a regular basis. There is nothing illegal about them, but the SEC hates them and you'll be responding to questions all the time, you just have to ask yourself is that really the posture you want to have with the SEC." (#267)

One lawyer said:

> One of the increased risks today is because of the advocacy organizations. For instance, take privacy, there are a number of advocacy organizations right now where even if the FTC doesn't necessarily take something up, one of the privacy advocacy organizations will start hammering in the press on their own website and pushing the FTC or other regulators and say, "Hey, you really need to go take this up." The swift sharing of information in our current world has speeded up and amplified those voices. [The result is

that] public relations is way more important [and lawyers include it in their advice]. (#139)

Many lawyers said that they regard advising on important nonlegal considerations as a basic part of their role. "I think if we're doing our job right," one said, "we're always looking at not just, can we do this or how do we do this particular task, but how does it impact the client?" This means that "even if they don't ask, I think our answer is usually like, 'All right, here are some of the other repercussions or implications here'" (#48).

Trusted advisors thus may not simply lay out the risks for clients, but may advise against proceeding in a way that would be legal but unwise. One lawyer said, "If I think it's a foul ball, I'll tell them, you know." There was then this exchange:

INTERVIEWER: A foul ball in the sense of being outside the bounds of the law or even within the law but not a very good idea?

PARTNER: Both, both. Because even if you go within the law but think it is not a very good idea, you have reputational risks, you have trust issues and they need to understand that they are going outside the bounds of those and I would not be doing my duty to my client if I didn't let them know that they may not go to jail, but they are not going to advance their cause. . . . I won't participate in something that I think is wrong, even if it's legal. (#69)

Another lawyer was asked whether he would "feel comfortable" suggesting that a client not do something that is legal but that "doesn't seem like the right thing to do." He replied, "Oh, yes" (#271). Another was asked whether he would advise a client that what it wanted to do was problematic even though it was legal. "Yes, I think that's right," he said. "I think we have an obligation to tell them about [how this would affect] their own mission, and not just answer the technical question. I do think that we have that role as well" (#265).

These comments identify two characteristics of a trusted advisor that relate to conceptions of professional responsibility. The first is willingness to discuss the spirit as well as the letter of the law. The second is willingness to advise on nonlegal considerations. A lawyer need not refer to either set of concerns to abide by the well-established standard conception of the lawyer's role known as the Neutral Partisan. The lawyer in this model is neutral in that she is not morally accountable for, nor must she pass moral judgment on, the morality of the client's ends as long as they are colorably legal. The lawyer is partisan in that she must do her utmost to help the client attain his ends without regard to the interests of anyone else. Loyalty to the client, and partiality to the client's legal interests, defines the scope of her responsibility. The Neutral Partisan therefore may advance any colorable interpretation of the law that favors her client, exploit the letter of the law regardless of its spirit, and be indifferent to the moral desirability of what the client seeks to achieve (Freedman 1975).

It is true that Model Rule of Professional Conduct 2.1 reads, "In representing a client, a lawyer shall exercise independent professional judgment and render candid advice. In rendering advice, a lawyer may refer not only to law but to other considerations such as moral, economic, social and political factors, that may be relevant to the client's situation." That provision, however, does not define "law," and a lawyer who does so according to the rule's literal language follows accepted convention within the profession. Furthermore, the rule permits, but does not require, a lawyer to advise on nonlegal considerations. A lawyer arguably does not violate the rule if she chooses not to do so.

The point is that partners whose conception of professional responsibility has contracted as a result of recent market pressures have perfectly acceptable rationales for embracing narrow understanding of their responsibilities. The fact that the partners in our interviews did not do so in describing the role of trusted advisor suggests, although it certainly does not prove, that many lawyers in large firms have retained a more robust understanding of their professional obligations.

One form of assistance that a trusted advisor may provide is to support inside counsel's efforts to persuade people within the client about the importance of certain initiatives. One lawyer who works on regulatory compliance, for instance, shared:

> [This involves] giving the people who are leading the organization the tools they need to help create a culture of compliance and also sometimes it's providing them support when they are trying to do it. Both the in-house lawyers and also sometimes the business leaders may say, "How do I convince people this is important?" and then you brainstorm with them and may say, "Here is one thing you could point to that is a danger." You just try to help them bulk up their argument. (#264)

An exchange with another lawyer described how this might occur:

> PARTNER: The client may say, "We've got the legal advice, now let's talk about our organization, you help us figure out maybe other ways to socialize [people] and to get things going."
> INTERVIEWER: So they are looking to you for support and reinforcement to help them with their internal task of persuading people?
> PARTNER: Yes, it's partly persuasion and it's partly education. (#151)

One lawyer said that he may serve not only to provide reinforcement but to "play the heavy." He continued:

> I can give you an example. I've got two projects that I'm working on right now where the Vice-President and General Counsel like our team to really kind of work with their team and subject matter experts directly, and say, "This is what you are going to do, this is how you have to do it and this is what [the regulator] expects. The people may not like it but the general counsel who pay the bills do." (#74)

The trusted advisor thus appears to provide advice that reflects what Eli Wald and Russell Pearce (2012, 2016) have described as a "relational" understanding of a client's interest. As they describe this orientation:

> [A] relational perspective recognizes that all actors, whether individuals or organizations, have separate identities yet are intrinsically inter-connected and cannot maximize their own good in isolation. Through the lens of relational self-interest, maximizing the good of the individual or business requires consideration of the good of the neighbor, the employee or customer, and of the public. Accordingly, relational lawyers advise and assist clients, colleagues, and themselves to take into account the well-being of others when contemplating and pursuing their own interests. (Wald and Pearce 2016, 601)

What Do Clients Want?

Partners' responses were mixed when asked whether there has been a decline in recent years in the extent to which clients ask for the kind of expansive professional advice that the trusted advisor provides. A few agreed, while some said that no decline had occurred at all. Most, however, said that some clients tend to ask less for such advice, but that there still remain many instances in which they do. Their responses suggest that Kronman relies on an overly simple dichotomy between handling all of a client's legal work and working on discrete matters involving no ongoing relationship with a client. The reality of practice tends to lie between these extremes, with opportunities to act as a trusted advisor varying based on the type of client, the size of its legal department, and the matter in question. Overall, while there has been some change, there does not appear to be a dramatic shift in the role of outside counsel from trusted advisor to service provider.

One partner was emphatic in saying that clients do not turn less often to outside counsel for wide-ranging advice:

> My experience is that we are absolutely still being used for broader professional judgment. Are we being looked at for technical advice? Of course, always have been, always will be, but I do believe that they are looking to us still for the broad professional judgment as well and I have not in my practice seen a change in that over the years. . . . I absolutely am still asked to give broad professional judgment. (#136)

Other partners said that lawyers involved in transactional work are expected as a matter of course to provide guidance that takes into account the business implications of legal advice. "The fact of the matter," one partner said, "is that when you are a transactional lawyer as I am they are all mixed issues. They don't ask me technically 'What is the bare minimum or what can we do?' They generally say 'What do you see?' So no, I don't see [a decline in client requests for broad professional advice] as being as much of a problem as I think I see in the press." When asked whether this means that the client relies on him to "figure out what is in its best interest, all things considered so to speak," he responded, "Yeah, I think that in so many ways in transactional practice . . . the role is still more counselor than attorney" (#170).

Still another partner who works on compliance issues said, "I have in-house lawyers who I talk to on a daily, weekly basis who email me, call me with one-off questions, we'll talk in the middle of the night you know and there is very much that trusted advisor role and that's very satisfying" (#37).

Another lawyer suggested that lawyers tend to play the role of trusted advisor less "with the larger companies." This is the case, he said, "as companies' legal shops have grown and they have added their own capabilities and specialties inside their firms." With smaller clients, however, "I have a lot more small to mid-tier clients where either I'm interacting directly with the business owner or I'm interacting with one lawyer in-house who is doing everything under the sun and I'm basically supporting him or her in whatever they are doing" (#103).

Another partner responded to the question whether clients are seeking more specialized technical advice by saying, "That one for me is a resounding maybe. It's kind of yes and no. It really depends on the client. [In] companies that have very large in-house legal departments, I do think there is a trend toward that." Medium-size and small companies, however, look "for both the lawyers that can give them specialized technical advice and the lawyers who can give them that broader piece of judgment [and] I still see that trusted advisor role happening" (#139).

The relationship between client size and complexity of advice, however, can vary. In some cases, companies with small legal departments may ask for more routine legal work from law firms than do clients with large departments. The latter group can perform basic legal tasks in-house and so turn to outside counsel for advice on complicated matters with multiple dimensions to consider.

Several lawyers suggested that the ostensible distinction between technical and professional advice is overstated. On all but the narrowest technical issues, lawyers are asked for their broader judgment and, even when not asked, the client welcomes them providing it:

> There are . . . clearly some cases in which it's broader professional judgment they're looking for, and there are some that are clearly more specialized advice like, "I want a patent application on this" and they don't want to talk about whether it is a good idea or not. But then there is a lot that is in the middle who want us to say, and even if they don't ask it, they are still very happy if we say, "You know, I think what you need to do is this other thing," and they seem to greatly appreciate that. I think that our job is to raise that kind of issue. So I don't think I've noticed particularly a change in that. (#48)

Another partner made the same point:

> [A client] may ask, "Here is what we're doing. How does that compare to what others are doing?" The essence of the question is, "What's your view

> on the marketplace?" There are other situations where it's really just much narrower and there are many, many that are in between where you get a narrower question but it wouldn't be appropriate to answer it without saying, "I know you only asked me about this but you should know that most people think of it a little bit differently." (#267)

One lawyer described her experience this way:

> There is this small technical question like, "Can you do this?" and there is what I think of as the broader question, "Should I do this?" [The latter] to me is closer to the professional end. There is a lot where either they ask, "Should we do it?" or our advice back is, "Yeah, you can do it, but it's a dumb idea," or "This would be difficult, but we think you should try it anyway because of some factors." So I do think we get asked about the bigger picture fairly regularly. (#48)

If inside counsel in large companies now is a sophisticated lawyer who has the best understanding of the client, what is the basis on which she turns to a law firm lawyer for expansive professional judgment? The answer is that outside counsel is familiar with a large number of different companies and thus may have a better sense than inside counsel of an overall industry. This includes knowledge of market conditions; how other companies are handling various issues; emerging best practices; and the views of stakeholders such as regulators, investors, suppliers, and customers.

Thus, a client may ask, "'How do we get this done internally, what have you seen other companies do? Given what you know about us what would you do?'" A client "will come in, they'll have a new task for us to do that is new to them but not to us because we've been through it with a number of other clients. They'll say, 'In our organization we need to figure out how to implement this and sell it to the various teams, can you help us figure out how to roll this out amongst our teams?' That is an issue requiring professional judgment" (#139).

As one lawyer put it, "it's the experience in the industry. I've seen this problem 25 times before and I have a pretty decent idea of what happens if we go down path A or what's going to happen if we go down path B" (#141). Another partner explained, "You can provide professional judgment, you can provide some judgment based on what you've seen in the market" (#160).

One lawyer described it this way:

> [O]ne thing when you're inside is that you are aware that you don't necessarily have the perspective that being outside will bring. So there is a great deal of respect for the perspective of that outside counsel. Very often somebody who is that trusted advisor inside will reach out to outside counsel and say, "Could you look to make sure I'm thinking about this right because I don't have the perspective of the way other companies are handling this."

He then provided an example of this type of request:

> A perfect example was just last week. A client public company called, a very, very, very thoughtful person, and just wanted some input on how different companies are handling the open trading window. This window is after you announce earnings, there is a period of time during which you can open a window and say it's safe to trade but that's a finite time period, sometimes it lasts for a matter of weeks, sometimes a month or two. [This person] just wanted to say, "Here is what we're doing, how does that compare to what others are doing?" (#121)

Another partner who works with private equity funds said that many clients look to outside counsel for what he called "market data." He described how this might occur:

> [W]e help fund sponsors set up and structure their funds and negotiate with investors and we also help investors negotiate their deal into these funds so that's sort of the bread and butter of what we do. Even if you're a large sophisticated fund, you know your fund documents, you know your investors, you sort of have a broad take of what the universe is, but it is still limited. Whereas we are counsel to many different clients and we see a lot of what is going on.
>
> So clients will come to us and say, "Technically make sure this works, what's the law here, how do we do this," but they'll also ask us, "What's market practice, where are people going, are you seeing this, that and the other thing?" Even if they don't ask that, I think in many cases the expectation is "I am expecting you to not just be my lawyer but also to guide me on the business terms as well. That is, being a partner in setting up the business arrangement." (#160)

Another lawyer was asked whether this sort of advice provides information on emerging best practices:

> Yeah, that's fair, or the wide range of best practices. Very often you can say, "Here is the best practice but you should also know there is a wide range of normal." It would be, if somebody said to me, "What's the best practice?" it would be this, but "It's neither illegal nor really wildly strange to be doing something that is a little bit different, and here is the full range; you just need to figure out where you want to be. Are you on the cutting edge of best practice or are you a follower, not an initiator, you would rather hang back a little bit?" (#267)

This perspective can lead even sophisticated inside counsel to turn to outside counsel to ensure that the former's deep involvement in an issue doesn't unduly limit her judgment. "One of the hardest things about being inside," a lawyer said, "is how you can be both an advocate for your team and an objective person, so therefore it's really useful when you are inside to be able to call to outside counsel and just get some perspective." Inside counsel may say, "The way that I'm going to make this decision is really going to impact a lot of things, including people who work for me, so I just would appreciate your listening to this thinking about this and give me your objective perspective." He added, "You are able to be a little more objective when you are outside than inside because you first are outside the organization looking in and that brings some objectivity, and second you have more than one client so you are a little less tied to [the one client]" (#121). Another lawyer echoed this: "because companies are so complex and because there is so much going on the collective experience of outside counsel is still going to be valued" (#69).

Thus increased specialization in law firms does not necessarily mean fewer opportunities to provide expansive professional advice. One lawyer, when asked whether, notwithstanding her specialty, clients look to her for broad advice on "what their regulatory environment is like and what other firms have done," replied, "Absolutely" (#74). Another said that her specialization means that she now deals less in large companies with the general counsel and more with specialized in-house counsel. In these cases, "your trusted advisor role has shifted to the relevant attorney whose portfolio includes your specialization." Notwithstanding greater in-house expertise, she is "still a trusted advisor" because of the broader perspective she can provide on industry conditions and best practices (#95).

One partner suggested that the emerging model is that inside and outside counsel now often collaborate to play complementary trusted advisor roles.

"My observation," he says, "is that the partnership between that inside trusted advisor and outside trusted advisor now is the key way to deliver the combined advice." He explained:

> [W]hen you are inside you don't really have a wide view of what others are doing in the industry. When you are outside you have a great view of what others are doing in the industry but you don't have an intimate view of how it applies to the enterprise that you are advising. The role that the outside advisor brings is not just that technical expertise in their areas, but . . . the ability to understand what the market is, how are people handling these different things. [These] help you reason your way to an approach for a particular company.

In such cases, "it's the integration of that advice" that is the key to providing the best guidance to the client (#267).

Our interviews thus indicated that partners regard serving as a trusted advisor as a role in which they can fulfill their distinctive social obligations as a member of the legal profession. This role involves providing advice not simply on the letter but the spirit of the law, as well as on nonlegal considerations as appropriate.

As the next section describes, partners regard commitment to the client as crucial in obtaining opportunities to play this role and to performing it effectively. This is in striking contrast to prominent theories of legal ethics that view such commitment with suspicion, on the ground that it threatens a lawyer's ability to look to broader concerns beyond the client's desires. The next section provides partners' descriptions of how commitment to the client enables them to serve as a trusted advisor who provides expansive counsel.

Commitment and Trust

Numerous interviewees said that the ability to offer expansive advice to the client depends crucially on the client's belief in the lawyer's genuine commitment to advancing the best interest of the client. Furthermore, several described a relationship with a client that is built on such trust as an especially rewarding source of professional fulfillment.

One lawyer, for instance, said that "with that type of relationship it is much harder in some ways because it's like your friend, you don't want to tell your friend bad news, but in some ways it's easier because they trust you and so they come to us for this advice and they know that there is some possibility we're going to come back and say, 'Don't do this,' but I do think [overall] they like that a lot" (#261). Another lawyer was asked whether he regarded his basic role as "being independent of the client and having a duty to look out for broader public concerns." He replied, "I don't think of myself or other lawyers that I interact with as being some sort of independent arbiter. Rather, we typically are involved in trying to forge some sort of agreement with a party across the table that works for everyone within the confines of custom and practice" (#170).

One partner put it this way:

> You do have to have a relationship with the client in order to be able to communicate to the client and yet it doesn't mean that you can't be objective. I think the line is that you need to have that relationship in order to be a good communicator, and yet you also need to be thinking with one part of your brain at all times, "Is the question that I'm being asked leading to the right place, is the question I'm being asked something that is one where I should question the question and say, 'Gosh, yes we could get that solution but let's just step back and think do you really want to go to that solution?'" Sometimes the answer is no and those are the most satisfactory conversations where you engage the client and they say, "Oh you're right, I hadn't really been thinking about that," and it goes in a slightly different direction. (#267)

Another partner emphasized the importance of commitment rather than distance in this way:

> I've always viewed our responsibility, and my sense is that the clients would prefer this, [to say], "I know what you want to do, I know what you are trying to accomplish, how can we accomplish that within the framework of the law and get you a solution that works." The more you are not distanced from the needs and the desires of the client, the more you really understand them, the better your solutions are going to be, and the more likely you are to be able to come up with one that works. So I feel like this aloof independence of the distanced arm's length advisor is really not an accurate depiction of what my role has been [in doing this]. (#272)

Lawyers thus regard commitment to the client as fostering the trust that enables them to advise the client on a wide range of considerations. They also find this type of relationship with a client as a deeply rewarding source of professional reward.

The lawyers with whom we spoke do not regard their commitment to the client as unqualified. Acting as a trusted advisor means sometimes giving the client unwelcome advice. The client may push back, which can lead to a more extended discussion that may include consideration of alternative courses of action. Lawyers draw the line in accommodating the client, however, at anything they regard as outside the bounds of the law.

One partner said that it is important that the client know that "'I'm not a person in your organization who is a yes man, I can't be, that's not what you're hiring me to be, if that is what you wanted, you know, buy a puppet and they'll say whatever you want it to say.'" He continued, "At the same time you absolutely need to be a part of their team that has their best interests at heart. They have to trust that you have their best interests at heart and sometimes simply serving their best interest is to disagree with a direction that someone in a position of authority would like to go" (#268).

Another partner expressed it this way: "I tell it like it like it is, and I'm a compliance lawyer so sometimes the answer is just, 'No, you can't do that,' and sometimes the answer is, 'You've got to do something about this because of the significant legal liability that you are facing, and I am not going to create a way around it, the law is what the law is'" (#104). Another said, "I give advice sometimes that is not popular at all—I mean at all—and sometimes it's, 'Look I don't have a silver bullet for you, I can't solve this problem. You are in a problem right now, it is not going to end in a great way, so we've just got to talk about really mitigating the downside of what is currently going on.' And, you know, that doesn't go over very well but you have to" (#136).

One lawyer, when asked what distinguishes her as a professional, said:

> I think that one of the differentiating factors of being a lawyer is that we have an ethical commitment to put ourselves in the client's shoes but at the same time we have an ethical commitment to tell them what we think the legal advice is even if they don't want to hear it. I think that others who provide services are not circumscribed by the same ethical requirements regarding the nature of the advice and the services that we render. If you are a good

> lawyer, sometimes you do have to tell the clients information that they don't want to hear.

She described one way in which this might play out: "For example, you may have a client, and you are not sure whether employee A or B knew that the widget was going to Iran. The company says, 'We think he really didn't know.' Well, can you really file that [submission]? Sometimes I have to say, 'Look, unless we can talk to him and look at his emails and whatever, we're really not going to be in a position to help you with this matter. If that is not how you want to do it, then you need to go to somebody else'" (#265).

Another lawyer explained:

> If a client is asking a hard question that may lead to a negative outcome, we need to walk them through what their question means and what the answer might mean, because once I start looking, I have a duty to tell you what the answer is. I had a client that we sent a memo to yesterday, they asked for a memo. I said, "Hey, here's your memo and now you've got a document in your files [that says] I'm recommending to you to do an internal investigation. Sorry, but you asked a question so I've got to tell you what I think you should do."
>
> So I think that lawyers even in today's world of [competitive pressures] understand that our kind of special place in the professional universe is that we have that right as well as that obligation to you not to let our client [violate the law] and/or not let our clients put their heads in the sand. (#103)

Such comments illustrate the pervasive view among the lawyers with whom we spoke that legality establishes a hard boundary to a lawyer's commitment to a client. As one lawyer put it, "[A]s a lawyer I would never be in a position and never will put myself in a position to advise a client that it's okay to run a red light" (#69). Another said, "We can never give advice that is not legally sound . . . that's bad news for everybody" (#160). That is not to say that issues of legality are always black and white. There are gray areas that admit of different reasonable interpretations, but this raises questions of risk and wisdom rather than pure legality.

Commitment and Distance

As the interviews indicated, the trusted advisor plays a more expansive role than prescribed by the model of the Neutral Partisan. Partners' emphasis on commitment to the client, however, is at odds with prominent scholarly alternatives to the Neutral Partisan. These conceive of the lawyer's role as involving commitment to interests beyond the client, such as ordinary moral values or the interests of justice. Thus, for instance, David Luban (1988) argues that in scenarios outside of criminal defense the lawyer should be guided by ordinary moral demands rather than the legal interests of the client. She should serve as a "moral activist" who engages clients about the moral desirability of their goals and should refuse to assist them in achieving their aims if she finds them morally problematic.

Similarly, William Simon (1999, 9) prescribes that "[l]awyers should take those actions that, considering the relevant circumstances of the particular case, seem likely to promote justice." As he explains, "Justice' here connotes the basic values of the legal system and subsumes many layers of more concrete norms" (138). On what he describes as the "Contextual View," a lawyer should assess factors such as the reliability of procedures designed to provide an authoritative legal determination in a given instance, the underlying purpose of a legal rule, and any other relevant considerations in determining what justice requires (139).

Emphasizing commitment to the client also is in tension with a revised version of the Neutral Partisan offered by Brad Wendel (2010). Wendel accepts that a lawyer may be partial to a client over other interests because of her role as an agent of the political system in a democracy. Law in that system enables peaceful coexistence among persons with different moral commitments by providing an authoritative resolution of disagreements that otherwise would be intractable. As such, it provides reasons and justifications that rest not on contestable moral claims but on the outcomes of a legal system whose authority to play this role is regarded as legitimate.

Wendel argues that a lawyer's role is to effectuate the operation of this system through her commitment to secure for clients the benefits to which they are legally entitled. Thus, "the legal entitlements of clients, not client interests, ordinary moral considerations or abstract legal norms such as justice, should be the object of lawyers' concerns when acting in a representative capacity" (49). Wendel differentiates this from "the lawyers' version of the Principle of Partisanship," which is "the view that client interests . . . are paramount in determining what actions lawyers should take on behalf of clients" (31).

This model appears more accepting of lawyer commitment to the client as a core feature of the lawyer's role. It subtly distinguishes, however, between commitment *to the client* and commitment to *enabling the client to secure her legal interests.* It is the latter, not the former, that is appropriate, which establishes at least some distance between lawyer and client.

These models are meant not simply to provide theoretical accounts of the role of the lawyer but to guide actions. They prescribe how a lawyer should think of herself and how this self-understanding should influence her daily work. To varying degrees, they maintain that it is crucial for a lawyer to distance herself from the client to play her social role.

This emphasis is consistent with Robert Rosen's (2010, 43) observation that "[i]t is part of legal culture that corporate lawyers and law firms are analyzed, by researchers at least, through the lens of independence. The fundamental research question asks whether lawyers can resist client demands and whether law firms can sustain such independence." This reflects the fear that becoming too close to the client risks compromising the lawyer's professional identity by subjecting her to "client capture" (Dinovitzer, Gunz, and Gunz 2014a).

Rosen challenges this way of thinking about lawyers' professional obligations. Instead, he argues, "I propose that corporate lawyers and their firms be studied by thinking of them as committed to their clients and inquiring how they handle these commitments" (34). Rather than asking "whether lawyers can withstand the needs of their clients," we should "ask how they are organized to serve their clients." This allows us to "treat the firm and the corporation as partner organizations, enabling a view of how power flows between them and how their interests are jointly determined." Rosen maintains that this understanding of ethical behavior conceives of it as emerging from participating in a relationship rather than conforming to an ideal that is external to it. "Asking how they elaborate their relationships to clients," he says, "may better describe the choices facing corporate lawyers than thinking about them as attempting to maintain independence from clients" (35).

Whether or not their behavior comports with theory, Rosen argues, law firm lawyers naturally are committed to their clients. By contrast, he argues: "Thinking through [the lens of] independence segregates lawyers from clients" (35). The consequence, Rosen maintains, is that "[i]n the absence of research that shows that corporate lawyers are committed to their clients and the consequences of these commitments, there is no way of thinking about corporate lawyers except through independence. As a result, we have the dead-end of attributing independence to lawyers and then debunking their independence" (38). From this perspective, lawyers will always fall short of their professional obligations.

Rosen suggests that "[a]sking how they elaborate their commitments to clients may better describe the choices facing corporate lawyers than thinking about them as attempting to maintain independence from clients" (35). Acknowledging law firm lawyers' commitments to their clients conceives of ethics as forged on an ongoing basis in the course of these relationships, as lawyers bargain, compromise, advise, constrain, and empower their clients with respect to the pursuit of their interests. In this conception, the lawyer is not a moral activist or minister of justice who jealously guards her distance from the client but a collaborator who is involved in a joint enterprise that may call for complex ethical judgment.

This is consistent with Rebecca Roiphe's (2016, 679) suggestion that the modern conception of the professions is not as a source of objective authority to which patients or clients must voluntarily submit, but as "one way in which individuals (both the professionals and those they serve) are bonded into comprehensive and stable relationships and these groups and communities enable individuals to make sensible choices and understand their role in a broader context." Similarly, Dana Remus (2017, 866) observes, "relational dynamics—trust, loyalty empowerment, and service—are as important as independent judgment in attaining and sustaining a framework of stable law. Lawyers can only serve as gatekeepers and protectors of such a framework if they gain their clients' trust and a broad understanding of their clients' circumstances." This formulation is consistent with Wald and Pearce's (2016, 624) argument that lawyers can better play a distinctive social role by engaging in "relational counseling that stems not from purporting to take a moral high ground divorced from lawyers' and clients' understanding of the lawyer's role, but rather that is inherent to lawyers' conception of their job."

What would this shift in focus entail in assessing lawyers' conduct? As Rosen (2010, 65) suggests:

> Understanding committed corporate lawyers would require examination of the elaboration of client power. The focus would be on how lawyers engage their clients and bargain and compromise with them. Having made their commitments, corporate lawyers would be asked how they have served these commitments. They would be asked how they addressed the blinders of their own commitments and the value of others' commitments."

Lawyers thus would be asked, Rosen says, to account for how their commitments distinguished "between tolerable and intolerable partiality" (54).

Empirical research by Ronit Dinovitzer, Hugh Gunz, and Sally Gunz (2014a, 2014b, 2014c) on ethical decision making by lawyers in corporate firms is explicitly premised on Rosen's suggestion. "Instead of asking whether lawyers are really independent," they note, "we ask how they engage with their clients and their projects" (Dinovitzer, Gunz, and Gunz 2014b, 6). This directs attention to "how professionals operate in an uncertain world in which complete compliance with abstract rules is not always, and perhaps seldom, possible" (674). This reflects a conception of the lawyer as what Susan Silbey and her colleagues have called "the sociological citizen" (Silbey, Huising, and Coslovsky 2009; Parker and Rostain 2012). This concept focuses on how

> agents' activities extend beyond . . . scripted responsibilities and how they are invented to fit specific contexts, although sometimes also [they] develop a pattern or toolkit of adaptable processes. This very practical, experimental approach recognizes no simple script or singular way of doing the work, but rather relies on the lively interactive relations to provide informational feedback for self-correction—back and forth between goals and means . . . approaching institutionally and organizationally legitimate goals. (Silbey 2011, 6)

For Dinovitzer, Gunz, and Gunz, this perspective opens up inquiry into the numerous resources on which a lawyer may draw, and the various factors that may influence her, in her effort to navigate relationships with clients in ways that are reasonably consistent with professional responsibility. Their work, for instance, illuminates how a lawyer's colleagues within a firm may contribute to pressure to accede to a client's wishes (2014a), and how lawyers' responses to ethical vignettes may vary across two dimensions (2014c). These responses can be characterized in terms of whether a lawyer is "more or less inclined to talk in terms of the collectivity of the firm or others in the firm," and whether she tends "to reference law versus experience to explain their behavior or decisions" (688). The result is a typology of four "identities" that represent different approaches that lawyers use in working through relationships with clients. Consistent with Rosen's admonition, this perspective treats fulfilling professional responsibility as a fluid and dynamic process forged in the context of relationships with others.

For the partners with whom we spoke, it is commitment to the client that provides professional meaning when they get out of bed in the morning, put in long hours addressing difficult problems, and fall into bed at a late hour. One partner described the professional satisfaction that comes from collaborating with a sophisticated in-house lawyer to solve a problem:

> The client thinks of you and wants you and so you always have to be embedded with your client. [This means] you know their business, you know they get deals, you're willing to really go the extra mile to help them, they trust you, they know that if one of their underlings is making a mistake you'll make sure it gets fixed or they know about it. If they have a competitive person within the organization who doesn't tell them everything, they know you'll fill them in. It's all human nature but you have to be special to be doing it. That's the key to client relationships. (#36)

Partners appreciate that their identity as lawyers imposes an ultimate limit on this commitment, in the sense that the law sets the limits of what they are willing to do for their clients. In this respect, they conform most closely to Wendel's model of the Neutral Partisan whose role is to secure her client's legal entitlements. As a phenomenological matter, however, this appears to be background rather than foreground—an internalized limit. An athlete is aware of the boundaries of the playing field; she focuses her attention, however, not on those boundaries but on trying to do her best within them. Similarly, the bulk of the trusted advisor's day is spent trying to make good on her commitment to her client, not focusing on the conditions that set ultimate limits on it.

In addition, it is commitment to the client that appears to give partners the opportunity even to advance some of the goals contained in broader conceptions of the lawyer's role, such as furthering ordinary moral values (Luban 1988) or the interests of justice (Simon 1999). This opportunity, however, does not arise through a conception of their role as maintaining enough distance from a client to enable them to evaluate the moral worth or justice of their client's goals. Rather, they believe that earning the trust of a client by exhibiting commitment can open the way for conversations about the spirit of the law and about concerns beyond the law.

The conceptual model that this approach most approximates may be Charles Fried's notion of "the lawyer as friend" (1976). Fried regards this model as furnishing justification for a lawyer favoring her client's interest over others and over society. He roots it in the more general idea that moral sensibility begins with awareness of oneself as a concrete individual who can express oneself as a moral agent in interaction with other particular individuals. In such interactions, "the effects which I can produce upon people who are close to me are qualitatively different from those produced upon abstract, unknown persons" (1070).

This moral authority to be partial is most apparent in family and friendship relationships. Fried maintains, however, that we can conceive of the lawyer as a "limited-purpose friend . . . in regard to the legal system." As such, the lawyer "adopts your interests as his own" (1071). The scope of the lawyer's concern is more limited than in other relationships, in that its animating purpose is "to preserve and express the autonomy of his client vis-à-vis the legal system" (1074). The role of "legal friend," says Fried, furthers the "due liberty of each citizen before the law" and "exemplifies, at least in a unilateral sense, the idea of personal relations of trust and personal care which (as in natural friendship) are good in themselves" (1075).

Partners' description of the trusted advisor's willingness to provide expansive counsel is consistent with the idea that genuine concern for a friend's interests leads to assessment of a range of considerations beyond what the law may technically permit her to do. As Fried insists, "it is no part of my argument to hold that a lawyer must assume that the client is not a decent, moral person, has no desire to fulfill his moral obligation, and is asking only what is the minimum that he must do to stay within the law." Thus, "it would be absurd to contend that the lawyer must abstain from giving advice that takes account of the client's moral duties and his presumed desire to fulfill them" (1088). This is true no less for a corporate executive than it is for any other individual. Indeed, the complexity of concerns that the former needs to take into account on behalf of a company arguably makes acting as a trusted advisor even more urgent in that setting.

Firm Culture and the Trusted Advisor

Our study did not engage in the type of focused analysis on ethical judgment that might ground conclusions about what features of law firms might support decision making in accordance with a robust version of the trusted advisor. Our very preliminary and unscientific impressions, however, are that firms that regard nonfinancial values as intrinsically important may be especially likely to have a culture that provides such support. While partners who had an expansive view of the trusted advisor's role practiced in various types of firms, they tended to belong to firms that emphasized collaboration and other professional goods for their own sake. The latter included a conception of lawyers as having distinctive ethical obligations.

It seems at least plausible that there may be such a correlation between firms with these characteristics and support for the model of trusted advisor. An organization's culture with respect to ethical behavior generally is not distinguishable from its overall culture (Regan 2013). As one group of scholars observes, "*All* management policies, priorities and initiatives—formal or informal, and explicitly stated or implicitly assumed—can either undermine or support ethical practice within a firm" (Parker et al. 2008, 161) (emphasis in original). This is because, as Tom Tyler (2005, 1303–04) observes, "people are motivated to align their behavior with the rules of organizations or groups they belong to when they view those groups as being legitimate and consistent with their own sense of right and wrong."

Thus, for instance, research indicates a strong connection between behavior consistent with an organization's ethics and compliance program and perceptions by members that an organization treats people fairly, as well as members' identification with and commitment to the organization (Killingsworth 2012; Treviño, Weaver, and Reynolds 2006, 967). Social cognition theory indicates that people tend to store information in broad conceptual categories, which they use to "interpret incoming information and to retrieve information from memory." The category of ethics tends to include concepts such as justice, fairness, rights, and obligations. When an organization directs attention to ethics, "this is likely to cue a cognitive connection with the ethical issues that are salient to employees" (Weaver and Treviño 2001, 115).

With respect to law firms, one dynamic could be that partners in firms that are seen as genuinely valuing nonfinancial rewards may be less likely to be guided by narrow self-interest and may cultivate a more other-regarding perspective. This may make them more receptive to playing the role of the trusted advisor, rather than a narrowly conceived role of the Neutral Partisan. In addition, to the extent that collaboration fosters the institutionalization of clients, a partner may be less moved by the desire to retain a client at any cost. Finally, a firm that is seen as genuinely respecting professional values relating to cooperation may also reinforce the professional value of fulfilling the lawyer's social role. Much more systematic research would be necessary to explore these hypotheses, but they could be a fruitful focus of inquiry.

A Cautionary Note

Practicing lawyers regard commitment to the client as essential in playing their social role as trusted advisor. Our interviewees believed this was a more realistic model than one in which they mediate between the client and society, which requires a certain distance from the client. At the same time, if psychological realism leads us to regard commitment to the client as a reasonable orientation, it should also prompt us to identify the practical risks of adopting that approach.

At least two concerns may arise when lawyers base their professional self-concept on commitment to the client, implicitly bounded by respect for the law. First, conversations about the broader impacts of client behavior that commitment makes possible are often framed in language of risk rather than morality. Looking out for the client's best interest, even expansively understood, means focusing on how actions affect the client, not stakeholders. This suggests a cost-benefit orientation that considers adverse impacts on others only if they will result in damage to a company's reputation or its relationship with regulators, investors, or creditors.

From this perspective, harm to others is only instrumentally, not intrinsically, problematic. If the relevant stakeholders cannot protest in a sufficiently visible way or if the benefits to the company outweigh the harm they suffer, then the best interests of the client would counsel moving ahead with a course of action. This is what leads the United Nations Guiding Principles on Business and Human Rights (2011, 18) to emphasize, "Human rights due diligence can be included within broader enterprise risk management systems, provided that it goes beyond simply identifying and managing material risks to the company itself, to include risks to rights-holders." Getting a client to internalize that certain action is wrongful, rather than imprudent, ultimately is the best way to protect those who may be adversely affected by its actions.

It is reasonable to feel uneasy about companies' demonstrating concern about the adverse impacts of their operations only when their businesses incur costs as a result. One response is that we should encourage any approach that broadens the perspective of corporate clients to include concerns beyond immediate profitability and return to shareholders. Even an instrumental orientation can limit to some extent the harm done to stakeholders.

A second response is that considering potential reputational damage requires moral imagination, as decision makers must anticipate *why* taking certain action might lead people to condemn the company on moral grounds.

Regularly considering the possible responses of various stakeholders thus may generate greater sensitivity to their perspectives and concerns in a process that is akin to internalizing the view that certain actions are simply wrongful. As Regan and Hall (2016, 2032) suggest:

> Th[e] process of taking the perspective of persons outside the company requires imaginative evaluation of the company's operations according to moral considerations rather than simply self-interest. That evaluation may initially be for the purpose of determining whether public moral reactions will result in criticism of the company. It seems plausible to imagine, however, that the habit of consulting ordinary morality will lead to moral standards being a direct, rather than derivative, influence on behavior.

At the same time, the tendency to focus on risk underscores that the ability of the trusted advisor to counsel the client about the broad impacts of its actions will depend on the ability of third parties to impose financial or reputational costs on harmful corporate behavior. These parties may be government agencies, nongovernmental organizations, or other groups in civil society, as well as market actors such as creditors, investors, and contracting parties. The prospect of adverse action by these groups constitutes the risks to which the advisor can refer in her conversation with the client. Expansive advice by the lawyer thus is not a substitute for action by other parties in producing socially responsible corporate behavior—the latter is in fact an important precondition for the former.

A second concern is that emphasizing commitment to the client creates the risk that a lawyer will pay insufficient attention to the limits of legality. This risk need not materialize in the form of willingness to counsel breaking the law. More subtly, it can affect how the lawyer interprets the law—that is, where she locates the limits of legality. As Donald Langevoort (2011, 495) notes, "When lawyers speak, they sometimes use the term 'get comfortable' to describe the thought process by which they conclude that what the client wants to do is permissible—that is, does not generate unacceptable legal risk." Langevoort suggests that the danger in this process is that a lawyer may lose her "cognitive independence" because "a large cluster of behavioral traits works to enable people to see what they want to see, and feel as 'right' that which they are motivated to prefer, objective evidence notwithstanding" (496). A lawyer who sees herself mainly as committed to the client may understand that legality sets limits to this commitment, but she may be subtly inclined to construe those limits more expansively than would a lawyer who conceives of her role as ensuring that clients receive only those legal benefits to which they are entitled.

This also is a reasonable—and realistic—concern. It is natural that someone who sees herself as committed to the client would begin to see the world through the client's eyes. Indeed, this would seem to enhance the ability to serve as an effective trusted advisor. At the same time, the lawyers we interviewed indicated that adopting this orientation is a condition for the opportunity to advise the client on considerations beyond technical legality.

Partners indicated that a lawyer who held in the foreground a conception of herself as an impartial arbiter of the client's legal entitlements would be viewed more as a "cop" than as a "counsel," to use the terms of Nelson and Nielsen (2000) in their study of in-house counsel (462). The cop serves as a gatekeeper, ensuring that the client stays within the law. As the term suggests, clients tend to view the lawyer who plays this role as policing their behavior. As Nelson and Nielsen describe, one risk of this approach is that clients may avoid including in their decision-making process lawyers whom they perceive in this way. They may forgo legal advice or, more likely, approach a lawyer whom they regard as more committed to helping them achieve their aims. The cost of adopting a role that emphasizes independence and distance from the client therefore can be that a lawyer is marginalized. While such a lawyer may possess great professional judgment, she may have limited opportunities to provide it.

By contrast, the lawyers in our study see themselves as playing the role of counsel. This role "implies a broader relationship with business actors that affords counsel an opportunity to make suggestions based on business, ethical, and situational concerns" (464). Such a lawyer is more likely to be regularly consulted by business clients. When she is, the client may be more receptive to advice from her than from a lawyer who is not perceived as genuinely committed to the client. The client's trust that the lawyer has its best interest at heart allows the lawyer to raise concerns that relate to the spirit of the law, as well as to those that go beyond the law entirely. The potential cost of adopting this role, however, is the loss of cognitive independence.

Nelson and Nielsen emphasize that the roles they describe are ideal types, and that lawyers may move back and forth between them. Nonetheless, their typology suggests that each role carries distinctive benefits and risks. The cop may have impeccable independent judgment that is rarely requested. The counsel may have several opportunities to provide expansive advice, but that advice may be subtly shaped by what the client wants to hear. The partners in our interviews believe that the second role is more effective because the lawyer is more likely to be at the table when important decisions are made. As we have suggested, this suggests that models of the lawyer's role should accept commitment to the client as a legitimate orientation, and then focus on how the lawyer works through the demands of that commitment.

Conclusion

Our interviews indicate that many lawyers believe that serving as a trusted advisor is how they can play a distinctive social role as a professional. They also believe that opportunities remain to play this role despite changes in the market that have provided clients with more bargaining power. They do not see the trusted advisor as an impartial moral activist or instrument of justice. They see her instead as someone who is justifiably partial, committed to helping further the client's best interest. They regard that interest as bounded by what is legal, but not confined to that. The trusted advisor may go beyond technical legality to counsel a client on the spirit as well as the letter of the law, and on considerations that transcend the law altogether. In this respect, they do not subscribe to the narrow view of the Neutral Partisan model.

While the trusted advisor closely resembles Wendel's model of fidelity to law, she differs subtly from that model by being oriented on a daily basis by commitment to the client, not to determining the client's plausible legal entitlements. As a psychological matter, those entitlements serve as background constraints, not animating motivation. It is her commitment that engenders client trust that in turn gives her the opportunity to provide expansive advice. In this respect, the trusted advisor resembles Fried's notion of the lawyer as a limited-purpose friend.

We believe that accepting, rather than lamenting, the fact that law firm lawyers are committed to their clients is a more realistic approach to legal ethics that directs attention to how professional independence is dynamically forged in the course of interactions between lawyer and client. The trust that such commitment engenders both provides opportunities for a lawyer to render expansive advice and poses subtle risks that she may uncritically internalize the client's perspective. Research that investigates how law firm lawyers manage this tension has the potential to provide rich insights into the process through which professional identify is forged on an ongoing basis.

Conclusion

Money and Meaning in the Modern Law Firm

This book asks questions designed to explain the daily experience of law practice in large law firms and the self-concepts of partners within them. What concerns and pressures do law firm partners face in their practices? How do they think about the firms in which they work? Do they understand themselves as professionals, as persons engaged in business, or as some combination of the two? If the latter, do they see these aspects of identity as complementary or antagonistic? We began our research without any specific theory or analytical framework in mind, in the hope that the interviews would reveal meaningful themes and patterns.

We were mindful, however, of pervasive claims that modern large law firm practice has lost its character as a profession and is now simply one type of business activity. The premise of this contention is that a greater focus on financial performance means a corresponding diminution in commitment to nonfinancial professional values. In other words, business and professional orientations are inherently antagonistic.

Our interviews indicate a more complex experience and self-understanding, however, than is captured by a sharp dichotomy between business and profession. This finding led us to look to accounts that conceptualize professions as occupations that inevitably contain a mixture of business and professional features. From this perspective, the inquiry is to what extent these features are complementary or antagonistic. We found helpful two analytical frameworks that adopt this approach. The first is Eliot Freidson's notion of a profession as a way of organizing the work of an occupation as opposed to market and bureaucratic principles. The second is the institutional logics perspective, which, when applied to professional organizations, assumes that an organization will mix business and professional elements in dynamic relationship. By situating an occupation and its organizational forms within the market, these theories suggest that we should focus on the balances that law firms are able to strike between business and professional features under different market conditions.

The interviews also suggest that modern market forces continue to gain momentum, with the potential to drain law firms of distinctive features as they become more interchangeable business enterprises. A firm that seeks to avoid this outcome by building a distinctive culture must find a way to gain the commitment and loyalty of its lawyers by conveying the sense that the firm is a common cooperative venture. This can both minimize defections to other firms and encourage cooperative rather than narrowly self-interested behavior. This insight led us to the concept of firm-specific capital, which enables a firm to provide a place to work that is more rewarding than other firms.

Our interviews indicate that partners seek both financial and nonfinancial professional rewards in their practices. That is, they seek both money and meaning. Attending to financial rewards means that a firm must solve a collective action problem, or a Prisoner's Dilemma, by convincing partners that commitment to the firm and cooperating to further success will be more financially rewarding than narrowly self-interested behavior. Attention to the desire for professional rewards means that a firm must credibly communicate that it stands for something more than simply financial success. Conveying this message effectively enables a firm to solve an Assurance Game. The strength of commitment to the firm that this can foster in turn can further the firm's financial success, as partners are willing to work harder and go the extra mile for a firm they believe in. In this way, solving both challenges can initiate a virtuous cycle in which business and professional concerns reinforce one another.

The strongest form of culture results from a firm's success in solving both of these challenges. Solving only the Prisoner's Dilemma will create financial incentives for loyalty and cooperative behavior, but those will operate only as long as alternative behaviors are not more financially rewarding. Solving only the Assurance Game creates the risk that a firm with a clear commitment to professional values may not be financially successful enough to survive in an intensely competitive market for law firm services. The modern firm that hopes to establish and maintain a distinctive culture that balances business demands and professional values therefore must be *both* a well-run business that provides financial rewards and an organization that provides nonfinancial professional rewards.

These analytical frameworks suggest a fruitful way to think about the evolution of the large law firm from the late nineteenth to the early twenty-first century. From its emergence in the late nineteenth century until the last decades of the twentieth century, large firms operated in a market characterized by long-term client relationships. This assurance of ongoing business lessened the need for firms to focus explicitly and aggressively on measures that insured competitive financial performance. This in turn allowed firms to organize their work in accordance with their partners' desires for nonfinancial professional rewards. The result was that firms possessed firm-specific capital that made partner commitment to the firm both financially rational and professionally satisfying. This capital served as a means to solve both the Prisoner's Dilemma and the Assurance Game, respectively. It provided the stability necessary to establish a distinct organizational culture in which professional values could flourish.

Market conditions for firms have dramatically changed over the past few decades, however. The loss of long-term client relationships means more intense competition for business. The result is that firms have had to focus more deliberately on measures to ensure economic competitiveness. These measures reflect greater attention to business logic within the firm. This in turn means that firms seeking to sustain a distinct culture that reflects commitment to professional values must act more explicitly to communicate such commitment. Without this, the default likely will be toward expanding influence of business logic as firms become business enterprises less distinguishable from one another.

The precondition for establishing a culture with common expectations and norms is relative stability. Modern firms, however, no longer have firm-specific capital in the form of long-term client relationships that provide such stability. Firms therefore need to develop other sources of firm-specific capital that promote stability by encouraging partners to commit to the firm and to cooperate in furthering its success rather than pursuing only their self-interest. Under modern market conditions, they must solve the Prisoner's Dilemma by convincing partners that acting cooperatively will provide greater financial rewards than are available at other firms and that would accrue from purely individualistic behavior. Doing so enhances stability by providing economic reasons for commitment to the firm and its welfare.

Purely economic incentives can be fragile, however, if leaving the firm or not acting cooperatively becomes more individually profitable. Our interviews indicate the importance to partners of the nonfinancial professional values that a firm can provide. Belief that a firm is committed to these values can reinforce economic incentives and create an even stronger tie to the firm. Credibly conveying this commitment to partners is the challenge posed by the Assurance Game. In various ways, a firm must credibly communicate that it regards nonfinancial values as intrinsically important.

The next section situates this analytical framework within the scholarly debate over what, if anything, can hold large law firms together under modern market conditions.

Searching for Firm-Specific Capital

Larry Ribstein's (2010) work has been skeptical about large law firms' ability to create and sustain the firm-specific capital necessary to establish secure ties between partners and firms. Ribstein argues that clients traditionally purchased services from large firms rather than from individual lawyers or small groups of them because clients rely on the reputation of these firms to compensate for the difficulty of assessing the quality of legal services. Clients assume that firms will carefully screen and monitor their lawyers to preserve this reputational bond. This in turn requires that firms "motivate their lawyers to provide the mentoring, screening, and monitoring that supports the firm's reputation" (754).

Ribstein suggests that the rise in influence and sophistication of corporate counsel have reduced or eliminated the information asymmetry that creates the need for reputational bonding. Thus, "[w]hen clients have the technical expertise to dispense with specialists and can figure out on their own which individual lawyers are reliable and meet their specific needs, they will have less need to buy outside legal services based on personal relationships with individual lawyers or to rely on a stable of 'preferred provider' Big Law firms" (761). This approach is reflected in the common corporate client assertion that "we hire lawyers, not law firms." Ribstein argues that the movement of more legal work to inside the company, greater reliance on technology, and the rise of nonlawyer alternative providers of more routine services all reduce even further client reliance on large firms.

The result, as we note in this book, is that firms now find it more difficult to provide their lawyers with a steady stream of work from regular clients, which can undermine lawyers' ties to the firm. A lesser sense of connection in turn can erode lawyers' incentives to spend time in those functions that support a firm's reputation. As Ribstein notes, "The problem is that lawyers constantly must allocate time and effort between building the firm's reputation and building their own clienteles. If the ties binding lawyers to firms unravel, lawyers' temptation to build their personal human capital and client relationships may outweigh their incentive to invest in building the firm. The firm then may become just a collection of individuals sharing expenses and revenues that has little or no value as a distinct entity" (754).

Ribstein expresses pessimism about the large law firm's surviving in anything like its present form.

> [T]hese firms need outside capital to survive, but lack a business model for the development of firm-specific property that would enable the firms to attract this capital. These basic problems have left Big Law vulnerable to client demands for cheaper and more sophisticated legal products, competition among various providers of legal services, and national and international regulatory competition. The result is likely to be the end of the major role large law firms have played in the delivery of legal services. (813)

Work by Bernard Burk and David McGowan (2011) and by Emmanuel Lazega (2001) suggest that resource interdependencies among partners in the modern law firm may provide at least some amount of glue that helps counter the many centrifugal forces to which firms are subject.

Burk and McGowan (2011, 65) note that "since the 1980s, it is both a mantra and largely true that clients hire lawyers, not firms." As a result, the reputations of individual lawyers generally have become more important than firms' reputations. Thus, "referrals no longer come in a generalized inquiry from the client to its outside firm, but rather to a particular partner whose reputation, experience, or prior proof of reliability has attracted the call." As they elaborate:

> A client choosing the lead partner for a particular matter typically accepts, more or less blindly, the team the partner will bring to the task to assist her. The client largely assumes that the lead partner who has proven to have the most appropriate skills and experience will have access to, and know how to choose and deploy, the colleagues and subordinates . . . with the knowledge,

> skills, and experience necessary to get the job done right. Similarly, the contact partner who receives a call seeking assistance on a matter outside his expertise proves worthy of the caller's trust by pointing the way to suitable expertise, the ultimate quality of which will reflect on his reliability and judgment in the eyes of the client. (67)

The authors suggest that "out of this web of incentives emerges a model of a professional partnership as an internal referral network, with both the partnership and the firm structured to maximize the value of each individual partner's relational and other human capital" (69). This function of the network can serve as a source of glue that ties partners to the firm. At the same time, this glue may be relatively weak, because

> nothing in the partners' personal relational capital that powers a firm's internal referral network is highly firm-specific: An individual partner's relational capital should lose little value if the partner withdraws it to move to another partnership whose members have personal capital that is similar, greater, or "better" (e.g., more complementary or less prone to creating conflicts of interest) than the partners in the old firm. (73)

Lazega's (2001) ethnographic study of a corporate law firm examines co-workers, advisors, and friendship relationships among partners of different status levels and in different offices and specialties. He argues that these networks of exchange can provide a stabilizing force that furthers organizational integration:

> Dyads or small groups of co-workers cut across status boundaries and countered the centrifugal effects of stratification. Small cliques of mutual advisers cut across geographical boundaries and countered the effects of distance and differences between offices. Small cliques of friends cut across practice boundaries and countered the effect of the division of work. This shows that, at least in the informal structure of the firm, there was no single strongest relational basis for integration of the organization. Each type of relationship contributed in a specific way to the cohesion of the firm. (185)

Burk and McGowan, along with Lazega, thus maintain that large firms may still have means available to build some amount of firm-specific capital that creates incentives for lawyers to commit to particular firms. They caution, however, that there are limits to the ability of such capital to create a strong connection between partners and the firm.

Based on the interviews in our study, our view is that Ribstein's perspective is important in highlighting challenges that modern firms face in creating and maintaining firm-specific capital. He is right to note the potential risk that partners will choose to devote time to building their own practices at the expense of efforts to strengthen the firm. We believe, however, that he expresses too pessimistic a view about the ability of firms to create modern forms of firm-specific capital. As sophisticated as inside counsel have become, they still rely on law firms for a considerable amount of work. Overall firm reputation may be a less important factor in deciding to whom to give this work since the assumption is that any firm under serious consideration will provide high-quality services. Nonetheless, firms still can establish collaborative teams and processes whose integrated expertise and responsiveness to client needs give them an edge in competing for work. Unlike long-term relationships with clients, this form of capital must be constantly replenished and demonstrated because of the potentially centrifugal forces of intense competition. To the extent that a firm consistently does so, however, it has at least an opportunity to provide the financial rewards and professional satisfaction that can elicit partner loyalty.

Burk and McGowan's sophisticated analysis reflects an appreciation of important dynamics that shape modern firms. They are right that ties based on referral relationships can be weak to the extent that they are assessed on the basis of their financial returns. These returns provide a common metric that can be used on an ongoing basis to evaluate ties within an existing firm compared to those in a prospective new firm. Firm-specific capital in the form of referral relationships therefore will be fragile and contingent. In this respect, referral networks offer one solution to the Prisoner's Dilemma, but a relatively weak one.

As we suggest above, however, referral networks are only one type of firm-specific capital that a firm may provide. A firm may be able to assemble several kinds of resources that can be difficult to replicate elsewhere. These may include junior lawyers, nonlawyer experts, staff, information technology support, complementary practices, ways of organizing and providing work, and processes and systems. This combination of resources may create a more robust form of firm-specific capital that can establish stronger economic ties between lawyers and the firm than a referral network alone can engender.

Lazega's work reflects some appreciation of the varied types of relationships that may help integrate lawyers into a firm, although he focuses mainly on connections between individuals rather than processes and systems.

In addition, the collaboration required to form this type of firm-specific capital can provide intrinsically valuable nonfinancial professional rewards such as collegiality, intellectual stimulation, and opportunities to refine professional knowledge and skills. A firm that can demonstrate to its partners that it is committed to providing these types of rewards can build even stronger ties by solving the Assurance Game.

Meeting the Challenge

Chapters 3 through 8 discuss various measures that firms have adopted to respond to increasing market competition and to avoid being dominated by business logic by solving the Prisoner's Dilemma and the Assurance Game. Chapter 3 describes the emphasis on partners being entrepreneurial to ensure that the firm has a steady stream of business. Obtaining new clients is the form of entrepreneurial behavior that is most handsomely rewarded, but partners also can generate new business from existing clients by selling their services to colleagues within the firm. This chapter also discusses the particular challenges that women may face in meeting the expectation of being entrepreneurial.

Chapter 4 notes that encouraging an entrepreneurial ethos carries the risk of leading partners to eschew cooperative behavior in an effort to develop their own self-sufficient practices. Solving the Prisoner's Dilemma therefore requires that the firm stress that being entrepreneurial is a collaborative rather than a solo enterprise. One way to do this is to attempt to "institutionalize" clients by involving numerous partners on work for each client. This can create an obstacle to defecting to another firm because a partner cannot be certain that clients will follow. This makes remaining at the firm more individually profitable than practicing at another firm and highlights the financial benefits of working collaboratively. A firm also can emphasize the economic benefits of collaborating by giving significant weight to collaborative behavior in its compensation system and by reducing compensation because of selfish or uncooperative behavior.

A firm can solve the Assurance Game by credibly communicating to its partners that it regards collaboration as an intrinsic professional reward rather than simply as an instrument to enhance financial performance. One way to do this is to provide compensation credit for involvement in "citizenship" activities within the firm that strengthen it as an organization but do not immediately generate revenue. Another is to subsidize partners seeking to build new practices by maintaining compensation at a level that would not be strictly justified by application of the firm's compensation criteria because of time spent on nonbillable business development.

Chapter 5 describes the greater willingness of modern firms to terminate lawyers, including partners, for what is regarded as insufficient productivity. This development creates the risk of undermining any sense that a firm has a distinctive culture by suggesting that it is concerned only with the financial performance of the firm and its partners. This perception in turn can erode commitment to the firm and willingness to act cooperatively.

As Chapter 5 explains, solving the Prisoner's Dilemma in this case requires persuasively communicating to partners that the firm's policy ensures that everyone pulls equal weight on behalf of a common enterprise. Willingness to act cooperatively requires confidence that others will not take advantage of such behavior. Holding everyone accountable to common productivity standards thus can foster the trust that encourages cooperation, which in turn can generate firm-specific capital in the form of greater commitment to the firm. It is critical to this process that partners believe that everyone is held to the same standards, and that they are fairly applied.

Solving the Assurance Game can be especially challenging with respect to an increasing willingness to terminate partners for insufficient productivity. One approach that some firms take is to reduce the need for termination by providing a wide range of practices that vary in revenues and profitability. These firms accept greater differences in financial productivity than many other firms. They avoid the perception that all partners are not doing their share, however, by providing lower compensation to those with lower productivity. The choice to offer several different practices can also represent a business strategy to further a firm's financial goals by diversifying its risk. This underscores that policies sometimes may serve both business and professional ends.

Another measure aimed at solving the Assurance Game is to temper business logic by relying on longer-term financial metrics rather than short-term swings in productivity as the basis for termination decisions. Combined with early consultation with partners whose practices encounter a decline, this can allow a partner to improve performance or at least to adjust to eventually needing to leave. In addition, those partners asked to leave may be given a generous amount of time to depart to smooth the transition.

Chapters 6 and 7 explain how law firm compensation systems represent both a material and a symbolic economy, which distribute financial rewards and professional respect. They described how these economies operate on the basis of both a formal compensation process regulated by the firm and a largely unregulated, informal internal market. In broad terms, firms can attempt to solve the Prisoner's Dilemma by rewarding cooperative behavior that helps the firm build firm-specific capital based on teams and processes that deliver superior services to clients. It can seek to solve the Assurance Game by rewarding behavior consistent with traditional nonfinancial professional ideals such as the quality and creativity of a partner's work and willingness to devote nonbillable hours to responsibilities such as administrative tasks, mentoring junior lawyers, resolving ethical issues or business conflicts, and counseling new lateral partners.

Chapter 8 describes the tremendous increase in activity in the lateral market and the challenge this poses for efforts to build firm-specific capital. Ongoing departures and arrivals of partners to and from the lateral market can erode a sense of shared expectations and norms, and threaten to make financial performance the only common denominator. One measure that could respond to this risk by solving both the Prisoner's Dilemma and the Assurance Game is for a firm to seek laterals who expand a firm's "platform" rather than "buying a revenue stream" by simply pursuing those who are profitable. A second is to spend time screening prospective laterals to ensure that they will fit into the firm's culture, while a third is to devote significant resources to integrating a lateral both economically and culturally into the firm. Each of these practices can be financially beneficial for a firm, but each also can signal that the firm takes its culture seriously and is not willing to jeopardize it by hiring solely on the basis of financial productivity.

Finally, chapter 9 indicates that law firm partners also seek the professional satisfaction of serving as a trusted advisor to clients. This role may offer an opportunity to provide expansive advice that goes beyond the letter of the law, incorporating both its spirit and nonlegal considerations. This conception of the lawyer's role, and opportunities to play it, appear to have persisted despite mounting business pressures.

The chapter aims to describe the nuances of this professional self-understanding rather than to rigorously test its influence in practice or to explore in depth how law firm culture can support and reinforce it. It seems plausible to suggest that a firm that solves the Assurance Game by demonstrating genuine commitment to nonfinancial professional values may create a climate conducive to acting as a trusted advisor. Testing this tentative hypothesis through more focused research may be a fruitful line of inquiry.

The six firms on which we focused differ in the extent to which they seek deliberately to solve the Prisoner's Dilemma and the Assurance Game, and in the effectiveness with which they appear to do so. Interviews suggested that Firm 6 is especially effective in meeting this challenge, and that Firm 4 also has considerable success in doing so. Partners in both firms said that the firm's culture is an explicit topic of conversation, and that decisions at various levels often include the effect on culture as a consideration. Both firms deliberately offer a range of services with varying levels of revenues and profits, and compensate partners differently based in part on these metrics. Partners in both firms said that this reflects an effort to minimize the need for terminations, although both firms in recent years have needed to resort to this more often. They also said that this philosophy leaves money on the table, in the sense that a more tightly focused set of higher-end practices probably would be more profitable to the firm. In this way, the firm sends a credible message about the importance of nonfinancial professional values. It is worth noting that both firms had dissenters from this approach who fretted that it might not be the most prudent policy in an increasingly competitive market.

Firm 6 also emphasizes collaboration as an important factor in compensation, asking in the partner self-assessment both whom a partner has helped and which others have helped him. This enables it to be especially successful in institutionalizing clients, although there still remain challenges in doing so. Information about compensation is somewhat more widely shared in Firm 4 than in Firm 6, but there is a sense in both firms that those in managing positions have taken less compensation than the amount that they could claim. This is regarded as another example on the individual level of leaving money on the table, which is another way of helping to solve the Assurance Game.

Firm 6 engages in some additional measures that contribute to fostering a reasonably distinct culture. It explicitly pursues only laterals who will help expand its "platform," rather than simply those who offer a lucrative book of business. It also involves a large number of partners in the process of vetting prospective lateral hires in an effort to ensure a good cultural fit. It chooses not to extend offers to those who are not seen as a good fit, even though they would help expand the platform and enhance the firm's financial performance.

Other firms have at least some success in sustaining a reasonably distinct culture. Firm 2 seems to use its pro bono program to help strengthen its culture. While there is not necessarily a strictly zero-sum relationship between billable hours and hours spent on pro bono work, strong commitment to the latter leaves at least some money on the table in the form of forgone billable hours. This appears to send a message both to current members of the firm and to prospective recruits, with the latter ideally resulting in self-selection into the firm's perceived culture.

Firm 2 also is notable for delaying opening a new office in a location with significant revenue potential. A typical way of establishing a presence in a new location these days is to merge with or acquire a firm in that location. Firm 2 instead waited in one instance until it could send an existing partner to open the office because it wished to integrate the office into the firm's culture. This also effectively helped solve the Assurance Game by leaving money on the table, in the form of forgone revenues from opening the office sooner.

Partners in Firm 3 emphasize a strong culture of collaboration in the firm. Interviews suggested that one factor that may contribute to this is the willingness of the compensation committee to reassign compensation credits if it believes that a partner has not been fair in claiming them. Partners also described occasions on which the firm asked a profitable partner to leave because of what was regarded as unacceptable behavior, which can result in at least a short-term shortfall in revenues. Finally, as we describe in chapter 8, the firm has a more formal program for lateral integration than the other firms we studied. We were not able systematically to survey partners about the effectiveness of this program, but it does at least formally signal the firm's commitment to the importance of the integration process.

While leaving money on the table emphasizes professional rather than business logic, it should be clear that the logics align in some instances. Rewarding collaboration and penalizing those who do not practice it, for instance, can enhance firm profitability while providing incentives to engage in professional relationships that partners find intrinsically rewarding. Fostering a collective rather than individualistic entrepreneurial ethos also can create both financial benefits and nonfinancial professional rewards. Hiring laterals who help strengthen the firm's "platform" rather than simply "buying a revenue stream" can enhance profitability as well as foster close relationships among partners.

Appreciating that some measures can further both profitability and professional values challenges the conventional dichotomy between business and professional principles. As we argue, understanding law firms requires moving beyond this framework. Consider, for instance, Jonathan Molot's (2014) suggestion that firms should be able to provide permanent equity to partners that can be cashed out upon retirement. The value of such equity would reflect some multiple of the partner's revenues.

If, for instance, a partner generates $10 million in revenue and $5 million in profits a year, he currently shares in profits only as long as he works for the firm. With an equity investment in the firm, the partner would be able to cash out and sell the practice for, perhaps, a multiple of 10, or $50 million. While the firm may distribute some of the partner's equity to others in the firm, "for a lawyer who earns several million dollars per year, the prospect of a nest egg upon retirement worth tens of millions of dollars could well be life-altering." This would create an incentive for the partner to assist the firm in institutionalizing his relationships with clients:

> [T]he market value of such a law practice would tend to be inversely related to just how important its senior lawyer is to its continued success and, thus, directly dependent upon how well it could function upon the departure or retirement of that lawyer. An entrepreneur who builds a business that is able to function without him—such that the business has intrinsic value independent of his or her labor—is likely to be able to sell that business for more than an entrepreneur whose business depends upon his or her continued labor. (Molot 2014, 26)

In this way, equity investment can give partners a long-term stake in the firm that enhances partner loyalty, encourages meaningful professional development of associates, and provides more intrinsic professional satisfaction by mitigating emphasis on short-term performance. Thus, a measure that seems inherently to express business logic can further professional logic. Dismissing it simply on the ground that it will change law firm practice from a profession to a business ignores this possibility (Regan 2008). The question is the extent to which a measure is likely to align business and professional values or to create tension between them.

Conclusion

Our interviews indicate that law firm partners maintain a sense of themselves as distinctive professionals, notwithstanding a significant intensification of business pressures on both law firms and law firm partners in recent years. They continue to seek nonfinancial professional rewards from the practice of law that matter to them. In some respects, this should not be surprising. It is consistent with the idea that those who apply to law school are motivated by a variety of goals other than financial success (Stetz 2018). Even though much can happen between applying to law school and becoming a law firm partner, our interviews indicate that many partners retain this orientation. This continues to be the case despite general skepticism that professionalism remains a useful concept in the practice of law (Morgan 2010).

Nothing ensures, however, that these values will continue to survive, that these rewards will always be available, or that partners will continue to pursue them. Relentless competitive pressures require that firms focus more explicitly on financial performance, and that they adopt policies that further this goal. A firm that desires to provide a unique culture in which professional rewards are available must think carefully about whether measures to promote business success can complement professional values or are antagonistic to them. Without sensitivity to this issue, a firm may drift toward a culture dominated by business logic that is indistinguishable from other firms.

Until a generation ago, many firms possessed firm-specific capital in the form of long-term client relationships that enabled them to align business and professional logic. Under modern market conditions, capital in this form no longer is available. Firms must create new ways of eliciting commitment and loyalty from their partners. As we suggest, accomplishing this task is possible but increasingly difficult. The extent to which large firms are able to succeed in doing so will determine whether they can continue to provide both money and meaning for the partners within them.

APPENDIX ON THE RESEARCH PROJECT

Our study involved interviews with 259 partners, and an additional 20 second interviews with partners in that group, for a total of 279 interviews. The numbers cited in the book are to one of the 279 interviews. All first interviews were conducted between July 2009 and August 2014. The second interviews were conducted in July 2016.

Of the 259 partners interviewed, 244, or 94 percent, were from six firms. Five of those firms were in the AmLaw 100 and had at least 900 lawyers at the time of the interviews. The sixth firm was in the AmLaw 200 and had more than 400 lawyers at the time of the interviews. Of the additional 15 partners interviewed, 12 were in AmLaw 100 firms. Interviews were conducted at what is considered the home office of each of the six core firms, as well as other firm offices. These were at offices on the East Coast, the West Coast, and in the Midwest. The number of partners interviewed in each of the five firms in the AmLaw 100 was 26, 39, 40, 51, and 62. We interviewed 26 partners in the firm in the AmLaw 200.

Some 37 percent of partners had joined their firm as laterals from other firms. Eighty of our interviews, or about 31 percent, were with female partners. This is higher than the percentage of female income partners (30 percent) and female equity partners (20 percent) reported in the 2018 National Association of Women Lawyers survey of AmLaw 200 firms. While we interviewed some African American, Hispanic, and Asian American partners, these were too few to permit us to draw any conclusions about the possible effects of ethnic background on experiences and attitudes.

The number of years since the interviewees had graduated from law school is as follows:

7–10 years: 7.6%
11–15 years: 15.8%
16–20 years: 12.5%
21–25 years: 14.6%
26–30 years: 19.8%
31–35 years: 13.4%
36–40 years: 11.7%
More than 40 years: 3.2%

The median years since graduation was 25. If we make a rough assumption that individuals on average spent 8 years in practice before making partner, the median interviewee had been a partner about 17 years.

All but one of the original 259 partner interviews were in person, with one on the telephone. All 20 of the second interviews were by phone. All of the 244 interviews with partners in the six firms were tape recorded, with each partner's consent. Interviews were conducted by one or two interviewers, using a semi-structured interview format. Interviews ranged from one to two hours, with an average of just under ninety minutes.

All interviews with partners in the six main firms were arranged with the cooperation of firm management. Partners were selected to provide a range of interviewees by practice area, seniority, gender, ethnic background, office location, management responsibilities, and lateral market status. We spoke to the managing partners of all six of the main firms in our study and to the current or former managing partner of three other AmLaw 100 firms.

ACKNOWLEDGMENTS

We would like to express our deep appreciation to the Law School Admissions Council for a generous grant that enabled us to conduct the research that forms the basis for this book. We are also grateful to Charles Myers at the University of Chicago Press, and series editors Lynn Mather and John Conley, for their insightful guidance, encouragement, and patience as we completed the manuscript. Betsy Kuhn at Georgetown University Law Center provided extraordinary editorial assistance that greatly enhanced the clarity and accessibility of the book.

We have incurred many debts along the way to those who read or discussed portions of the manuscript with us. Elizabeth Chambliss was an original participant on the project but had to withdraw at an early stage because of other commitments. She nonetheless made important contributions during her time on the project, as well as afterward, that helped sharpen our thinking about the research. John Darley and Ann Tenbrunsel also were original participants whose commitments required them to withdraw, but they were helpful in shaping our focus as well. In addition, Avani Sood provided valuable assistance during her time as a doctoral student at Princeton. For valuable comments and conversations through the course of the project, we are grateful to Ronit Dinotitzer, Heidi Gardner, Kath Hall, Neil Hamilton, Vivien Holmes, Leslie Levin, David Luban, Jim Jones, Ashish Nanda, Bob Nelson, Dana Remus, Rob Rosen, Tanina Rostain, Nancy Sachs, Carole Silver, Lisa Smith, Kristin Stark, Joyce Sterling, Eli Wald, Brad Wendel, and David Wilkins. Portions of chapters 6 and 7 previously were published as our article

"Money and Meaning: The Moral Economy of Law Firm Compensation," *University of St. Thomas Law Journal* 10, no. 1 (2012): 74–151.

This book would not have been possible without the cooperation of senior management in several large law firms. These leaders informed their partners of our project and encouraged them to speak with us, without any attempt whatsoever to influence what they would say or to learn what they said. We are enormously grateful to the many partners who agreed to arrange their very busy schedules to meet with us, who were unfailingly generous with their time, and who offered candid and reflective responses to every question asked. This book simply would not have been possible without their participation.

Mitt dedicates this book to Nancy; to Rebecca, Ben, and Bryan; and to Liam and Dash, the most recent generation in the family. Their love, patience, humor, irreverence, playfulness, and deep compassion enrich my life incomparably. I could not be luckier to be part of their lives. I'm sure that none of them will mind if I say that Nancy is my center and foundation: a loving companion with her own impressive accomplishments; someone who nurtures and challenges me in ways that enlarge my awareness; and a partner with a gift for continuously making the world seem new and promising with each day that we share.

Lisa would like to acknowledge her colleagues, especially Lisa Smith and Kristin Stark, and clients at Fairfax Associates for their conversations and insights about the legal profession. She would also like to thank her doctoral advisor and mentor Ashish Nanda at Harvard Business School for introducing her to the rewards of telling stories through case studies and qualitative research. Finally Lisa is blessed to have her family—Gavin and Maddie have been a source of patience, laughter, and love. And J.J. has been a faithful supporter of Lisa's career, always overflowing in his love and generosity through rewards and challenges. Without J.J., this would not have been possible.

NOTES

Introduction

1. We provide details of the research in the appendix.

Chapter 1

1. Our interviews indicate that partners also regard serving as a trusted advisor to clients as a distinctive professional reward. This includes providing advice with regard for the law and sometimes considerations beyond the law. This reward has less to do with interaction among partners and between partners and the firm, so we discuss it in chapter 9.

Chapter 2

1. Assumes an average of $450/hour in collected fees, which was the average in the Thomson Reuters/Georgetown (2020) report.

Chapter 3

1. Although "productivity" sometimes is used to refer specifically to billable hours, we use the term here in a broader sense.

Chapter 5

1. When Milbank increased its starting associate salary from $160,000 to $190,000 in June 2018, not as many firms immediately matched it as had done so in the past (Simmons 2018b; Zaretsky 2018a, 2018b), although Cravath increased midlevel and senior associates by $5,000 and $10,000 more, respectively, than Milbank's increases (Tribe 2018). A healthy number, however, did do so, including some in the lower part

of the AmLaw 100 that generally do not realistically compete with Milbank for high-end client matters and associates. Such firms want to preserve at least the possibility that they will be in the upper tier of any emerging market segmentation.

Chapter 6

1. Law firms tend to place much greater weight on revenue than profitability in the compensation process. Traditionally, the profitability of matters and clients was difficult to determine due to disagreements over the distribution of firm-wide costs such as office space, administrative assistance, and so on.

Chapter 7

1. It is noteworthy that a comprehensive recent survey of law firm compensation declares that "[c]ronyism continues to be, by far, the most significant reason for dissatisfaction with compensation satisfaction, outpacing all of the other enumerated reasons combined" (Lowe 2012, 7).

2. Class and Collective Action Complaint at 10, Tolton v. Jones Day, No. 1:19-cv-00945-RDM (D.D.C. Apr. 3, 2019).

3. Id. at 10–11.

Chapter 8

1.Jacob v. Norris, McLaughlin & Marcus, 607 A.2d 142, 147 (N.J. 1992).

REFERENCES

Adams, J. S. 1963. "Toward an Understanding of Inequity." *Journal of Abnormal Psychology* 67, no. 5 (November): 422–36.

Altonji, Joseph B. 2009. "Who Broke the Two-Tier Model?" (unpublished manuscript on file with authors).

Amabile, Teresa M., and Steven Kramer. 2011. *The Progress Principle: Using Small Wins to Ignite Joy, Engagement, and Creativity at Work*. Boston: Harvard Business Review Press.

American Bar Association. *Report of the Twentieth Annual Meeting of the American Bar Association*. 1897. Philadelphia: Dando.

———. Commission on Professionalism. 1986. "'. . . In the Spirit of Public Service': A Blueprint for the Rekindling of Lawyer Professionalism." Chicago: ABA.

American Lawyer. 1895. "The Commercializing of the Profession." January 1895, 84.

———. 1989. "The AmLaw 100." July/August 1989.

———. 2018. "The 2018 AmLaw 100." April 24, 2018.

Atkinson, Rob. 1995. "A Dissenter's Commentary on the Professionalism Crusade." *Texas Law Review* 74, no. 2 (December): 259–343.

Babcock, Linda, Michele Gelfand, Deborah Small, and Heidi Stayn. 2006. "Gender Differences in the Propensity to Initiate Negotiations." In *Social Psychology and Economics*, edited by David De Cremer, Marcel Zeelenberg, and J. Keith Murnighan, 239–59. Mahwah, NJ: Lawrence Erlbaum.

Babcock, Linda, and Sara Laschever. 2003. *Women Don't Ask: Negotiation and the Gender Divide*. Princeton, NJ: Princeton University Press.

Beiner, Theresa M. 2008. "Not All Lawyers Are Equal: Difficulties That Plague Women and Women of Color." *Syracuse Law Review* 58, no. 2: 317–34.

Berle, Jr., A. A. 1933. "Modern Legal Profession." In *Encyclopaedia of the Social Sciences*, edited by Edwin R.A. Seligman and Alvin Johnson. London: MacMillan.

Besharov, Marya L., and Wendy K. Smith. 2014. "Multiple Institutional Logics in Organizations: Explaining Thleir Varied Nature and Implications." *Academy of Management Review* 39, no. 3: 364–81.

Bévort, Frans, and Roy Suddaby. 2016. "Scripting Professional Identities: How Individuals Make Sense of Contradictory Institutional Logics." *Journal of Professions and Organization* 3, no. 1: 17–38.

Bond, James T., and Families and Work Institute. 2003. *Highlights of the National Study of the Changing Workforce*. New York: Families and Work Institute.

Bowles, Hannah Riley. 2012. "Psychological Perspectives on Gender in Negotiation." RWP12-046. Faculty Research Working Paper Series. Harvard Kennedy School.

Bowles, Hannah Riley, Linda Babcock, and Lei Lai. 2007. "Social Incentives for Gender Differences in the Propensity to Initiate Negotiations: Sometimes It Does Hurt to Ask." *Organizational Behavior and Human Decision Processes* 103, no. 1: 84–103.

Bowles, Hannah Riley, Linda Babcock, and Kathleen L. McGinn. 2005. "Constraints and Triggers: Situational Mechanics of Gender in Negotiation." *Journal of Personality and Social Psychology* 89, no. 6: 951–65.

Brandeis, Louis D. 1905. "The Opportunity in the Law." Presented at the Harvard Ethical Society, Harvard University, May 4, 1905. https://louisville.edu/law/library/special-collections/the-louis-d.-brandeis-collection/business-a-profession-chapter-20.

Bristol, George W. 1913. "The Passing of the Legal Profession." *Yale Law Journal* 22, no. 8: 590–613.

Brock, David M. 2006. "The Changing Professional Organization: A Review of Competing Archetypes." *International Journal of Management Reviews* 8, no. 3 (2006): 157–74.

Brock, David, C. R. Hinings, and Michael Powell. 1999. *Restructuring the Professional Organization*. London: Routledge.

Bruch, Nicholas. 2018. "Associate Salary Increases: Don't Follow Milbank's Lead." Law.com, June 5, 2018.

Bruch, Nicholas, Michael A. Ellenhorn, and Howard Rosenberg. 2019. *Risky Business: Rethinking Lateral Hiring*. New York: ALM Intelligence. https://decipherglobal.com/wp-content/uploads/2019/03/RethinkingLateralHiring_Web.pdf.

Burk, Bernard A., and David McGowan. 2011. "Big but Brittle: Economic Perspectives on the Future of the Law Firm in the New Economy." *Columbia Business Law Review* 2011, no. 1: 1–117.

Campello, M., J. R. Graham, and C. R. Harvey. 2010. "The Real Effects of Financial Constraints: Evidence from a Financial Crisis." *Journal of Financial Economics* 97:470–87.

Carruthers, Bruce G., and Wendy Nelson Espeland. 1998. "Money, Meaning, and Morality." *American Behavioral Scientist* 41, no. 10 (August): 1384–1408.

Cassens Weiss, Debra. 2012. "Law Firm Consultant Predicts 'Absolutely' More Layoffs and as Many as Five BigLaw Dissolutions." *ABA Journal*, September 6, 2012.

Chandler, Mark. 2007. "The State of Technology in the Law." *Legal Evolution*, November 11, 2017. https://www.legalevolution.org/2017/11/mark-chandler-speech-january-2007-035/.

Chen, Chao C., Jaepil Choi, and Shu-cheng Chi. 2002. "Making Justice Sense of Local-Expatriate Compensation Disparity: Mitigation by Local Referents, Ideological Explanations, and Interpersonal Sensitivity in China-Foreign Joint Ventures." *Academy of Management Journal* 45, no. 4: 807–17.

Cipriani, Gina. 2018. "Volatility Is Now a Fact of Life for America's Biggest Firms." *American Lawyer*, April 24, 2018.

Clay, Thomas S., and Eric A. Seeger. 2018. *Law Firms in Transition: An Altman Weil Flash Survey*. Altman Weil.

Connelly, Brian L., S. Trevis Certo, R. Duane Ireland, and Christopher R. Reutzel. 2011. "Signaling Theory: A Review and Assessment." *Journal of Management* 37, no. 1: 39–67.

Cooper, David J., Bob Hinings, Royston Greenwood, and John L. Brown. 1996. "Sedimentation and Transformation in Organizational Change: The Case of Canadian Law Firms." *Organization Studies* 17, no. 4: 623–47.

Cotterman, James D. 2009. "Law Firm Compensation Practices Update." *Report to Legal Management*, Altman Weil Inc., July/August.

Daly, Mary C., and Carole Silver. 2007. "Flattening the World of Legal Services? The Ethical and Liability Minefields of Off-Shorting Legal and Law-Related Services." *Georgetown Journal of International Law* 38:401.

Dau-Schmidt, Kenneth G., Marc S. Galanter, Kaushik Mukhopadhaya, and Kathleen E. Hull. 2009. "Men and Women of the Bar: The Impact of Gender on Legal Careers." *Michigan Journal of Gender and Law* 16, no. 1: 49–146.

DeLong, Thomas J., John J. Gabarro, and Robert J. Lees. 2007. *When Professionals Have to Lead: A New Model for High Performance*. Cambridge, MA: Harvard Business Press.

Dinovitzer, Ronit, Hugh Gunz, and Sally Gunz. 2014a. "Corporate Lawyers and Their Clients: Walking the Line between Law and Business." *International Journal of the Legal Profession* 21, no. 1: 3–21.

———. 2014b. "Reconsidering Lawyer Autonomy: The Nexus Between Firm, Lawyer, and Client in Large Commercial Practice." *American Business Law Journal* 51, no. 3: 661–719.

———. 2014c. "Unpacking Client Capture: Evidence from Corporate Law Firms." *Journal of Professions and Organization* 1, no. 2: 99–117.

Dinovitzer, Ronit, Nancy Reichman, and Joyce Sterling. 2009. "The Differential Valuation of Women's Work: A New Look at the Gender Gap in Lawyers' Incomes." *Social Forces* 88, no. 2: 819–64.

Donnell, Cathlin, Joyce Sterling, and Nancy Reichman. 1998. *Gender Penalties: The Results of the Careers and Compensation Study*. Denver: Colorado Women's Bar Foundation.

"DuPont Case Study: Joining the Interests of Panel Law Firms and Client." 2011. *Times of London*, June 9, 2011.

Economist. 2011. "A Less Gilded Future." May 5, 2011.

Festinger, Leon. 1954. "A Theory of Social Comparison Processes." *Human Relations* 7, no. 2: 117–40.

Flaherty, Scott. 2018. "The 200-Partner Tour: Reducing Lateral Risk the Old-Fashioned Way." *American Lawyer*, January 28, 2018.

Flom, Barbara M. 2012. *Report of the Seventh Annual NAWL National Survey on Retention and Promotion of Women in Law Firms*. Chicago: National Association of Women Lawyers Foundation.

Freedman, Monroe. 1975. *Lawyers' Ethics in an Adversary System*. Indianapolis: Bobbs-Merrill.

Freidson, Eliot. 2013. *Professionalism: The Third Logic*. Hoboken, NJ: Wiley, 2013.

Fried, Charles. 1976. "The Lawyer as Friend: The Moral Foundations of the Lawyer-Client Relation." *Yale Law Journal* 85:1060–89.

Furnham, Adrian, and Michael Argyle. 1998. *The Psychology of Money*. London: Routledge.

Galanter, Marc, and William Henderson. 2008. "The Elastic Tournament: A Second Transformation of the Big Law Firm." *Stanford Law Review* 60, no. 6 (April): 1867–1929.

Galanter, Marc, and Thomas Palay. 1991. *Tournament of Lawyers: The Transformation of the Big Law Firm*. Chicago: University of Chicago Press.

———. 1994. "The Many Futures of the Big Law Firm, Conference on the Commercialization of the Legal Profession." *South Carolina Law Review* 45, no. 5: 905–28.

Gardner, Donald G., Linn Van Dyne, and Jon L. Pierce. 2004. "The Effects of Pay Level on Organization-Based Self-Esteem and Performance: A Field Study." *Journal of Occupational and Organizational Psychology* 77, no. 3: 307–22.

Gardner, Heidi K. 2013. *The Collaboration Imperative for Today's Law Firms: Leading High-Performance Teamwork for Maximum Benefit*. Cambridge, MA: Harvard Law School Center on the Legal Profession.

———. 2015. "When Senior Managers Won't Collaborate." *Harvard Business Review* 93, no. 3: 74–82.

———. 2016. *Smart Collaboration: How Professionals and Their Firms Succeed by Breaking Down Silos*. Boston: Harvard Business Review Press.

Garth, Bryant G., and Joyce S. Sterling. 2018. "Diversity, Hierarchy, and Fit in Legal Careers: Insights from Fifteen Years of Qualitative Interviews." *Georgetown Journal of Legal Ethics* 31:123–74.

Gerhart, Barry, and Sara L. Rynes. 2003. *Compensation: Theory, Evidence, and Strategic Implications*. Thousand Oaks, CA: Sage.

Gilson, Ronald J., and Robert H. Mnookin. 1985. "Sharing among the Human Capitalists: An Economic Inquiry into the Corporate Law Firm and How Partners Split Profits." *Stanford Law Review* 37, no. 2 (January): 313–92.

Glendon, Mary Ann. 1994. *A Nation under Lawyers: How the Crisis in the Legal Profession Is Transforming American Society*. New York: Farrar, Straus, and Giroux.

Gordon, Robert W. 1983. "Legal Thought and Legal Practice in the Age of American Enterprise, 1870–1920." In *Professions and Professional Ideologies in America*, edited by Gerald L. Geison, 70, 110. Chapel Hill: University of North Carolina Press.

———. 1984. "The Ideal and the Actual in the Law: Fantasies and Practices of New York City Lawyers, 1870–1910." In *The New High Priests: Lawyers in Post–Civil War America*, edited by Gerard W. Gawalt, 51–74. Contributions in Legal Studies 29. Westport, CT: Greenwood Press.

Gorman, Elizabeth H., and Julie A. Kmec. 2009. "Hierarchical Rank and Women's Organizational Mobility: Glass Ceilings in Corporate Law Firms." *American Journal of Sociology* 114, no. 5: 1428–74.

Gough, Margaret, and Mary Noonan. 2013. "A Review of the Motherhood Wage Penalty in the United States." *Sociology Compass* 7, no. 4: 328–42.

Green, Mark J., and Ralph Nader. 1978. *The Other Government: The Unseen Power of Washington Lawyers*. New York: W. W. Norton.

Greenwood, Royston, C. R. Hinings, and John Brown. 1990. "'P2-Form' Strategic Management: Corporate Practices in Professional Partnerships." *Academy of Management Journal* 33, no. 4: 725–55.

"Guiding Principles on Business and Human Rights: Implementing the United Nations 'Protect, Respect and Remedy' Framework." 2011. HR/PUB/11/04. Geneva: Office of the High Commissioner, United Nations Human Rights.

Habte, Samson. 2017. "Law Firms Take Aim at Outside Counsel Guidelines, Irking Clients." *Bloomberg News*, June 14, 2017.

Hagan, John, and Fiona M. Kay. 2010. "The Masculine Mystique: Living Large from Law School to Later Life." *Canadian Journal of Law and Society* 25, no. 2: 195–226.

Halgren, Guy. 2018. "The 200-Partner Tour: Reducing Lateral Risk the Old-Fashioned Way." *American Lawyer* (online), January 28.

Harper, Steven J. 2013. "Big Law's Troubling Trajectory." *New York Times*, June 24, 2013.

Harter, J. K., F. L. Schmidt, and Corey L. M. Keyes. 2003. "Well-Being in the Workplace and Its Relationship to Business Outcomes: A Review of the Gallup Studies." In *Flourishing: Positive Psychology and the Life Well-Lived*, edited by Jonathan Haidt and Corey L. M. Keyes, 205–24. Washington, DC: American Psychological Association.

Henderson, William, and Christopher Zorn. 2013. "Playing Not to Lose." *American Lawyer*, March 1, 2013.

Hildebrandt Consulting, LLC, and Citi Private Bank. 2013. "2013 Client Advisory."

Ho, Karen Zouwen. 2009. *Liquidated: An Ethnography of Wall Street*. Durham, NC: Duke University Press.

Hobson, Wayne K. 1986. *The American Legal Profession and the Organizational Society: 1890–1930*. New York: Garland.

Hochschild, Arlie, and Anne Machung. 2012. *The Second Shift: Working Families and the Revolution at Home*. New York: Penguin.

Hodges, Melissa J., and Michelle J. Budig. 2010. "Who Gets the Daddy Bonus? Organizational Hegemonic Masculinity and the Impact of Fatherhood on Earnings." *Gender and Society* 24, no. 6: 717–45.

Hoffman, Jan. 1994. "Oldest Law Firm Is Courtly, Loyal and Defunct." *New York Times*, October 2, 1994.

Jasper, Colin, and Susan Lambreth. 2016. "Law Firm Pricing: Focusing on the Right Problem." *Law Firm Management* (blog), Thomson Reuters. April 27, 2016.

Kay, Julie. 2012. "Greenberg CEO Richard Rosenbaum Discusses Finances, Internal Controls and the Future." *American Lawyer*, August 20, 2012.

Kelly, Michael. 1994. *Lives of Lawyers: Journeys in the Organizations of Practice*. Ann Arbor: University of Michigan Press.

———. 2007. *Lives of Lawyers Revisited: Transformation and Resilience in the Organizations of Practice*. Ann Arbor: University of Michigan Press.

Kim, W. Chan, and Renée Mauborgne. 2003. "Fair Process: Managing in the Knowledge Economy." *Harvard Business Review* 81, no. 1: 127–36.

Killingsworth, Scott. 2012. "Modeling the Message: Communicating Compliance Through Organizational Values and Culture." *Georgetown Journal of Legal Ethics* 25:96.

Koltin Consulting Group. 2014. "Lateral Hiring Study: First Half."

Krause, Elliott A. 1996. *Death of the Guilds: Professions, States, and the Advance of Capitalism, 1930 to the Present*. New Haven, CT: Yale University Press.

Kronman, Anthony T. 1993. *The Lost Lawyer: Failing Ideals of the Legal Profession*. Cambridge, MA: Harvard University Press.

Krueger, David W. 1986. "Money, Success and Success Phobia." In *The Last Taboo: Money as Symbol and Reality in Psychotherapy and Psychoanalysis*, edited by David W. Krueger, 3–16. New York: Brunner/Mazel.

Kulik, Carol T., and Maureen L. Ambrose. 1992. "Personal and Situational Determinants of Referent Choice." *Academy of Management Review* 17, no. 2: 212–37.

Langevoort, Donald C. 2011. "Getting (Too) Comfortable: In-House Lawyers, Enterprise Risk and the Financial Crisis." *Wisconsin Law Review* 2012, no. 2: 495–519.

Lat, David. 2013. "Nationwide Layoff Watch: Major Cuts Come to Weil Gotshal." *Above the Law*, June 24, 2013.

Lattman, Peter. 2013. "Mass Layoffs at a Top-Flight Law Firm." *New York Times*, June 25, 2013.

Lazega, Emmanuel. 2001. *The Collegial Phenomenon: The Social Mechanisms of Cooperation among Peers in a Corporate Law Partnership*. Oxford: Oxford University Press.

Lee, Raymond T., and James E. Martin. 1991. "Internal and External Referents as Predictors of Pay Satisfaction among Employees in a Two-Tier Wage Setting." *Journal of Occupational Psychology* 64, no. 1: 57–66.

Levine, Samuel J. 2013. "The Law: Business or Profession?: The Continuing Relevance of Julius Henry Cohen for the Practice of Law in the Twenty-First Century." *Fordham Urban Law Journal* 40, no. 1: 1–32.

Lewinsohn-Zamir, Daphna. 1998. "Consumer Preferences, Citizen Preferences, and the Provision of Public Goods." *Yale Law Journal* 108, no. 2: 377–406.

Liebenberg, Roberta D., and Stephanie A. Scharf. 2019. *Walking Out the Door: The Facts, Figures, and Future of Experienced Women Lawyers in Private Practice*. Chicago: American Bar Association and ALM Intelligence Compass.

Lindsey, Jon, and Jeffrey A. Lowe. 2014. "Lateral Partner Satisfaction Survey" Major, Lindsey & Africa.

Linowitz, Sol M. 1994. *The Betrayed Profession: Lawyering at the End of the Twentieth Century*. New York: Charles Scribner's Sons.

Llewellyn, K. N. 1931. Review: *A Lawyer Tells the Truth*, by Morris Gisnet. *Columbia Law Review* 31, no. 7: 1215–20.

Lok, Jaco. 2010. "Institutional Logics as Identity Projects." *Academy of Management Journal* 53, no. 6: 1305–35.

Longstreth, Andrew, and Nate Raymond. 2012. "Fat Guarantees Helped Weaken Dewey & LeBoeuf." Reuters (Business News Edition), May 4, 2012.

Lowe, Jeffrey. 2013. *2012 Partner Compensation Survey*. Washington, DC: Major, Lindsey & Africa. https://www.mlaglobal.com/publications/research/compensation-survey-2012.

———. 2014. *2014 Partner Compensation Survey*. Washington, DC: Major, Lindsey & Africa. https://www.mlaglobal.com/en/knowledge-library/research/compensation-survey-2014.

———. 2016. *2016 Partner Compensation Survey*. Washington, DC: Major, Lindsey & Africa. https://www.mlaglobal.com/publications/research/compensation-survey-2016.

———. 2018. *2018 Partner Compensation Survey*. Washington, DC: Major, Lindsey & Africa. https://www.mlaglobal.com/en/knowledge-library/research/2018-partner-compensation-report.

Luban, David. 1988. *Lawyers and Justice: An Ethical Study*. Princeton, NJ: Princeton University Press.

MacEwen, Bruce. 2013. *Growth Is Dead: Now What?* New York: Adam Smith, Esq.

Maister, David H. 1997. *Managing the Professional Service Firm*. New York: Free Press Paperbacks.

McLellan, Lizzy. 2018. "How Morgan Lewis Grew into a Powerhouse on Its Own Terms." *American Lawyer*, April 24, 2018.

McQueen, M. P. 2016. "Perpetual Motion." *American Lawyer* 38, no. 2 (February): 38–41.

Mitchell, Terence R., and Amy E. Mickel. 1999. "The Meaning of Money: An Individual-Difference Perspective." *Academy of Management Review* 24, no. 3: 568–78.

Moliterno, James E. 2012. "Crisis Regulation." *Michigan State Law Review* 2012, no. 2: 307–46.

Molot, Jonathan T. 2014. "What's Wrong with Law Firms? A Corporate Finance Solution to Law Firm Short-Termism." *Southern California Law Review* 88:1.

Morgan, Thomas D. 2010. *The Vanishing American Lawyer*. New York: Oxford University Press.

Nanda, Ashish, and Lisa Rohrer. 2012a. "Robinson & White (A): Pay for Performance." Cambridge, MA: Harvard Law School. https://casestudies.law.harvard.edu/robinson-white-a-pay-for-performance/.

———. 2012b. "Robinson & White (B): Compensation Review." Cambridge, MA: Harvard Law School. https://casestudies.law.harvard.edu/robinson-white-b-compensation-review/.

National Association of Law Placement. 1989. *Directory of Legal Employers*. Washington, DC: NALP.

———. 2019. "Employment for the Class of 2018—Selected Findings." *Jobs & JDs*. https://www.nalp.org/uploads/SelectedFindingsClassof2018_FINAL.pdf.

National Law Journal. *National Law Journal Law Firm Rankings*. 2007–2012. Washington, DC: ALM.

Nelson, Robert L. 1988. *Partners with Power: The Social Transformation of the Large Law Firm*. Berkeley: University of California Press.

Nelson, Robert, Ronit Dinovitzer, Gabriele Plickert, Joyce Sterling, and Bryant G. Garth. 2014. *After the JD, Wave 3: A Longitudinal Study of Careers in Transition, 2012–2013, United States* (ICPSR 35480). Ann Arbor, MI: Inter-university Consortium for Political and Social Research.

Nelson, Robert L., and Laura Beth Nielsen. 2000. "Cops, Counsel, and Entrepreneurs: Constructing the Role of Inside Counsel in Large Corporations." *Law and Society Review* 34, no. 2: 457–94.

Newsham, Jack. 2019. "The Growing Nonequity Tier Is Forcing a Conversation on Partnership." *American Lawyer*, July 31, 2019.

Noonan, Mary C., Mary Corcoran, and Paul N. Courant. 2008. "Is the Partnership Gap Closing for Women? Cohort Differences in the Sex Gap in Partnership Chances." *Social Science Research* 37, no. 1: 156–79.

Ostrow, Ellen. 2010. "Great Expectations: Lateral Integrations." *New York Law Journal* 243, no. 20: 6.

Packel, Dan. 2018. "'The Wave of the Future': Law Firm Panels Are Creating a New In-Crowd." *American Lawyer*, July 29, 2018.

———. 2019. "Law Firms Are Reimagining Origination Credit." *American Lawyer*, January 3, 2019.

Parker, Christine, and Tanina Rostain. 2012. "Law Firms, Global Capital, and the Sociological Imagination." *Fordham Law Review* 80:2347.

Parker, Christine, Adrian Evans, Linda Haller, Suzanne Le Mire, and Reid Mortensen. 2008. "The Ethical Infrastructure of Legal Practice in Larger Law Firms: Values, Policy and Behaviour." *UNSW Law Journal* 31, no. 1: 158–88.

Parnell, David J. 2018. "The Battle for Talent Is Disrupting the Business of Law." Law .com, August 15, 2018.

Pearce, Russell G. 1995. "The Professionalism Paradigm Shift: Why Discarding Professional Ideology Will Improve the Conduct and Reputation of the Bar." *New York University Law Review* 70, no. 6: 1229–76.

Pearce, Russell G., and Eli Wald. 2012. "Rethinking Lawyer Regulation: How a Relational Approach Would Improve Professional Rules and Roles." *Michigan State Law Review* 2012:513–36.

Peery, Destiny. 2018. *2018 National Association of Women Lawyers Survey on Retention and Promotion of Women in Law Firms*. Chicago: NAWL.

Percheski, Christine. 2008. "Opting Out? Cohort Differences in Professional Women's Employment Rates from 1960 to 2005." *American Sociological Review* 73, no. 3: 497–517.

Pinansky, Thomas Paul. 1987. "The Emergence of Law Firms in the American Legal Profession." *University of Arkansas at Little Rock Law Review* 9, no. 4: 593–640.

Pinnington, Ashly, and Jorgen Sandberg. 2013. "Lawyers' Professional Careers: Increasing Women's Inclusion in the Partnership of Law Firms." *Gender, Work and Organization* 20:616.

Pollock, Ellen Joan. 1990. *Turks and Brahmins: Upheaval at Milbank, Tweed: Wall Street's Gentlemen Take off Their Gloves*. New York: American Lawyer Books/ Simon and Schuster.

Press, Aric. 2011. "A Chasm with Consequences: Despite Recovery, Market Forces Creating Challenges for Am Law 200 Firms." *Legal Intelligencer*, June 6, 2011.

———. 2014. "Special Report: Big Law's Reality Check." *American Lawyer*, October 29, 2014.

Randazzo, Sara. 2019. "Being a Law Firm Partner Was Once a Job for Life. That Culture Is All but Dead." *American Lawyer*, August 9, 2019.

Rapp, Richard. 2016. "Understanding the Lateral Hiring Frenzy." Adam Smith, Esq. March 11, 2016. https://adamsmithesq.com/2016/03/understanding-the-lateral -hiring-frenzy/3/.

Regan, Milton C., Jr. 1999. "Law Firms, Competition Penalties, and the Values of Professionalism." *Georgetown Journal of Legal Ethics* 13, no. 1: 1–74.

———. 2004. *Eat What You Kill: The Fall of a Wall Street Lawyer*. Ann Arbor: University of Michigan Press.

———. 2008. "Lawyers, Symbols, and Money: Outside Investment in Law Firms." *Penn State International Law Review* 27, no. 2: 407–38.

———. 2010. "Taxes and Death: The Rise and Demise of an American Law Firm." In *Law Firms, Legal Culture, and Legal Practice*, edited by Austin Sarat. Studies in Law, Politics, and Society 52. Bingley, UK: Emerald.

———. 2013. "Nested Ethics: A Tale of Two Cultures." *Hofstra Law Review* 42, no. 1: 143–74.

Regan, Milton C., Jr., and Kath Hall. 2016. "Lawyers in the Shadow of the Regulatory State: Transnational Governance on Business and Human Rights." *Fordham Law Review* 84, no. 5: 2001–37.

Regan, Milton C., Jr., and Palmer Heenan. 2010. "Supply Chains and Porous Boundaries: The Disaggregation of Legal Services." *Fordham Law Review* 78, no. 5: 2137.

Regan, Milton C., Jr., and Lisa H. Rohrer. 2012. "Money and Meaning: The Moral Economy of Law Firm Compensation." *University of St. Thomas Law Journal* 10, no. 1: 74–151.

Rehnquist, William H. 1987. "The Legal Profession Today Dedicatory Address." *Indiana Law Journal* 62, no. 2: 151–58.

Reichman, Nancy J., and Joyce S. Sterling. 2002. "Recasting the Brass Ring: Deconstructing and Reconstructing Workplace Opportunities for Women Lawyers." *Capital University Law Review* 29:923.

———. 2004. "Sticky Floors, Broken Steps, and Concrete Ceilings in Legal Careers." *Texas Journal of Women and the Law* 14, no. 1: 27–76.

———. 2013. "Parenthood Status and Compensation in Law Practice." *Indiana Journal of Global Legal Studies* 20, no. 2: 1203–22.

Remus, Dana. 2017. "Reconstructing Professionalism." *Georgia Law Review* 51, no. 3: 807–77.

Rhode, Deborah L. 2011. "From Platitudes to Priorities: Diversity and Gender Equity in Law Firms." *Georgetown Journal of Legal Ethics* 24:1041.

———. 2014. "Diversity and Gender Equity in Legal Practice." *University of Cincinnati Law Review* 82, no. 3: 871–900.

Ribstein, Larry, E. 2010. "The Death of Big Law." *Wisconsin Law Review* 2010, no. 3: 749–815.

Ridgeway, Cecilia L. 2011. *Framed by Gender: How Gender Inequality Persists in the Modern World*. New York: Oxford University Press.

Rikleen, L. 2013. *Closing the Gap: A Road Map for Achieving Gender Pay Equity in Law Firm Partner Compensation*. Chicago: American Bar Association.

Rogers, Abby. 2013. "Law Firm Partners Can Expect Major Layoffs This Year." *Business Insider*, January 8, 2013.

Rohrer, Lisa, and Nicole DeHoratius. 2015. "SeyfarthLean: Transforming Legal Service Delivery at Seyfarth Shaw." Case Study HLS 15-13. Boston: Harvard Law School. https://casestudies.law.harvard.edu/seyfarthlean-transforming-legal-service-delivery-at-seyfarth-shaw/.

Roiphe, Rebecca. 2016. "The Decline of Professionalism." *Georgetown Journal of Legal Ethics* 29:649–82.

Rose, Joel A. 2010. "Administering Partner Compensation Systems." *Compensation and Benefits for Law Offices* 10, no. 10–12: 1–11.

Rosen, Robert Eli. 2010. "Rejecting the Culture of Independence: Corporate Lawyers as Committed to Their Clients." In *Law Firms, Legal Culture, and Legal Practice*, edited by Austin Sarat. Studies in Law, Politics, and Society 52. Bingley, UK: Emerald.

Rostain, Tanina. 2010. "Self-Regulatory Authority, Markets, and the Ideology of Professionalism." In *The Oxford Handbook of Regulation*, edited by Robert Baldwin, Martin Lodge, and Martin Cave, 169–200. Oxford: Oxford University Press.

Rozen, Miriam. 2018. "The NLJ 500: Career-Nurturing Firms Win High Rankings on Women-in-Law Scorecard." *National Law Journal*, June 28, 2018.

Rudman, Laurie A. 1998. "Self-Promotion as a Risk Factor for Women: The Costs and Benefits of Counterstereotypical Impression Management." *Journal of Personality and Social Psychology* 74, no. 3: 629–45.

Ryan, Richard M., and Edward L. Deci. 2000. "Intrinsic and Extrinsic Motivations: Classic Definitions and New Directions." *Contemporary Educational Psychology* 25, no. 1: 54–67.

Sako, Mari. 2010. "Make-or-Buy Decisions in Legal Services: A Strategic Perspective." Conference Presentation. Law Firm Evolution: Brave New World or Business as Usual, Georgetown University Law Center, Washington, DC, March 21–23, 2010.

Scheiber, Noam. 2013. "The Last Days of Big Law." *New Republic*, July 21, 2013.

Seal, Ben. 2019. "What Helps the Super Rich Maintain Their Success?" *American Lawyer*, April 23, 2019.

Shelton, George F. 1901. "Law as a Business." *Yale Law Journal* 10, no. 7: 275–82.

Silbey, S. 2011. "The Sociological Citizen: Pragmatic and Relational Regulation in Law and Organizations." *Regulation and Governance* 5:1–13.

Silbey, S., R. Huising, and S. Coslovsky. 2009. "The Sociological Citizen: Recognizing Relational Interdependence in Law and Organizations." *L'Année Sociologique* 59:201–229.

Silverstein, Silvia Hodges. 2014. "White Paper: Gender Study." Sky Analytics.

Simmons, Christine. 2018a. "Fewer Firms Expected to Follow Milbank's Associate Pay Boost." *American Lawyer*, June 4, 2018.

———. 2018b. "Milbank Boosts Associate Salaries with $190K Starting Pay." *American Lawyer*, June 4, 2018.

———. 2018c. "The Super Rich Are Getting Richer." *American Lawyer*, April 24, 2018.

Simon, William H. 1999. *The Practice of Justice: A Theory of Lawyers' Ethics*. Cambridge, MA: Harvard University Press.

Simons, Hugh. 2017. "Global Lateral Hiring by the Numbers: A Look Behind the High 5-Year Attrition Rate." *American Lawyer*, February 3, 2017.

———. 2019. "Equity and Nonequity Partners Are on Divergent Paths." *American Lawyer*, April 17, 2019.

Simons, Hugh, and Bruch, Nicholas. 2018. "Success in the Am Law 100 Is Being Driven by Management." *American Lawyer*, April 24, 2018.

Sloan, Karen. 2013. "ABA Issues Toolkit, Aiming to Eliminate Gender Pay Gap." *National Law Journal*, March 18, 2013.

Smets, Michael, Paula Jarzabkowski, Gary T. Burke, and Paul Spee. 2014. "Reinsurance Trading in Lloyd's of London: Balancing Conflicting-yet-Complementary Logics in Practice." *Academy of Management Journal* 58, no. 3: 932–70.

Smets, Michael, T. Morris, S. Carroll, and N. Malhotra. 2009. "Orchestrating for a Winning Performance: Re-Thinking Strategy in Professional Service Firms." Working paper, Novack Druce Centre for Professional Service Firms, Said Business School, University of Oxford, Oxford, UK.

Smigel, Erwin Orson. 1964. *The Wall Street Lawyer. Professional Organization Man?* 2nd prtg. New York: Collier-Macmillan.

Smith, Jennifer. 2014. "Female Lawyers Still Battle Gender Bias." *Wall Street Journal*, May 4, 2014, US ed.

Smith, Reginald Heber. 1940. "Law Office Organization, IV." *ABA Journal* 26, no. 8: 648–51.

Solomon, Rayman L. 1992. "Five Crises or One: The Concept of Legal Professionalism, 1925–1960." In *Lawyers' Ideals/Lawyers' Practices: Transformations in the American Legal Profession*, edited by Robert L Nelson, David Trubek, and Rayman L. Solomon, 144–74. Ithaca, NY: Cornell University Press.

Sommerlad, H. 2015. "The "Social Magic" of Merit: Diversity, Equity, and Inclusion in the English and Welsh Legal Profession." *Fordham Law Review* 83, no. 5: 2325–47.

Sommerlad, H., and P. Sanderson. 1998. *Gender, Choice and Commitment: Women Solicitors in England and Wales and the Struggle for Equal Status.* London: Routledge.

Stein, Jacob A. 2010. "Legal Spectator: Finders, Minders, and Grinders." *Washington Lawyer*, April 2010.

Sterling, J., and N. Reichman. 2016. "Overlooked and Undervalued: Women in Private Law Practice." *Annual Review of Law and Social Science* 12:373–93.

Stetz, Mike. 2018. "Why Go to Law School? Most Go to Help Others." *PreLaw*, October 12, 2018. http://www.nationaljurist.com/prelaw/why-go-law-school-most-go-help-others.

Stevens, Mark. 1987. *Power of Attorney: The Rise of the Giant Law Firms.* New York: McGraw-Hill.

Stone, Harlan F. 1934. "The Public Influence of the Bar." *Harvard Law Review* 48, no. 1: 1–14.

Strom, Ray. 2019. "Big Law Is Humming, but Collections Keep Tumbling." *Bloomberg Law*, September 19, 2019.

Strom, Roy, and Christine Simmons. 2018. "The Top 5 Strategies Behind Law Firms' Lateral Hiring—And Whether They Work." *American Lawyer*, January 28, 2018.

Strong, Theron George. 1914. *Landmarks of a Lawyer's Lifetime.* New York: Dodd, Mead.

Suddaby, Roy, and Royston Greenwood. 2005. "Rhetorical Strategies of Legitimacy." *Administrative Science Quarterly* 50, no. 1: 35–67.

Sullivan, William M. 2005. *Work and Integrity: The Crisis and Promise of Professionalism in America.* San Francisco: Jossey-Bass.

Susskind, Richard. 2008. *The End of Lawyers? Rethinking the Nature of Legal Services.* Oxford: Oxford University Press.

Terry, Laurel S. 2008. "The Future Regulation of the Legal Profession: The Impact of Treating the Legal Profession as 'Service Providers.'" *Journal of the Professional Lawyer* 2008:189–211.

Thomson Reuters Legal Executive Institute and Peer Monitor, and Georgetown University Law Center. 2017. *Alternative Legal Service Providers: Understanding the Growth and Benefits of these New Legal Providers.* Thomson Reuters, January 1, 2017.

———. 2018. *2018 Report on the State of the Legal Market.* Thomson Reuters, January 18, 2018.

———. 2019. *2019 Report on the State of the Legal Market.* Thomson Reuters, January 8, 2019.

———. 2020. *2020 Report on the State of the Legal Market.* Thomson Reuters, January 6, 2020.

Thomson Reuters Legal Executive Institute, Georgetown Law, Said Business School at University of Oxford and Acritas. 2019. *Alternative Legal Service Providers 2019: Fast Growth, Expanding Use and Increasing Opportunity.*

Thornton, Patricia H., and William Ocasio. 1999. "Institutional Logics and the Historical Contingency of Power in Organizations: Executive Succession in the Higher Education Publishing Industry, 1958–1990." *American Journal of Sociology* 105, no. 3: 801–43.

———. "Institutional Logics." 2008. In *Sage Handbook of Organizational Institutionalism,* edited by Royston Greenwood et al., 99–129. London: Sage.

Treviño, Linda K., Gary R. Weaver, and Scott J. Reynolds. 2006. "Behavioral Ethics in Organizations: A Review." *Journal of Management* 32:951–90.

Tribe, Meghan. 2018. "Cravath Sets New High in Associate Salary Race." *American Lawyer,* June 11, 2018.

———. 2019. "Baker McKenzie Moves Toward Black Box System for Equity Partner Pay." *American Lawyer,* March 12, 2019.

Triedman, Julie. 2007. "The AM LAW 100 2007 Top Design." Law.com, May 1, 2007.

———. 2012. "House of Cards, Part III: A Perfect Storm." *American Lawyer,* July/August 2012.

Trotter, Michael H. 1997. *Profit and the Practice of Law: What's Happened to the Legal Profession?* Athens: University of Georgia Press.

Tyler, Tom R. 2005. "Promoting Employee Policy Adherence and Rule Following in Work Settings: The Value of Self- Regulatory Approaches." *Brooklyn Law Review* 70:1287–1312.

Tyler, Tom R., and Steven L. Blader. 2002. "Autonomous vs. Comparative Status: Must We Be Better than Others to Feel Good about Ourselves?" *Organizational Behavior and Human Decision Processes* 89, no. 1: 813–38.

Vaughan, Steven, and Claire Coe. 2015. *Independence, Representation and Risk: An Empirical Exploration of the Management of Client Relationships by Large Law Firms*. Birmingham, UK: Solicitors Regulation Authority.

Wald, Eli. 2010. "Glass Ceilings and Dead Ends: Professional Ideologies: Gender Stereotypes, and the Future of Women Lawyers at Large Law Firms." *Fordham Law Review* 78, no. 4: 2245–88.

———. 2015. "BigLaw Identity Capital: Pink and Blue, Black and White." *Fordham Law Review* 83, no. 5: 2509–56.

Wald, Eli, and Russell G. Pearce. 2016. "Being Good Lawyers: A Relational Approach to Law Practice." *Georgetown Journal of Legal Ethics* 29:603.

Weaver, Gary R., and Linda Klebe Treviño. 2001. "The Role of Human Resources in Ethics/Compliance Management: A Fairness Perspective." *Human Resources Management Review* 11:113, 115.

Wendel, W. Bradley. 2010. *Lawyers and Fidelity to Law*. Princeton, NJ: Princeton University Press.

Wesemann, Ed, and Nick Jarrett-Kerr. 2012. *The Edge International 2012 Global Partner Compensation System Survey*. London: Edge International.

Wilkins, David B. 1992. "Who Should Regulate Lawyers?" *Harvard Law Review* 105, no. 4 (February): 799–887.

Williams, Joan. 2001. *Unbending Gender: Why Family and Work Conflict and What to Do About It*. New York: Oxford University Press.

Williams, Joan C., Marina Multhaup, Su Li, and Rachel Korn. 2018. "You Can't Change What You Can't See: Interrupting Racial and Gender Bias in the Legal Profession." Executive Summary. Chicago: ABA/MCCA.

Williams, Joan C., and Veta Richardson. 2010. "New Millennium, Same Glass Ceiling—The Impact of Law Firm Compensation Systems on Women." *Hastings Law Journal* 62:597.

Williams-Alvarez, Jennifer. 2017. "Legal Departments Keep Huge Percentage of Work In-House. Here's Why." *Corporate Counsel*, June 26, 2017.

Wolinsky, Asher. 1993. "Competition in a Market for Informed Experts' Services." *RAND Journal of Economics* 24, no. 3: 380–98.

Zaretsky, Staci. 2018a. "Are Layoffs Looming If Some Firms Match Milbank's Associate Salary Increase?" *Above the Law*, June 5, 2018.

———. 2018b. "Salary Wars Scorecard: Which Firms Have Announced Raises and Bonuses? (2018)." *Above the Law*, June 5, 2018.

Zelizer, Viviana. 1994. *The Social Meaning of Money*. Princeton, NJ: Princeton University Press.

INDEX

A page number in italics refers to an illustration.

THE CHICAGO SERIES IN LAW AND SOCIETY
Edited by John M. Conley and Lynn Mather

Series titles, continued from front matter:

The Myth of the Litigious Society: Why We Don't Sue
by David M. Engel

Policing Immigrants: Local Law Enforcement on the Front Lines
by Doris Marie Provine, Monica W. Varsanyi, Paul G. Lewis, and Scott H. Decker

The Seductions of Quantification: Measuring Human Rights, Gender Violence, and Sex Trafficking
by Sally Engle Merry

Invitation to Law and Society: An Introduction to the Study of Real Law, Second Edition
by Kitty Calavita

Pulled Over: How Police Stops Define Race and Citizenship
by Charles R. Epp, Steven Maynard-Moody, and Donald Haider-Markel

The Three and a Half Minute Transaction: Boilerplate and the Limits of Contract Design
by Mitu Gulati and Robert E. Scott

This Is Not Civil Rights: Discovering Rights Talk in 1939 America
by George I. Lovell

Failing Law Schools
by Brian Z. Tamanaha

Everyday Law on the Street: City Governance in an Age of Diversity
by Mariana Valverde

Lawyers in Practice: Ethical Decision Making in Context
Edited by Leslie C. Levin and Lynn Mather

Collateral Knowledge: Legal Reasoning in the Global Financial Markets
by Annelise Riles

Specializing the Courts
by Lawrence Baum

Asian Legal Revivals: Lawyers in the Shadow of Empire
by Yves Dezalay and Bryant G. Garth

The Language of Statutes: Laws and Their Interpretation
by Lawrence M. Solan

Belonging in an Adopted World: Race, Identity, and Transnational Adoption
by Barbara Yngvesson

Making Rights Real: Activists, Bureaucrats, and the Creation of the Legalistic State
by Charles R. Epp

Lawyers of the Right: Professionalizing the Conservative Coalition
by Ann Southworth

Arguing with Tradition: The Language of Law in Hopi Tribal Court
by Justin B. Richland

Speaking of Crime: The Language of Criminal Justice
by Lawrence M. Solan and Peter M. Tiersma

Human Rights and Gender Violence: Translating International Law into Local Justice
by Sally Engle Merry

Just Words, Second Edition: Law, Language, and Power
by John M. Conley and William M. O'Barr

Distorting the Law: Politics, Media, and the Litigation Crisis
by William Haltom and Michael McCann

Justice in the Balkans: Prosecuting War Crimes in the Hague Tribunal
by John Hagan

Rights of Inclusion: Law and Identity in the Life Stories of Americans with Disabilities
by David M. Engel and Frank W. Munger

The Internationalization of Palace Wars: Lawyers, Economists, and the Contest t
o Transform Latin American States
by Yves Dezalay and Bryant G. Garth

Free to Die for Their Country: The Story of the Japanese American Draft Resisters in World War II
by Eric L. Muller

Overseers of the Poor: Surveillance, Resistance, and the Limits of Privacy
by John Gilliom

Pronouncing and Persevering: Gender and the Discourses of Disputing in an African Islamic Court
by Susan F. Hirsch

The Common Place of Law: Stories from Everyday Life
by Patricia Ewick and Susan S. Silbey

The Struggle for Water: Politics, Rationality, and Identity in the American Southwest
by Wendy Nelson Espeland

Dealing in Virtue: International Commercial Arbitration and the Construction of a Transnational Legal Order
by Yves Dezalay and Bryant G. Garth

Rights at Work: Pay Equity Reform and the Politics of Legal Mobilization
by Michael W. McCann

The Language of Judges
by Lawrence M. Solan

Reproducing Rape: Domination through Talk in the Courtroom
by Gregory M. Matoesian

Getting Justice and Getting Even: Legal Consciousness among Working-Class Americans
by Sally Engle Merry

Rules versus Relationships: The Ethnography of Legal Discourse
by John M. Conley and William M. O'Barr

www.ingramcontent.com/pod-product-compliance
Lightning Source LLC
Chambersburg PA
CBHW060029030426
42334CB00019B/2247

9780226742137